The
Great
Powers
and Global
Struggle

1490-1990

The Great Powers

and Global Struggle

1490-1990

Karen A. Rasler &
William R. Thompson

THE UNIVERSITY PRESS OF KENTUCKY

Copyright © 1994 by The University Press of Kentucky

Scholarly publisher for the Commonwealth,
serving Bellarmine College, Berea College, Centre
College of Kentucky, Eastern Kentucky University,
The Filson Club, Georgetown College, Kentucky
Historical Society, Kentucky State University,
Morehead State University, Murray State University,
Northern Kentucky University, Transylvania University,
University of Kentucky, University of Louisville,
and Western Kentucky University.

Editorial and Sales Offices: Lexington, Kentucky 40508-4008

Library of Congress Cataloging-in-Publication Data

Rasler, Karen A., 1952-
    The great powers and global stuggle / Karen A. Rasler & William
R. Thompson.
       p.   cm.
    Includes bibliographical references and index.
    ISBN 0-8131-1889-1 (acid-free)
    1. World politics. 2. World politics—1945- 3. Geopolitics.
I. Thompson, William R. II. Title.
    D31.R37   1994
320.1'2—dc20   94-31406

For Cam and Lieu

Contents

Tables

Figures

Preface

In March 1992 a U.S. Defense Department planning document on post-cold war strategy stated that the first objective of the United States was to block the emergence of new regional powers that might threaten its global position.

Our first objective is to prevent the re-emergence of a new rival, either on the territory of the former Soviet Union or elsewhere, that poses a threat on the order of that posed formerly by the Soviet Union. This is a dominant consideration underlying the new regional defense strategy and requires that we endeavor to prevent any hostile power from dominating a region whose resources would, under consolidated control, be sufficient to general global power. [*New York Times*, May 24, 1992, p. 1]

Lest this passage be interpreted as being solely oriented toward the former Soviet Union, a second paragraph clarified the more generic policy message:

The U.S. must show the leadership necessary to establish and protect a new order that holds the promise of convincing potential competitors that they need not aspire to a greater role or pursue a more aggressive posture to protect their legitimate interests. In non-defense areas, we must account sufficiently for the interests of the advanced industrial nations to discourage them from challenging our leadership. . . . We must maintain the mechanism for deterring potential competitors from even aspiring to a larger regional or global role. [*New York Times*, May 24, 1992, p. 5]

Specifically named as potential threats were Japan in East Asia, Germany in Western Europe, and India in South Asia. The policy message, however, proved to be too blunt. Two months later the first objective described above had been demoted to a third rank:

Our most fundamental goal is to deter or defeat attack from whatever source. . . . The second goal is to strengthen and extend the system of defense arrangements that binds democratic and like-minded nations together in common defense against

aggression, build habits of cooperation, avoid the renationalization of security policies, and provide security at lower costs and with lower risks for all. Our preference
for a collective response to preclude threats, or, if necessary, to deal with them is a
key feature of our regional defense strategy. The third goal is to preclude any hostile
power from dominating a region critical to our interests, and also thereby to strength-
en the barriers against the re-emergence of a global threat to the interests of the U.S.
and our allies. [*New York Times*, May 24, 1992, p. 5]

Hence, the objective of suppressing the global ascendance of regional
powers seemed to remain, but it was now to be more subtly stated. The
reaction to the overly direct and insensitive initial statement was not particularly surprising, but what should we make of this concern with regional
threats? It might have been a qualification of the heady triumphalism associated with winning the cold war. Or was it, more cynically, a rationale for
maintaining a large number of armed forces personnel in uniform? Could it
have been as well a manifestation of the anxieties of a declining superpower?
And yet President George Bush went out of his way in a May 1992 Southern
Methodist University commencement address to assure his audience that
the United States was not in decline, in spite of what all the "declinists"
were saying. Or was he protesting too much?

No doubt, the best answer to these questions is all of the above. More
important for our purposes, however, a global leader's concern with suppressing regional threats before they become global threats is a critical key
to understanding world politics. During the past five hundred years, conflicts between declining global leaders and ascending regional leaders have
triggered a sequence of global wars. The outcomes of these wars, as well as
the combat associated with them, have shaped our modern world. This
statement is not timeless, but it is as applicable to the late twentieth century as it was to the sixteenth, seventeenth, eighteenth, and nineteenth
centuries.

A process that is so fundamentally central and all-pervasive needs to be
recognized and understood. That is the principal aim of this book. We develop a theory that explains what these global conflicts are about, when and
under what circumstances they are most likely to occur, and what the pivotal
causal processes are that act as engines of change. These are ambitious
goals. All we need to explain is why the world works the way it does. We do
not claim to have all the answers that may be germane to such a question,
but we think we do have a powerful and empirically substantiated explanation of why global wars occur and why major powers rise and fall. Indeed, it
is impossible to account for one without the other. Rise-and-fall dynamics
lead to wars. Wars contribute to rise-and-fall dynamics. Therefore, the preventive regional security concerns of a superpower with declining relative
economic capabilities and an increasing number of competitors should not

be dismissed as entirely unrealistic or merely budgetary rhetoric. The concerns are easy to ground in the macrohistory of world politics.

An overview of our understanding of what drives global conflict is advanced in chapter 1. After outlining the basic processes, we will focus in subsequent chapters on the various components of the explanation. Chapter 2 traces the history of rising and descending regional and global powers between 1494 and the present. A case is also made for carefully distinguishing between regional actors and their theaters of operation and global actors oriented primarily toward the global political economy and transoceanic commercial transactions.

Appendix B differentiates global wars—wars of succession fought to determine whose rules and policies will predominate in the management of global transactions—from other types of conflicts by demonstrating that only a few wars qualify as agents in the reconcentration of capabilities within the global political economy. Other wars are not unimportant. They simply play different roles in our story. Chapters 3 and 4 specify, at regional and global levels of analysis, the linkages between positional change and the onset of global wars, including their timing and structural contexts. Power transitions and the levels of global and regional concentration have a prominent function in these chapters.

Once we establish the context of structural change and actor incentives in which global wars take place, we need to take a step back and ask how and why the structural change occurs. Chapter 5 makes a case for technological innovation in commercial and industrial activities as the main motor for global power and leadership. The causal linkages among technological innovation, economic leadership, naval leadership, and war are modeled empirically.

Chapter 6 surveys the ways in which observers have sought to account for the rise and decline of powerful states over several thousand years. A negative case, again based in part on empirical analysis, is made in chapter 7 for the often asserted primary role of tradeoffs between investment and various types of consumption. The argument in chapter 8 also speaks against overextension as a primary cause of relative decline at the global level. Overextension is important for understanding the defeat and decline of regional powers. In general, though, tradeoffs and overextension, we argue, are at best secondary factors, especially in comparison with the centrality of technological innovation.

Chapter 9 reassembles the various components of our model and explicitly contrasts the argument with alternative explanations. One last question is raised in chapter 10: Have we accounted for processes of structural changes that have themselves been made obsolete by other, more recent structural changes? Chapter 10 reviews six "endism" arguments that contend that the probability of future warfare between major powers is exceedingly low. While the prospects for global conflict may well appear diminished for the very near future, we conclude that the world has not yet changed so radically as to preclude the possibility of major power conflict somewhere down the road.

One final warning about what is to follow is probably necessary. We and others have constructed a number of verbal models explaining how these processes of structural change and conflict operate. We could stay at this level of discourse and hope that our arguments were so persuasive that readers would accept our interpretations over those of other analysts. However, we have a strong preference for empirical evidence as the arbiter of competing arguments. Thus, wherever possible, we will attempt to buttress our arguments with appropriate indicators and statistical examinations that test the validity of the theoretical statements advanced. We realize we run some risk of alienating readers who are uncomfortable with quantitative approaches. But we see no alternative, for our argument finally hinges on how well the evidence corresponds to our assertions. We have made some stylistic compromises by placing as much of the technical details as seemed feasible in notes and appendices. Readers can choose whether to read these sections or not. For that matter, we would like to believe that even readers who find any numbers, besides those indicating the order of the pages, repugnant could choose to skip over passages that contain enumeration and still find some value in our interpretation. Ultimately, only our readers can assess whether this belief is warranted.

Acknowledgments

The analyses reported in chapters 6 and 7 were assisted by a 1985-87 grant from the National Science Foundation. Earlier versions of the chapters have benefited from comments at presentations in various forums, including seminars and colloquia at the Claremont Graduate School; Harvard University; Texas A & M; University of California, Los Angeles; University of California, Riverside; and the University of Michigan. We have also benefited from specific comments on earlier versions of various chapters from Jeremy Black, Terry Boswell, Christopher Chase-Dunn, Paul Diehl, Charles Doran, Richard Eichenberg, Suzanne Frederick, John Freeman, Joshua Goldstein, Paul Huth, Stephen Krasner, Jacek Kugler, Jack Levy, Michael McGinnis, George Modelski, James Morow, David Rapkin, Bruce Russett, Frank Wayman, and a bevy of anonymous reviewers. None of them can be blamed for what we did with their advice. On the editorial side of this process, we have been extremely well served by Angela G. Ray. We could not ask for better help in disseminating our arguments.

We are also grateful to the following organizations for permission to use portions of earlier publications: to Sage Publications for permission to publish material from William R. Thompson and Karen A. Rasler, "War and Systemic Capability Reconcentration" (*Journal of Conflict Resolution* 32 [June 1988]) and Rasler and Thompson, "Technological Innovation, Capability Positional Shifts and Systemic War" (*Journal of Conflict Resolution* 35 [Sept. 1991]); to Lynne Rienner Publishers for permission to publish material from Rasler, "Spending, Deficits, and Welfare Trade-Offs; to MIT Press for permission to publish material from Thompson, "Long Waves, Technological Innovation, and Relative Decline"; to Blackwell Publishers for permission to publish material from Rasler and Thompson, "Relative Decline and the Overconsumption-Underinvestment Hypothesis" (*International Studies Quarterly* 35 [Sept. 1991]); to Routledge Publishers for permission to publish material from

Rasler and Thompson, "Politico-economic Tradeoffs and British Relative Decline" (in Steve Chan and Alex Mintz, eds., *Defense, Welfare and Growth: Perspectives and Evidence* [London: Routledge, 1992]); to Johns Hopkins University Press for permission to publish material from Thompson, "Dehio, Long Cycles, and the Geohistorical Context of Structural Transitions" (*World Politics* 43 [Oct. 1992]); to Westview Press for permission to publish material from Thompson, "The Past and Future of Transitional Warfare" (in James Burk, ed., *The Military in New Times: Adapting Armed Forces to a Turbulent World* [Boulder, Co.: Westview Press, 1994]).

1.

An Overview of the Argument: Ascent, Decline, Transition, and War

Stated most simply, our thesis is that states rise and fall in the pecking order of world politics. Ascending states fight one another as well as descending states, and descending states fight one another as well as ascending states. To a great extent, these conflicts are structurally inspired. It is not that states that happen to be experiencing status mobility find issues to contest. Rather, states fight because they are, or wish to be, moving up or down in status. We do not claim, however, that all conflict can be traced to structural change. States do quarrel about such things as territorial control, access to resources, and ideologies. Sometimes they choose to fight over these issues. In many cases, a structural interpretation simply may not be useful.

Nevertheless, the most intense conflicts in world politics tend to involve dynamics of structural change. Territory, resources, and ideology may be at stake in these conflicts as well. But the issues in contention are fought out within the context of ascent and decline trajectories. Nor is it any state's ascent and decline that is of most interest. The most significant wars, which also tend to be among the most deadly ones, take place within the context of ascent and decline among the world system's most powerful state actors. It is movement toward and away from the apex of the world system's status hierarchy, and the associated costs and benefits associated with leading positions, that cause so much trouble.

Other analysts have made similar assertions. What we do that is different is to suggest that the most critical historical pattern of structural change has been one of attempted transitions between an ascending and expansionist regional leader (in Western Europe) and a declining global leader specializing in long-distance, interoceanic transactions. Not only do we wish to document this pattern and explore its implications for such topics as balances of power and concentration, but we also wish to explain why ascent and decline occur at the apex of the system. To do this we focus predominantly on the role of successive pioneering innovations that shape the world's economy, consumption-investment tradeoffs, and overextension. The life cycle of returns from innovating activity, we contend, is paramount to an understanding of the rise and fall of leadership at the global level. Tradeoffs and overextension are genuine policy problems, but they are also manifestations of decline more than its original sources.

We recognize that these are strong and controversial assertions. In the hope of going beyond mere assertion, we propose to test our version of the roots of transitional warfare. But before we move on to the numerous tests we have in mind, a preliminary discussion of the components of our interpretation should facilitate the presentation of the argument and its underlying logic.

More and more scholars are focusing on gains and losses in the relative positions of rival nation-states as a critical factor in explaining patterns of conflict and cooperation. The basic insight is that states improving their positions have incentive structures, goals, and perspectives different from those of states experiencing positional losses. In addition, states that acquired their positions at earlier points control resources and prestige to which rising states aspire. As a consequence, rising states have some propensity to engage in conflict with declining states and vice versa. Cooperation, in general, becomes more difficult.

There are several ways to analyze this phenomenon of positional gains and losses. Monadic examinations ask whether, to what extent, or why a single state improved its position or suffered a decline. Why did Rome fall? Is the United States currently in decline? Is Japan the next heir apparent? Dyadic examinations study the interactions of rival powers. Athens versus Sparta, Carthage versus Rome, Britain versus France in the seventeenth and eighteenth centuries, Britain versus Germany in the late nineteenth century, and the United States versus the Soviet Union in the late twentieth century all exemplify some of the more popular Cain-Abel matches in the history of international relations. Multilateral inquiries look at a field of great powers, attempting to determine which powers are on first base, second base, and so on in different corners of the world. Ultimately, of course, the macrosystemic analyses are interested in the aggregate properties of resource concentration, the fluctuations in this systemic dimension, and its various consequences.

None of these alternative foci are inherently superior. Nor need they be pursued in mutually exclusive fashions. On the contrary, we prefer to see them pursued in integrated ways. We begin with certain systemic observations and then seek to account for the systemic regularities with a model that moves back and forth from the systemic to the monadic end of the analytical continuum.

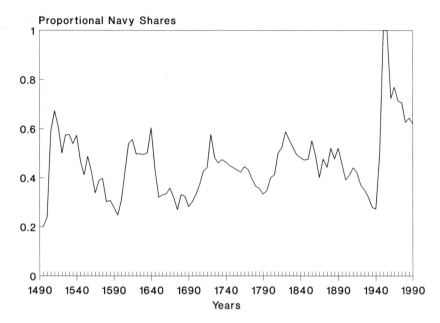

Figure 1.1 The Leadership Long Cycle

Capability Concentration and Systemic War

For the past five hundred years, the world's global political economy has experienced a repetitive sequence of capability concentration, deconcentration, and reconcentration. Figure 1.1 provides a quick sketch of the undulations in this process. Data on the year-to-year distribution of warships, an important indicator of global-reach capabilities, are available from 1494 to the present (Modelski and Thompson 1988). Figure 1.1 demonstrates one simple way to capture the degree to which this form of military resource is concentrated. A leading power is first identified for a specific period of time. Its share is then calculated and plotted. The basic pattern is one of increasing concentration in the early sixteenth, seventeenth, eighteenth, and nineteenth centuries and in the mid-twentieth century. Decreasing concentration is evident toward the ends of the sixteenth through the nineteenth centuries.

Not shown in figure 1.1 is the pattern of warfare related to the ups and downs of systemic capability concentration. War among the major powers is least prevalent when naval capabilities are most concentrated. Major power warfare is most prevalent when the naval capabilities are least concentrated. Moreover, many of the bouts of warfare that proved most serious as measured by battle deaths, geographic scope, number and political weight of the participants, duration, and consequences have regularly taken place in the intervals separating the periods of lowest and highest capability concentration.

The process began with the Italian and Indian Ocean Wars (1494-1516), continued through the Dutch-Spanish Wars (1580-1608), the Wars of the Grand Alliance (1688-1713), and the French revolutionary and Napoleonic wars (1792-1815), and most recently was manifested in a particularly lethal way in the two world wars of the twentieth century (1914-45). Thus, it is not difficult to argue that global war serves as a sort of systemic switching mechanism by facilitating the movement from phases of deconcentration to phases of reconcentration.

Fluctuations in capability concentration and systemic war are closely related. To explain systemic war, therefore, it is necessary to explain why systemic capability concentration fluctuates. Answers to this question certainly will not tell us everything we need to know about the onset of warfare. But an improved understanding of the deconcentration-reconcentration process, assuredly, would contribute significantly to the etiology of war and a number of other important forms of politico-economic behavior.

The Principal Agents of Concentration

One key, we believe, to the concentration-deconcentration process is that there is nothing particularly mysterious about who is most responsible for the systemic phases of concentration and deconcentration. Early in each century, one state has taken the political-military-economic-financial-cultural lead. Later in the century, that same state has experienced critical losses in its initial positional lead. Hence, one efficient way to explain why the world system goes through phases of greater and lesser concentration can be equated with accounting for the rise and fall of each century's global leader: Portugal in the sixteenth century, the United Provinces of the Netherlands in the seventeenth century, Britain in the eighteenth and nineteenth centuries, and the United States in the twentieth century.

Explaining the rise and relative decline of major powers does not entail raising entirely novel questions. The literature on Britain's late nineteenth-century decline, for example, is quite extensive. The literature on the current and near-future status of the United States is growing markedly. This latter development should hardly be surprising given the momentous implications of the relative decline of the world system's lead economy and politico-military actor. Despite the significance of the implications, however, we are not blessed with an abundance of theoretically justified models to explain ascent and decline. We do have some theories and models, but mostly we have bits and pieces of something resembling a comprehensive explanation. That is to say, we have plenty of generalizations and hypotheses, yet only a few of them have been subjected to systematic empirical scrutiny.

In this book we propose to integrate several literatures to form one general model of the linkages between positional changes and systemic war. One rather sparse literature seeks to explain why so few states have risen in the system to become major players in the transoceanic political economy. A second and rapidly expanding literature looks at the other side of the ascent coin—why these major players experience relative decline. The third literature seeks to account for long waves in technological innovation and production-commercial leadership. The fourth set of analyses focuses on why systemic wars occur.

Ascent Prerequisites

The first literature, with a few notable exceptions, is largely descriptive and easily the least extensive. What we have in mind are the discussions of the factors critical to the ascent of a given leading state. Naturally, many factors are idiosyncratic to a particular time and space. The Portuguese search for Prester John and the Dutch reliance on the herring fisheries are two obvious examples. A few factors, the prerequisites of ascent to systemic preeminence, however, tend to repeat themselves.

Mahan (1890) emphasized such factors as the ease of access to the sea and the quality of harbors as critical to the development of dominant sea powers. More recently, Wallerstein (1984), Keohane (1984), and Modelski (1987) have generalized about the conditions they believe are essential for the attainment of the status of hegemonic leader.[1] Our own interpretation of the ascent prerequisites overlaps these earlier arguments more than it contradicts them. In developing a model to explain why some European states developed regionally oriented geopolitical stances while others became full-fledged global powers, we have argued that three variables emerge as historically significant: location, size, and economic cohesion (Rasler and Thompson 1989).

Location was significant not merely for Mahan's appreciation of coastline quality. Geographic position also proved important for the development of Europe's long-distance trade network. It always helps to be in the right place at the right time. The advantages of protection from the attacks of neighboring rivals by some degree of insularity, whether assisted by canals, channels, or oceans, are an additional locational asset.

Size and cohesion have tended to be intertwined. Small states were less likely to resemble the crazy-quilt assemblage of multiple, poorly integrated subunits that characterized the expanding French and Spanish empires.

These subunits proved difficult to mobilize and to tax. Their multiple economic personalities (e.g., inland agrarian provinces competing with coastal ports) were not biased in favor of the triumph of long-distance commercial interests.

In contrast, the smaller states were comparatively more homogeneous, if only because they encompassed fewer people and less territory. The ones that became preeminent also had unusually good internal transportation networks. The resulting benefits for the cohesion of the political economy were enhanced further by the tendency for a single, dominant center to emerge, such as Lisbon, Amsterdam, and London.

The pronounced centrifugal threats of the multiple, poorly integrated subunits in the larger states placed a premium on coercive territorial consolidation and encouraged the tendency to engage in regular efforts at further territorial expansion. Administrative resources and large armies were required for control purposes. This development, in turn, necessitated greater efforts at resource extraction on the part of the state. Most of these problems were much less acute in the smaller, more maritime states. As a partial consequence, these states were less intrusive. At the very least, they were much less prone to interrupt maritime commercial developments than were the larger, continentally oriented powers that were continually distracted by immediate and local territorial problems.

The preeminent states (Portugal, the Netherlands, Britain, and the United States) were distinguished by a pronounced and consistent oceanic capability and orientation. Such an orientation presupposes an elite and dominant political coalition that is not biased against trade, navies, and the development of global reach. It also implies a preference for developing large-scale commercial networks over acquiring territory for its own sake. A less explicit, historical corollary is that these same states were the ones most likely to develop adequate fiscal and credit procedures to be able to take on and defeat their larger and nominally wealthier adversaries (Rasler and Thompson 1983, 1989). A victory in global warfare is another definite requirement for the ascent to preeminence.

Preeminent states emerged first as the commercial hubs of the post-1500 world economy. They were also early industry leaders in such sectors as shipbuilding and textiles. After the late eighteenth century, their industrial leadership, based on technological innovation, became even more pronounced and extensive. The relative significance of this source of preeminence and its implications, in comparison with those of some of the other factors discussed above, grew so dramatically after the Industrial Revolution that industrial innovation now clearly overshadows (and, in some cases, greatly reduces) the historical values of location, size, and economic cohesion.

Relative Decline

The second literature is considerably more extensive. We have many more discussions of why states fall than of why they rise in the first place. Perhaps this trait is related to the tendency to accept ascents as natural and even inevitable, at least after the fact, and the analogous tendency to regard decline as somehow less natural. Pervasive decline also tends to be an unpleasant topic or a pressing policy issue for those who write about it while experiencing its effects. Few analysts complain about ascent unless it appears to be occurring somewhere else. In these cases, there seems to be a stronger urge to worry about coping with or containing the rival's ascent than to place the specifics of a particular case within the more general context of the phenomena of rise and relative decline.

These observations only suggest that decline is a more emotional issue than ascent. Fortunately, we still have many highly useful and objective studies of what might be called decline episodes. The reasons for the decline of this or that state are discussed with sufficient frequency at least to facilitate what is more rare—the explicit comparison of factors thought to underlie the relative decline of preeminent powers. While the nature of the evidence makes it impossible to say that factor X deserves 35 percent of the credit or blame and factor Y is only responsible for 5 percent of relative decline, comparison helps to isolate those factors that appear to emerge in case after case, even if their guises vary. The analytical process is also aided by the outcomes of earlier examinations of comparative decline. Thus, we believe that we have sufficient information to construct what we call the relative decline syndrome, which we subdivide into internal and external components.

Innovation

No doubt the most telling point one can make about preeminent powers is that their rise to systemic centrality is predicated on innovational advantage. For a period of time, they possess a virtual monopoly in the control of either critical markets or the production of significant commodities. The Portuguese edge was associated with shipbuilding, navigation, and the Indian Ocean spice trade. The Dutch had herring, shipbuilding, and textiles, and they controlled much of the intra-European and European-Asian maritime commerce. The British claim was first predicated on shipbuilding, Atlantic commerce, and wool textiles. Later, cotton textiles, coal, steam engines, iron products, and then railroads lay at the heart of Britain's nineteenth-century centrality in the world economy. The American rise, in its turn, was based on automobiles, steel, and petroleum. More recently, these products were superseded to some extent by plastics, electronics, and aerospace industries.

The basic pattern thus is one of innovational waves. Each innovational era plays itself out. The Portuguese could not maintain their monopoly on navigational secrets or Asian spices. The Dutch could not dominate European maritime commerce forever. The British did not hold on to all of their Atlantic empire, nor were they able to make the transition to steel, chemicals, automobiles, and electrification smoothly. Each innovator is succeeded by another state that outperforms the old lead innovator in its specializations and introduces new areas of innovation as well. Different sources of energy are also involved. Wind and peat gave way to coal. Coal gave way to petroleum. No doubt petroleum eventually will give way to some new source.

Scholars have written an extensive literature on what drives these long waves. Different schools of thought promote the roles of investment spurts, profit trends, demographic shifts, food and raw material scarcity, price levels, technological innovation, and war as the primary movers of long-term economic fluctuations. Sorting these claims theoretically and empirically will constitute a major challenge, but not one that we need to pursue at this time. Instead, we will assume that whatever the relationships among these phenomena may be, innovation plays one of the more significant roles.

At this point, we do at least have fairly strong evidence for long waves of technical innovation. Figure 1.2 plots an aggregate index of leading-sector growth rates for the 1760-1980 period. Following the arguments of Schumpeter (1939) and Rostow (1978), production indicators for a dozen leading-sector commodities—raw cotton consumption, pig iron, railroad track, crude steel, sulfuric acid, electrical energy, motor vehicles, nitrogen fertilizer, plastics and resins, synthetic fibers, semiconductors, and civilian jet airframes—have been collected for the periods during which a given sector is thought to be leading, in the sense that its rate of growth exceeds the general rate of growth of industrial production. These data, which have been collected for Britain, France, the United States, Germany, and Japan, can be used to calculate relative shares of leading-sector production (Thompson 1988) and/or fluctuations in the pace of production. Figure 1.2 focuses on production fluctuations.

Figure 1.2 represents the splicing together of two aggregate leading-sector growth rate series. Before 1890 the data reflect British production fluctuations. After 1890 U.S. information is used exclusively. The reasons for this procedure are twofold. First, the focus is placed on the most active national economic zones in the world economy. The leads enjoyed by these economic spark plugs are based to a considerable extent on the nations' leads in technological innovation. Therefore, we contend, nineteenth-century Britain and the twentieth-century United States are the best places to observe the presence or absence of innovational waves. Yet, as we noted earlier, the principal

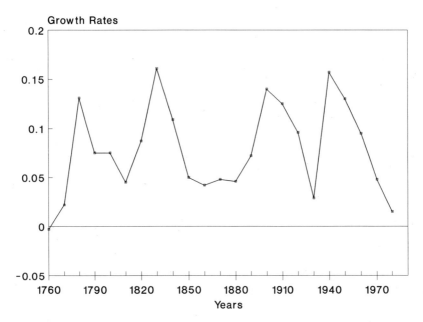

Figure 1.2 Leading-Sector Growth Rates in the Global Leader's Economy

source of innovation tends to shift. From a systemic point of view, therefore, the world economy's innovational rhythm should correspond to the rhythm of the lead units only as long as they retain their leadership. Hence, we have spliced the two national series in the late nineteenth century to correspond with the perceived shift in the location of the system's lead economy.

Four waves of leading-sector innovation are readily discernible. The first wave capitalizes on the Industrial Revolution in Britain in the late eighteenth century. The second wave is based largely on the development of railroads from the 1830s on. Wave 3 picks up late nineteenth-century breakthroughs in steel, chemicals, electricity, and automobiles. Wave 4 is a post-World War II phenomenon reflecting the revival of some earlier sectors, such as automobiles, and the appearance of several new ones, such as semiconductors and plastics.

Figure 1.2 provides support for the idea of fifty-year Kondratieff waves in technological innovation. These waves, however, are not restricted to the period after Britain's Industrial Revolution. Innovational waves can also be found in production and commercial series dating back at least to the early fourteenth century. The most prominent waves are those surges in innovation that propelled new lead economies to the front rank around the ends of the fifteenth, sixteenth, seventeenth, eighteenth, and nineteenth centuries (Thompson 1992; Modelski and Thompson forthcoming). At the very least, the findings do help solidify the linkages between technological innovation, national power, and shifting international pecking orders.

Implicit to the idea of successive waves of commercial and industrial innovation is a crude theory of relative decline. Relative decline takes two forms: decline in comparison with the achievements of other states (the comparative variety) and decline in contrast to historical standards of performance (the historical variety). The comparative type of relative decline is virtually inevitable, because the monopolies on which preeminence is based cannot be retained as national secrets for long. Individuals from the lead economy take their skills abroad. Individuals from other states learn the navigational tricks, the ways to build better ships, and the ways to produce lighter and more colorful fabrics or more reliable automobiles.

Critical technological innovations are diffused throughout the system. Other states catch up. Normally, their catch-up efforts are assisted by measures to protect their infant industries. These restrictions do little to help the original leader maintain its lead in the commodities that are affected by the protective legislation. Access to foreign markets, accordingly, becomes more difficult. The increased number of producers-competitors, some of whom are likely to be closer to significant markets, also reduces the original leader's market share.

Diffusion may be inevitable. Diminishing innovation need not be. Yet it does reoccur with some regularity. The principal sources of innovation shift in space and over time. Something else besides technological diffusion and catch-up must be taking place. That something else, we argue, has four internal components. First, the returns on a given innovation diminish with time. Thus, even if a leader could maintain its initial monopoly indefinitely, the value of the lead would likely decline. New means of transportation are invented. Artificial materials replace natural materials. Automation depreciates the value of labor. Second, leaders are apt to become complacent. At their peak, they have little in the way of competition. When competition does reemerge, the response of leading firms is likely to be slow and clumsy. The ways of competition need to be relearned. Institutional rigidities, a third factor, act as additional brakes on the pursuit of more appropriate responses to changing environments. Class lines harden. Labor unions and manufacturer associations, as well as other organizations, seek to protect their memberships.[2] Old ways of doing things are retained too long because they are known and offer some security in an increasingly uncertain world. Finally, a fourth factor, not unlike the complacency factor, stems from the very success of the preeminent. As the society becomes wealthier, production grows increasingly more expensive. As a consequence, production tends to move to areas where factor costs are cheaper. At one time, this process meant that urban industry would move to the countryside. Now it means movement from the First World to NIC production sites.

These factors constitute what we call the relative decline syndrome. Secondarily related to this syndrome are two other components: consumption-investment tradeoffs and overextension. Some analysts have stressed these phenomena as primary agents of relative decline. Gilpin (1981), for instance, argues that increasing public and private consumption squeezes out investment and the potential for future growth. Kennedy (1987b) emphasizes the historical propensity for great powers to acquire more territorial commitments than they are capable of defending.

We do not dismiss tradeoffs and overcommitments as illusory policy problems. They pose difficult choices for decision makers. They represent, in addition, underlying problems that are difficult to resolve. Nevertheless, for reasons that are explored more fully in chapters 7 and 8, we do not view them as primary causes of relative decline. While they may contribute to decline once it is under way, they usually become noticeable only after the onset of relative decline. In this respect, they are as much products of decline as they may be secondary causes.

Systemic War

The literature on why systemic wars occur is considerable, but fortunately, it has received ample discussion elsewhere (Siverson and Sullivan 1983; Levy 1985; Thompson 1988; Midlarsky 1988). We see systemic wars as contests between global powers and regional powers. While preliminary bouts occur in which global powers fight global powers (e.g., the Anglo-Dutch Wars), regional powers fight regional powers (the Hapsburg-Valois duel), and regional powers fight global powers inconclusively (the Seven Years' War), the most important systemic wars are those events that are resolved fairly conclusively. As we noted above, a small number of wars switch the system from a phase of deconcentration to one of reconcentration. This switch happens because a single sea power emerges victorious from a global war with an initial monopoly in economic and military global-reach capabilities.

Why do global powers fight regional powers every one hundred years or so? There is reason to anticipate conflict among actors whose positions are improving and actors whose positions are deteriorating. The ambitions of the former threaten the welfare of the latter. Declining actors, moreover, possess a variety of things desired by rising actors. Not coincidentally, the global wars singled out by leadership long cycle theory involve the confrontation of an ascending regional power and either an ascending global power or some combination of a declining global power and an ascending one. Invariably, a maritime coalition will also include at least one continentally oriented power that is weaker than the principal adversary.

A popular image in the literature on systemic war is one of dissatisfied challengers attacking defenders of a previously established status quo. We view this interpretation as accurate enough in a broad sense. Global wars become contests over whose version of the status quo will prevail, but they are not initiated by a challenger directly attacking a declining system leader. Rather, challengers usually attack weaker targets on the premise that they can do so without provoking a powerful countercoalition. When they err and global power leaders choose to intervene, then relatively limited, local wars escalate into global wars.

Thus, systemic deconcentration is an important contextual factor in the etiology of systemic wars. The challengers perceive the global political economy's principal leader in decline and therefore less capable of acting and less likely to act in opposition to regional expansion. A more direct attack may come later. The declining global leader, on the other hand, perceives that, if successful, the expansion of the challenger will improve its capability foundation for a future, direct challenge of control of the transoceanic political economy. Both challenger and declining global leader operate in a context of global deconcentration. Their perceptions and strategies are strongly influenced by the movement away from the certainties of an earlier, less ambiguous, hierarchical arrangement. Deconcentration and the relative decline of a global leader do not make global war inevitable, but they do seem to improve the probability of its occurrence, particularly if concentration in a pivotal region is happening at the same time.

The Model

In figure 1.3 we attempt to capture our perception of the interacting relationships in a broad-gauged fashion. The prerequisites for ascent and the relative decline syndrome feed directly into innovation, one of the prerequisites for ascent. Innovation is also the principal vehicle of decline. It is the return on innovative production that diminishes. It is the success generated by innovation that breeds complacency. It is innovation that diffuses, and it is the adoption of innovations customarily first generated elsewhere on which catch-up programs are largely premised.

The interrelationships among the processes listed under "Other Long-Wave Dynamics" are complicated and deserve far more attention than they have received to date. We have good empirical reasons to believe that systemic wars influence long wave-related phenomena such as prices, investment, and innovation. These relationships are portrayed as feedbacks in figure 1.3. The primary link between the long waves and systemic war, though, is less direct. Innovation, we argue, affects a state's relative economic and military positions. Infrequently, a major burst of innovation, assuming the prerequisite ingredients are present, catapults one state into a

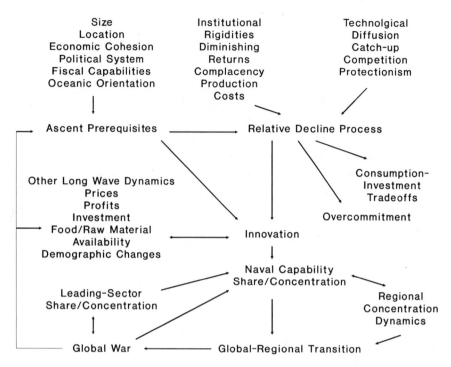

Figure 1.3 The Structural Transition Model

status of global preeminence. The relative decline syndrome works to undo the temporary era of high capability concentration. After a period of relative decline and deconcentration, in conjunction with ascent and resource concentration in a key region, systemic war erupts to resolve once again whose rules and policies will structure world politics and the manner in which the world economy functions.

Before we can proceed much further with this line of argument, we much first prepare a two-part empirical foundation. It needs to be established that there really were periods in which single states led their respective global and regional groups. To assist in validating our historical script, we need to be able to specify in advance the identities of these states and the approximate terms of their leadership. In other words, we need to demonstrate the predicted patterns of ascent and decline among the major powers of the past five hundred years. If we cannot do this, there would be little point in proceeding further. In chapter 2, therefore, we will tackle this foundational task.

A handle on rise-and-fall chronology is only a part of the foundation that needs to be laid. We also wish to relate patterns of warfare to the undulations in power concentration and deconcentration. Part of our argument is that some wars—global wars—are more important than others. As it happens, we will not always be content to confine our attention to these special wars. Our focus will depend on the nature of the hypothesis at stake. But we do need to establish the specialness of the structural consequences of global wars, so that we can focus exclusively on these consequences as justified subjects for explanation when it is theoretically appropriate to do so. We confront this task in appendix B. We have placed this discussion outside the main presentation of our argument because it represents a tangential test of one of our fundamental assumptions and because the nature of the examination is fairly technical. Readers may wish to examine the analysis in appendix B after reading chapter 2 or wait until a later time to evaluate this important tangent.

In the remainder of the book, we will focus on how and when major power warfare is related to structural change (chapters 3 and 4). Next we take a step back and ask why these structural changes occur in the first place. While there are limitations on how deeply we can pursue this question at the present time, it will help if we can at least establish a systematic relationship between our version of uneven growth and the wars examined in earlier chapters. This linkage is accomplished in chapter 5. Chapters 6, 7, and 8 focus on a popular alternative solution to the rise-and-fall puzzle—overconsumption and overextension arguments—which we regard as red herrings in the search for an understanding of the processes of relative decline. Chapter 9 reassembles the various threads of our argument and compares it with some of the other approaches available in the literature. Chapter 10 concludes by examining the question of whether the patterns of the past five hundred years or so are likely to have any relevance in the future.

2.

Tracing the Rise and Fall of Regional and Global Powers

In this analysis, leadership long cycle theory can be restricted to two sets of dynamics, one global and the other regional. Neither dynamic is viewed as a universal process. Both are conditioned by specific temporal and geographic parameters. The decade of the 1490s offers a convenient starting point for tracing the patterns of structural change that seem most important. The Western European region, in addition, has played a central role as a main arena for regional dynamics, just as European states have long dominated global processes.

Global processes focused on managing long-distance trade problems became particularly prominent after the Portuguese created an Atlantic path to the Indian Ocean. The management of intercontinental questions of political economy depends on the extent to which capabilities of global reach are concentrated in the control of the world system's lead economy. Historically, one state, the "world power," has emerged from periods of intense conflict in a position of naval and commercial-industrial preeminence. Naval power has served as one of the principal manifestations of global-reach capability. It has been, and continues to be, critical for projecting military force, for protecting commercial sea-lanes, and for denying extracontinental maneuverability to opponents. The ability to finance preeminent naval power, however, hinges in turn on grasping a commanding lead in economic innovation and reaping the profits that ensue from pioneering new ways of doing things (Modelski and Thompson 1992).

Winning a global war, a period of highly intensive struggle over whose policies will prevail in governing the global political economy, creates an unrivaled opportunity for imposing new rules or reinforcing old rules of global behavior. The world power and its allies have defeated the leader's rivals and reduced their capabilities, and at the same time the world power has improved its own economic and military capabilities.

Such opportunities come and go. The relative lead in naval power tends to decay. The returns from economic innovation peter out and frequently are not replaced by a new surge of creativity, at least in the same place. Old rivals rebuild. New rivals emerge. The coming together of these tendencies means that the leader's relative edge is gradually whittled away. The postwar concentration of global-reach capabilities, the foundations for political leadership and order, is eroded. It gives way to deconcentration and deteriorating order.

Within this context, one or more challengers to the world power's leadership will appear. The most dangerous challenger tends to be a state that either has already ascended or aspires to ascend to a dominating regional position through the development of its land power. From the perspective of the incumbent world power, regional hegemony, especially in Europe, is the first step to a direct attack on the global political economy. From the perspective of the ascending regional power, the world power, with its penchant for maintaining the status quo, is likely to thwart the prospects for further expansion. A clash becomes increasingly probable.

In the long run, then, global order is intermittent. Phases of relative order are followed by periods of relative disorder, punctuated by bouts of intensive combat to decide what type of order will be imposed. The regional processes of most interest overlap with the central global dynamic. Just as the global political economy has been characterized by successive peaks and troughs of capability concentration, so too has the European regional distribution of power.

The Global View

The leadership long cycle perspective argues that a global system emerged in the 1490s, after the Portuguese began to follow a new route for Eurasian trade. The governance of global politics, focusing primarily on the management of long-distance trade, depends on the concentration of capabilities of global reach. One state, the world power, emerges from a period of global war in a position of preeminence and with a commanding lead in these global-reach capabilities. The ability to pay for those capabilities is predicated in large part on leadership in prewar and postwar waves of economic innovation. Winning the global war and controlling a high proportion of the most valuable capabilities for global operations then enable the world power to develop policies and rules for the management of the world's economy. As the leader's capability position erodes over time, so too does its ability to supply global governance.

In distinguishing between global and regional levels of action, one must

Table 2.1 Global Wars and Their Participants

Long Cycle	Global War	Global Power Participation
1	Italian and Indian Ocean Wars, 1945–1516	Portugal + Spain + (England) vs. France
2	Spanish Wars, 1580–1608	Netherlands + England + France vs. Spain
3	Wars of the Grand Alliance, 1688–1713	Britain + Netherlands vs. France + (Spain)
4	French Revolutionary and Napoleonic Wars, 1792–1815	Britain + Russia vs. France + (Netherlands, Spain)
5	First and Second World Wars, 1914–1945	United States + Britain + Soviet Union + France vs. Germany + (Japan)

Source: Based on Modelski and Thompson 1988: 16.

Note: Global powers in parentheses are those with less than full participation during the periods indicated.

be careful to identify the set of elite actors associated with each level. Conventional lists of great or major powers mix global and regional powers. Global powers must demonstrate that they have the capability to operate over long, transoceanic distances by assembling at least a minimal naval capability (10 percent of the global capability pool). They must also demonstrate an interest in actually using their sea power beyond their local region. A navy that operates in only one sea—the Mediterranean or the Baltic, for instance—no matter how many ships it has, remains a regional power.

The global powers that historically have satisfied the minimal requirements remain a fairly small group: Portugal (1494-1580), Spain (1494-1808), England/Britain (1494-1945), France (1494-1945), the Netherlands (1579-1810), Russia/the Soviet Union/Russia (1714 to the present), the United States (1816 to the present), Germany (1871-1945), and Japan (1875-1945). To achieve the status of world power, a state's leaders must have controlled at least 50 percent of the global naval capability pool at the conclusion of one of the five global wars listed in table 2.1. Only four states have qualified: Portugal, the Netherlands, Britain, and the United States. Their principal opponents have been even fewer in number. France, Spain, and Germany have played the role of principal challenger over the past five hundred years.

Global wars are contests between two sides over whose version of world order will prevail. In this sense, they are succession struggles involving the challenger and its allies versus the incumbent world power and its allies. The successor, as often as not, is neither the challenger nor the old leader but one of the earlier world power's allies. Britain succeeded the Netherlands, and the United States succeeded Britain, in periods of global war. On only one occasion so far has a state managed to renew its global leadership status: Britain achieved this distinction in the Napoleonic Wars.

There appear to be four prerequisites for attaining the status of world power: geographic insularity, societal cohesiveness and openness, a preponderance of global-reach capability, and economic leadership (Modelski 1987). Insularity offers a number of advantages. Since borders are protected naturally, a preoccupation with land forces can be avoided. More resources are likely to be available for other activities, such as attaining global reach. Access to waterways is virtually assured. Maritime activities such as fishing, exploration, and trade are more likely to develop and to be seen as essential to economic survival. Naval protection, therefore, is more likely to receive a high priority.

The natural security advantages of insularity mean that invasion and occupation by enemies are less likely to occur. One by-product is greater cohesion and social stability. Cohesion and stability are important, because in their absence, societies tend to be preoccupied with domestic problems, leaving little in the way of time and resources for dealing with external affairs.

Naval power is one of the more important capabilities for achieving global reach. Naval power—as well as, more recently, aerospace power—has been absolutely necessary for a state to operate at the global level. Naval power is also particularly critical to global leadership. In times of war, a dominant navy is expected to exercise command of the sea. The other side's naval capability and long-distance, oceanic commerce will be either neutralized or destroyed. The home base is protected from attack, as are linkages between allies. Navies, of course, do not win global wars singlehandedly. Land forces and operations and allies with significant ground force capability are also crucial. Without a lead in naval capability, however, a state is highly unlikely to achieve global victory. That is one of the more important reasons that changes in the identity of the global leader are linked closely to shifts in the distribution of naval power. In peacetime, the preponderant navy continues to play vital roles. The need to protect the home base and sea-lanes persists. Would-be challengers are discouraged from mounting surprise attacks, and their intercontinental mobility is also severely restricted. In general, then, the lead navy bolsters the global status quo and political order (Modelski and Thompson 1988).

Leading-sector innovation has proved critical for fueling economic growth, developing elite interests in trade and global orientations, and generating the economic surplus to pay for naval power and efforts to manage global problems. Each world power is associated with two waves of innovation, one that immediately precedes and one that immediately follows a phase of global war (see table 2.2).

Table 2.2 Growth Spurts and Global Lead Industries

Growth Spurts	Global Lead Industries	Predicted Start-up Periods	Predicted High-Growth Periods
Portugal			
First	Guinea gold	1430–60	1460–94
Second	Indian spices	1492–1516	1516–40
Netherlands			
First	Baltic and Atlantic trades	1540–60	1560–88
Second	Eastern trade	1580–1609	1609–40
Britain I			
First	Amerasian trade (especially sugar)	1640–60	1660–88
Second	Amerasian trade	1688–1713	1713–40
Britain II			
First	Cotton, iron	1740–63	1763–92
Second	Railroads, steam	1792–1815	1815–50
United States			
First	Steel, chemicals, electric power	1850–73	1873–1914
Second	Auto, aviation, electronics	1914–45	1945–73

Source: Based on Modelski and Thompson 1992: 10b.

Between the fifteenth and early eighteenth centuries, the radical innovations that fueled the growth of the global leader and the world economy were associated with seaborne commerce. Toward the end of the eighteenth century, the emphasis shifted to industrial production. Whether commercial or industrial in nature, however, the waves of innovation were closely linked to global war and global leadership. The first wave made a global war more likely by accelerating uneven growth. The state whose economy was most responsible for the innovations was also the one most likely to develop the material and financial sinews of war essential to victory. Winning the global war greatly facilitated the second wave of radical innovation, which also helped underwrite a postwar phase of politico-military leadership.

Naval power, however, tends to decay. And since leading-sector innovations cluster in time and space, they are subject to long waves of prosperity and depression. The timing of the ascent of the world power and of its relative decline basically determines the rhythm of the long cycle of global leadership. A period of postwar leadership gives way to deconcentration and deteriorating order. Challengers emerge and become stronger. Thus, each successive leadership long cycle can be viewed as a four-phased process, or two processes, depending on whether one wishes to stress the dynamics of a world power's rise or decline. In table 2.3 we summarize the periodicity of these phases.

Table 2.3 Phases of the Leadership Long Cycle

Long Cycle Mode	Starting Date of Phase			
Rise:	Agenda Setting	Coalition Building	Macrodecision	Execution
Decline:	Delegitimation	Deconcentration	Global War	World Power
World Power:				
	1430	1460	1494	1516
Portugal				
	1540	1560	1580	1609
Netherlands				
	1640	1660	1688	1714
Britain				
	1740	1763	1792	1815
Britain				
	1850	1873	1914	1945
United States				
	1973	(2000)	(2030)	—

Source: Based on Modelski and Thompson 1992: 6b.

The macrodecision (global war) phase is one characterized by intense conflict over who will lead in the global system. It is also the phase that leads to a another phase, execution (world power), in which economic and military power are reconcentrated in the control of a global leader who establishes the ground rules for transoceanic transactions. The first phase of power erosion, agenda setting (delegitimation), is characterized by the development of new global problems and the raising of questions about the legitimacy of the global leader and its world order. A second phase of erosion, coalition building (deconcentration), follows. The decline of the incumbent leader accelerates as the leader falls further behind in a new upswing of growth. New coalitions at home and abroad become more likely. Serious challengers emerge and threaten to destabilize the global status quo.

The most dangerous challenger tends to be a hybrid power with mixed strategic orientations: primarily a land power with continental aspirations, it also makes some effort to acquire sea power. Signs begin to emerge of a nascent global strategic orientation, usually in direct conflict with the state's more traditional, local preoccupations. Others view victory in dominating the European continent as a first step to a direct threat to the leadership, rules, and order of the global political economy.

Yet another round of global war is triggered by a threat to the autonomy of a strategically located and prosperous zone of the global economy by an adjacent regional power. Control over the zone is interpreted as a stepping-stone to an assault on the global economy. Combat ensues among the global powers, who form alliances to decide once again who will determine policy for the global system.

The Regional View

Previous treatments of leadership long cycle theory have focused primarily on the global level, but there are good reasons to consider the intermittent intertwining of global and regional politics if we are to comprehend the etiology of systemic warfare. The principal source of our regional interpretation is Dehio (1962).[1] Dehio's approach is highly compatible with leadership long cycle theory. It is also highly complementary: while the two approaches share some common features, each one emphasizes some attributes that are treated lightly by proponents of the other approach.

The crux of Dehio's interpretation of world politics is associated with his contention that if Europe had been a closed system, some great power would eventually have succeeded in establishing absolute supremacy over the other states in the region. But the system was never entirely closed. Immediately before a would-be continental hegemon could unify the European region by coercion, counterweights emerged to deny a hegemonic victory by introducing new extraregional resources into the struggle for regional supremacy. The eastern wing of the continent supplied brute land force commanded by some form of "Oriental despotism." The western wing specialized in sea power, which was closely associated with its assumption of the principal commercial intermediary role between Europe and Asia and America. When both eastern and western counterweights operated simultaneously, they forced the aspiring regional hegemon to fight a resource-draining war on two fronts.[2]

The outcome was an intermittently renewed balance of European power as the regional system was opened to extraregional resources controlled by states on the region's main flanks. The periodicity of the balancing dynamic depended on an intermittent concentration of strength on land in the form of an aspiring regional hegemon.

France made the first bid for regional supremacy in 1494, by attacking Italy. It was resisted by Spain and then briefly by a unified Hapsburg entity led by Charles V. The second bid, this time in the name of Hapsburg regional hegemony, was stopped by a Franco-Ottoman coalition before the emergence of a functioning western maritime flank. Working in conjunction with the English, the Netherlands became the first western counterweight to Spain's bid for supremacy under Philip II.

By the middle of the seventeenth century, Spain had yielded its status as the primary continental power to a reascending France. Louis XIV's activities of the late seventeenth century ultimately threatened both the continental (regional) and the maritime (global) spheres. Another Anglo-Dutch coalition organized the first large-scale maritime encirclement of the continent and defeated the navy of the leading continental power at La Hogue in 1692. In the trough between La Hogue and Trafalgar (1805), the declining strength of the French kept the midcentury (1740s-80s) Anglo-French fighting from turning into a struggle over either continental or maritime supremacy.

The Spanish and first French ascents to continental domination and their subsequent declines were gradual, drawn-out affairs. The second French ascent, in 1792, "reared up abruptly out of the uttermost depths of the trough, only to crash down with equal abruptness" (Dehio 1962: 139). Russo-British probing and sparring along the Asian-Balkan imperial perimeter followed the exhaustion of Napoleonic France. The Russian forward momentum, frequently tentative in nature, was repeatedly checked by British containment strategies.

From Dehio's perspective, the ascending Germany of the late nineteenth century was seeking equality with other leading powers (rather than European supremacy) and an acceleration of Britain's relative economic decline. In response to a combination of commercial and naval rivalries and geographic proximity, Britain in turn identified Germany as its primary threat. The strategic circumstance of World War I combat then encouraged Germany to proceed as if it were indeed seeking regional supremacy. By the Second World War, both Germany and Japan had become more overt and ambitious in their assault on the status quo. The end of the war brought the territorial division of the losing European challenger as well as the division of the entire region into American and Soviet spheres. The European system of states and the distinctive modes of behavior associated with its functioning came to an end in 1945.

Dehio identified the principal dynamic of this system as the movement from a peak in the strength of the leading continental power through a long trough to the next peak and so on. The long troughs were characterized by leveling processes: the continental power that had earlier peaked was in gradual decline, and one or more other states were likely to be ascending. During the troughs, relative power relationships were unstable, making realignments likely. As phases of least likely resistance, the troughs provided windows of opportunity for the emergence of new land powers, and upwardly mobile aspirants were encouraged to challenge the status quo. Finally, Dehio contended, during the continental troughs, the strength of the western sea powers should be most concentrated.

Dehio's interpretation thus emphasizes the rhythms of two ongoing and dissynchronized cycles, or waves, centered on two different types of major powers: on land, the leading continental power rose and declined; at sea, the leading commercial intermediary and sea power rose and declined. For the most part, the one declined as the other peaked and vice versa.

Not only were the relative power trajectories of continental and sea powers dissynchronized with respect to one another, but they also represented totally different ways of life. The continental powers were seen as rising to regional primacy on the basis of absolute monarchies, large armies and bureaucracies, and the variable success of foreign policy strategies. Proximate adversaries were beneficial to the extent that they provided a motivation for developing military strength. In marked contrast, the maritime powers were successful in long-distance trade, to the extent that they were able to restrain their monarchies, develop large navies instead of large armies, and substitute some element of democracy for bureaucratic government. Their security depended on geographic insularity or the absence of proximate adversaries. Some type of water barrier—marshes, rivers, dikes, channels, oceans—was needed to provide protection against the predatory land powers.

As specialists in long-distance trade between different cultural regions, the maritime powers were primarily concerned with territorial and market expansion outside the European region. By contrast, the continental powers tended to be preoccupied with territorial expansion within the region. Operating on entirely different strategic vectors, maritime and continental powers, it would seem, had separate interests that were not inherently likely to conflict, at least not continually. Maritime powers had little interest in territorial expansion on the continent, and continental powers were unlikely to set the cultivation of long-distance trade as their highest priority.

Collisions over conflicting interests nevertheless occurred with impressive regularity, with the implications of achieving regional supremacy at the root of the problem. Once a continental power achieved regional supremacy, it was in an excellent position to acquire supremacy in the realm of intercontinental, maritime trade. The quest for regional supremacy invariably led would-be hegemons to seek control over adjacent sources of economic prosperity. Historically in Europe this meant attacking either northern Italy (in the late fifteenth and early sixteenth centuries) or the Low Countries. Successful expansion into these areas brought with it the promise of a quick fix for imbalances in wealth as well as significant improvements in maritime capabilities. Hence, the leading maritime power and would-be successors had strong incentives to prevent another power from achieving regional supremacy or hegemony, because that could threaten their own sphere of activities, the global economy.

Would-be regional hegemons were not always fully aware of the maritime implications of their continental stratagems, and this situation made occasional conflict with the western maritime powers even more likely. Furthermore, when the continental powers were explicitly interested in competing for control of long-distance trade, the potential for acute conflict at the regional and global levels was even greater. By contrast, collision between an aspiring regional hegemon and the counterweights on the eastern flank depended on the less subtle dynamics of mutually timed interests in expansion into the same territories.

Therefore, an aspiring regional hegemon that moved to expand toward the immediate north (the Low Countries) and toward the east, either simultaneously or sequentially, ran the risk of galvanizing resistance on both flanks. Dehio suggested that regional hegemons repeatedly made this same strategic error. Rebuffed in an unsuccessful clash with western maritime powers, continental powers would then attempt to compensate by attacking in the opposite direction. They doomed their own efforts time and again by creating the geostrategic preconditions for the extraregional interventions that would preserve the European balance of power.

Compensatory behavior is not the most compelling explanation for a consistent pattern of strategic irrationality. Dehio pointed out, however, that the maritime powers increasingly sought to contain hegemonic aspirants by encircling the European peninsula. If the leading continental power could expand to the southeast successfully, it might deal with two strategic problems with one offensive push. The maritime containment strategy could be defeated by outflanking the naval encirclement via land while also evading "the Russian colossus." But to work, this scheme required regional supremacy, a tautological assumption: it could not be a successful strategy to achieve supremacy if supremacy was assumed to be a prerequisite to success. As a result, in misconstruing its grand strategies, the aspiring hegemon often overextended itself and depleted its resources and energies.

In this fashion, the challenger to the regional and, potentially, the global status quo contributed to the maintenance of the regional balance of power by consistently developing strategies of attack that only increased the probability of failure. This sequence of events could not be repeated indefinitely: the proclivity to draw in the flanking powers and their resources concealed an important hidden cost. Each successive iteration of the balancing process further diminished the amount of power resident within the European region relative to what could be mobilized outside it.

The European regional system of states therefore had a finite life. Born in a struggle that had extinguished the autonomy of an even smaller region and the European system's prototypical predecessor, the Italian state system, it in turn was extinguished in another hegemonic struggle and replaced by a new bipolar, global system. Hence, the durability of the European regional system may have depended on a unique constellation of geohistorical factors. Would-be regional conquerors found themselves sandwiched between sea powers enriched by intercontinental trade on one flank and large reservoirs of military manpower on the other. Despite repeated attempts at achieving regional domination, challengers were unable to overwhelm the western and eastern flanks with their powerful resources. Simultaneously, and equally consistently, the continental strategies created to overcome these twin barriers to supremacy proved to be self-defeating. As a consequence, the European subsystem retained its basic pluralism and independence as long as it managed to maintain its central position in the larger system. Ultimately, however, the narrow regional stage came to be absorbed by the broader, global stage when the principal eastern and western flanking states divided the European region into their own spheres of influence.

Testing the Global and Regional Interpretations

The Hypotheses

Testing the leadership long cycle's interpretation of who the lead global actors have been since 1494 is reasonably straightforward. In table 2.3 we identify five peaks, as well as four global leaders: Portugal, the Netherlands, Britain, and the United States. Each peak is said to have occurred toward the end or immediately after a phase of global war (1494-1516, 1580-1608, 1688-1713, 1792-1815, and 1914-45). While ascent may be accelerated by wartime pressures, the relative decline of global lead actors is a gradual, protracted affair.

HYPOTHESIS 2.1: The global distribution of power historically has been characterized by a five-peaked pattern of concentration and deconcentration.

HYPOTHESIS 2.2: Waves of global concentration peak during or immediately after periods of global war and decay gradually.

Dehio also was quite specific about the shapes of the regional waves. Spain rose incrementally, peaked in 1585, and then gradually declined. France gradually rose as well, bypassing Spain by 1659-61 and peaking in 1692, before beginning a long and gradual decline in the eighteenth century. The second, revolutionary and Napoleonic rise of France was described as meteoric. Peaking just before another decisive sea battle in 1805, this wave crashed equally abruptly. Dehio described the fourth and final crest, Germany's in the first half of the twentieth century, as if it took place quite prematurely. Once World War I began, however, circumstances are said to have encouraged Germany to seek regional domination.[3] By contrast, German aspirations in World War II adhered more closely to the historical pattern of regional domination. Unlike the three earlier cases (one Spanish and two French), though, no decisive sea battle demarcated the apex of the German ascent.

A four-crested wave of regional power concentration and domination, with its delineation of peaks and troughs and waves of varying shapes certainly provides an explicit empirical focus. Yet Dehio's interpretation offers even more, arguing that each successive, would-be conqueror was in a relatively weaker position than its predecessors had been to achieve its regional objectives. Dehio proposed a metaphorical explanation for this negative trend: he said that by the eighteenth century the "outer-regions of West and East [had begun] to rob the ancient central region of light and air" (Dehio 1962: 139). In other words, the relative power potential of the European interior diminished as extra-European power potentials improved. Thus, we should expect the four-crested wave of regional power concentration to have an observable negative slope that becomes more noticeable after Louis XIV.

Finally, Dehio argued that western sea power was concentrated in the troughs of the continental power wave, although with the qualification that this was a post-Louis XIV phenomenon. Since Dehio's troughs are fairly long, the timing of the alternation of the peaks of continental and sea power is less than exact. Still, the notion of alternating peaks is quite novel. Nor is it intuitively obvious. Sea powers might peak, for example, in the process of blocking continental powers that are also peaking. Alternatively, one might not anticipate any consistent relational pattern between concentrations of the two types of power.

Yet the pattern of alternation is significant for Dehio's interpretation, for sea power becomes increasingly important to his scheme after the sixteenth century. Further, he credits declining sea power with encouraging assaults on the status quo in the twentieth century. Although this factor clearly cannot be said to have operated at constant strength from 1494 on, Dehio never made clear precisely when it became operative as an important feature.

In any event, the Dehio interpretation suggests at least three highly salient features that need to be examined empirically. We should expect to find a negatively sloped set of fluctuations in regional power distributions with four peaks, three of which are identified as occurring at 1585, 1692, and 1805. The first two waves should be gradual; the second two should be abrupt. The fourth wave should probably be the most difficult to discern. Finally, the concentration of sea (global) power, at least after 1714, should occur somewhere in between the peaks in continental (regional) power.

HYPOTHESIS 2.3: The modern European regional distribution of power historically has been characterized by a four-peaked, negatively sloped pattern of concentration and deconcentration.

Table 2.4 Basic Shifts in the Measurement of Naval Capability Concentration

Period	Indicators
1494–1654	The number of state-owned, armed sailing vessels capable of undertaking oceanic voyages
1655–1859	The number of ships of the line, subject to an escalating minimal number of guns carried to qualify as front-line fighting vessels
1860–1945	The number of first-class battleships, subject to escalating minimal attributes in ship and gun size (as in the case of pre- and post-Dreadnought battleships)
1816–1945	The level of naval expenditure, which is used to smooth the several abrupt technological changes experienced in the nineteenth and early twentieth centuries and which is given equal weight with the appropriate ship counts in a combined index
1946–93	The number of heavy or attack aircraft carriers and, after 1960, the number of nuclear attack submarines and the number of sea-based nuclear missile warheads weighted according to equivalent megatonnage (EMT) and counter military potential (CMP)—with carriers, attack submarines, EMT, and CMP given equal weight in a combined index

HYPOTHESIS 2.4: The first two waves of regional concentration, peaking in 1585 and 1692, were gradual; the last two waves, peaking in 1805 and around the First and Second World Wars, were abrupt.

HYPOTHESIS 2.5: After 1714, the concentration of global power alternates with the concentration of regional power.

Measuring Global and Regional Power

Dehio's continental powers are states that organize their resources, especially bureaucratic and military ones, to advance territorial, economic, and security interests in their roughly immediate neighborhoods. Thus, although continental or regional powers may have some interest in sea power, their primary orientation remains fixed on adjacent territorial concerns. One expects regional powers to have large armies and comparatively smaller navies, just as one typically associates states that are primarily maritime or global in their orientations with large navies and small armies. Therefore, a primary emphasis on developing armies should suffice as an indicator for comparing the relative strength of regional powers. Similarly, a primary emphasis on developing navies is used for comparing the relative strength of global powers.

There is already ample access to serial data on sea power concentration.

Table 2.5 Global and European Regional Powers

Global Powers	European Regional Powers
Portugal (1494–1580)	Spain (1490s–1800)*
Spain (1494–1808)	England/Britain (1490s–1945)
England/Britain (1494–1945)	France (1490s–1945)
France (1494–1945)	Austria (1490s–1918)*
Netherlands (1579–1810)	Netherlands (1590s–1800)
Russia/USSR (1714–)	Sweden (1590s–1809)
United States (1816–)	Prussia/Germany (1640s–1945)
Germany (1871–1945)	Italy (1860s–1943)
Japan (1875–1945)	

*Between 1520 and 1555, Spain and Austria were merged in a united Hapsburg identity.

Table 2.4 lists the changing indicators used by Modelski and Thompson (1988) to develop a series measuring the concentration of naval capability among global powers. Basically, the argument is that the measurement principles must shift with evolving changes in naval practice and technology. Armed but otherwise unspecialized vessels gave way to ships of the line, which in turn were replaced by iron and steel battleships. More recently, the battleship was superseded by aircraft carriers and nuclear submarines as first-line combat ships.

What is needed is a similar series for regional power distributions. The most direct and probably the most time-honored way to measure armies is to count personnel. Army size need not be correlated with efficiency, combat readiness, élan, or the general quality of the soldiers. Nor need we assume that a large army can overwhelm a technologically superior, if less numerous, foe. Thus, army size is admittedly a crude indicator, but it does seem to correspond closely to the notion of continental power.

The major regional and global powers that form the pools for calculating the leader's shares, listed in table 2.5, overlap to some extent. As noted earlier in this chapter, to qualify as a global power, a state must possess a minimum share of the world's naval capabilities (10 percent of total global power warships) and demonstrate oceangoing activity, as opposed to regional sea or coastal defense activities. If these thresholds were attained between periods of global war, the status is backdated to the conclusion of the preceding global war. The global power status is retained until the state is defeated or exhausted in global war and no longer qualifies as a global power in the post-global war era.

These global power membership rules are considered liberal, in the sense that some states are introduced earlier and others retained longer than might normally be expected. We have done this to minimize the amount of disturbance to the distribution of capabilities introduced by entrance and exit from the elite. When states are introduced relatively early—such as, most obviously, in the case of the United States (1816)—their capability shares are so small that the weight of their presence in the data set, as in real life, is minimal. Only as their foreign policy ambitions increase should we expect to see their capability shares begin to register.

The same philosophy but a different approach was used in developing the regional list. For the most part, Levy's (1983) guidelines on identifying great powers have been followed, although in a few cases, again to minimize the impact of entrance, we have granted regional elite status earlier than might be considered conventional. We have also imposed a Western European location as an additional requirement. Here we are assuming that Western Europe became the world system's principal region and source of regional challengers between 1494 and 1945. Hence, the United States and Japan are in the global list but not in the regional list.[4]

While these exclusions from the regional list should not be controversial, two others (the Ottoman Empire and Russia/USSR) may be more so. There are four reasons for their omission. The most important one is theoretical. In our framework, these two states served as the external, eastern balancers. Occasionally they chose to intervene in the affairs of Western Europe.[5] They were able to intervene because they could assemble very large armies drawn from manpower resident outside the region. As states located on the fringe of Europe, they also had more degrees of freedom in choosing when to become involved in Western Europe. They also had important and diverting interests in other regions of Eurasia and Africa. Therefore, the second reason for omission is an operational one. We do not regard the Ottoman Empire and Russia/USSR as indigenous members of the Western European region.

A third reason is a matter of comparability. The Ottomans in the fifteenth and sixteenth centuries, and the Russians thereafter, were quite capable of putting together armies larger than any of those of the Western European states. Even so, the numbers mobilized were always misleading. For much of the period with which we are concerned—certainly for the first half of it—the Ottoman and Russian armies represented large hordes of fighting men who were often poorly armed and organized. Rarely were the Ottoman and Russian leaders able to mobilize and place in the field many of the men who might be counted as their troops. Both imperial states also had significant garrison obligations and non-European security concerns that further reduced the number of men available for combat. As a consequence, it would be awkward to compare Ottoman and Russian army sizes with their Western European counterparts, who experienced organizational modernization much earlier.

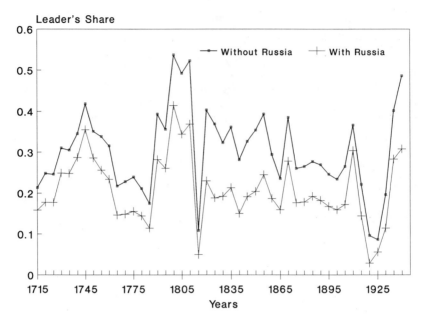

Figure 2.1 Regional Army Concentration in Western Europe

Finally, the fourth reason is a matter of convenience. We have no serial information on sixteenth-century Ottoman army sizes. Even if we wanted to include Ottoman data, we would be hard pressed to do so.[6] We do have a full series of Russian/Soviet army data, but anyone who insists that Russia/USSR must be considered a full member of the Western European region would be forced to discount systematically Russian army sizes. It is not clear what the size of the discount should be, and for that matter, it is no more clear whether one discount would work equally well in the eighteenth, nineteenth, and twentieth centuries.[7]

In the absence of some discounting mechanism, the Russian numbers tend to overwhelm the size of Western European armies, even though the same outcome was rarely realized on many European battlefields. Nonetheless, it is not clear that the exclusion of Russian/Soviet data at the regional level is as critical as one might imagine. In figure 2.1 we plot two versions of the regional leader's share index between 1715, the point at which Russian army data might begin to be considered if one were so inclined, and 1944. One series includes the Russian data in the total; the other excludes it. Visually, the two series look very much alike. Not surprisingly, they are highly correlated ($\underline{r}$ = 0.942). Excluding the Russian data, therefore, need not pose too great a threat to the validity of analyses calculating regional leader shares.

Table 2.6 Peaks in Global Power

| Leading | Peaks | |
Global Power	Expected	Observed
1 Portugal	after 1516	1510s
2 Netherlands	after 1608	1610s
3 Britain	after 1713	1720s
4 Britain	after 1815	1820s
5 United States	after 1945	1950s

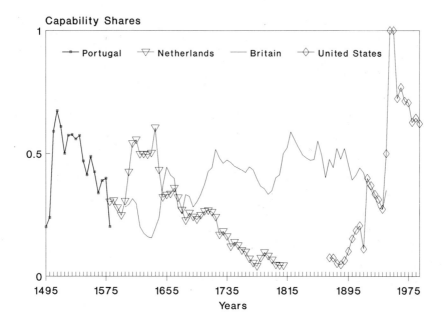

Figure 2.2 Successive Global Leaders

Inevitably, more data are available for some armies than for others. The worst case is the Ottoman Empire, for which little specific information on army size exists. In general, data availability improves after the sixteenth century and is best for the most prominent land powers (France and Prussia/Germany). The availability of data on states such as the Netherlands, Sweden, Austria, and Russia varies from period to period; for some periods there is very little data. In these cases, barring bouts of warfare, army size is assumed to be fairly stable between the better documented periods.

The limitations of the available information base preclude providing data for each year from the 1490s on. Rather, observations encompassing five-year intervals (for example, 1490-94, 1494-99) are about the best that can be expected. The army data, the sources from which they have been culled, and some additional details on collection procedures appear in appendix A.

Analyzing the Propositions

Figure 2.2 provides information necessary to evaluate the first two hypotheses presented above. The naval shares of Portugal, the Netherlands, Britain, and the United States are plotted for five-year intervals beginning in 1490-1494 and ending in 1985-1989. Hypothesis 2.1 predicts five peaks of concentration, and that is the pattern delineated in figure 2.2. Each of the four specified actors listed in table 2.6 peak when they are predicted to do so: Portugal in the 1510s, the Netherlands in the 1610s (although there is a brief spike in the early 1640s attributable to the destruction of the Spanish fleet at the 1639 battle of Downs), Britain in the 1720s and 1820s, and the United States in the 1950s. Finally, each of the decline trajectories are fairly protracted. Certainly none crash abruptly.

But what of the naval fortunes of Spain and France? Both of these states are popularly thought to have exercised considerable naval power to defend and expand their far-flung territorial empires. How did their shares compare with the designated global leaders? Figure 2.3 helps to answer this question by plotting their shares and Germany's over most of the same period covered in figure 2.2. Spain and France each enjoyed one brief burst of naval leadership; Germany had none. Spain's burst occurred after its absorption of Portugal and during a phase of global warfare. It had little in the way of state naval resources (other than Mediterranean galleys) before the 1580s. Nor did Spain's naval lead endure beyond a short window of global combat. France's naval story is similar. Its one real claim to naval leadership occurred briefly in the years just before the outbreak of global war in 1688. Its naval forces fared no better in the ensuing wars of 1688-1713 than did Spain's in the preceding global war. Making matters even more asymmetrical at sea, both states in their respective centuries of challenge also had to contend with the same imposing maritime coalition of England and the Netherlands in global wartime.

In figure 2.4 we plot data for the first two of Dehio's propositions. The proportional army sizes of Spain, France, and Prussia/Germany are plotted for five-year intervals beginning in 1490-94 and ending in 1940-44. Information on Prussia before 1840 is not plotted, solely to aid in the interpretation of the figure. We are looking for four crests at about Dehio's peaks, with each successive peak lower than the one that preceded it. The plot of the first forty years in the figure indicates some oscillation of position between France and Spain, with Spain's relative position definitively passing France's in the first half of the 1530s.

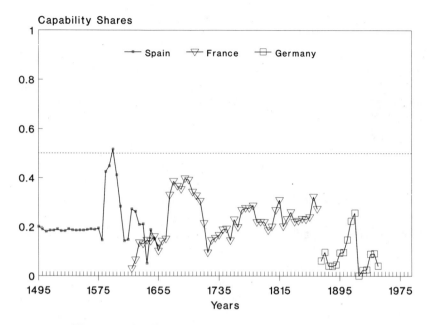

Figure 2.3 Sea Power Standings of the Regional Leaders

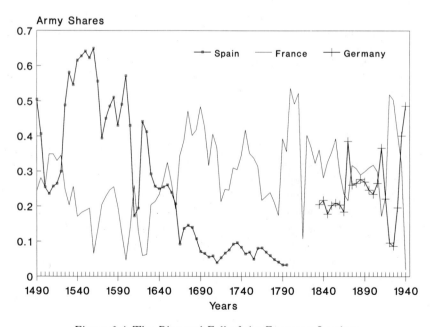

Figure 2.4 The Rise and Fall of the European Leaders

The first peak in the series, that of Spain, is reached in the late 1560s. Spanish decline then continued more or less through 1800. The rate of decline was slow until the early 1600s. What appears to be an early French gain in the interval 1610-14 actually reflects a short-term, rapid demobilization on the part of the Spanish during the Dutch-Spanish truce of 1609-21. France's upward trajectory genuinely intercepts the Spanish downward trajectory about 1645-49.

A second peak is discernible at 1690-94. It too is followed by a drawn-out process of decline. Whereas the Spanish decline essentially moved steadily downward, the equally prolonged French decline was interrupted by a rally in the mid-eighteenth century that peaked at 1745-49. This peak is, however, noticeably lower than the first French peak and the last one at 1800-1804 in the midst of the French Revolution and the Napoleonic Wars. As predicted, the last French peak was abrupt and brief.

The second half of the nineteenth century and the first half of the twentieth are characterized by an oscillation between France and Germany. Germany first passed France, though not decisively, in relative army size during the Franco-Prussian War (1870-71). German positional passage is depicted as occurring again in both of the world wars of the twentieth century. Not shown in figure 2.4 are the other major states both within and outside of the region. Their inclusion would demonstrate that the positional rivalries of this period were more complex than the simpler Hapsburg-Valois feud and certainly more complicated than the continental seesaw between France and Germany shown in the figure.

Nevertheless, figure 2.4 illustrates a series of wavelike regional transitions that closely accords with the expectations set by the Dehio perspective and hypothesis 2.3. Although the proportional army size peaks delineated in table 2.7 do not always coincide with the predicted years, they do fall quite close (always within two decades) to the critical sea battles used by Dehio as peak markers. The identity of the states and the shapes of their waves are predicted well. So too is the roughly negative trend in the height of the wave peaks (hypothesis 2.4). Yet it should be kept in mind that the third and fifth peaks that interrupt the pattern were highly episodic in nature. The third peak (at a proportion of 0.537) is higher than the second (0.484). The fourth peak (0.366) is the lowest of the set. The fifth peak (0.486) is slightly higher than the second peak (0.484). So the overall negative trend, practically guaranteed by the very high first peak (0.649) is not linear. Even so, Dehio's first two predictions are supported by the fluctuations in regional power as measured by army size.

Figure 2.5 is useful for evaluating the third Dehio prediction of alternating concentrations in regional and global power after 1714. Two chronological series, one for regional power and one for global power, are plotted here.

Table 2.7 Peaks and Transitions in Regional Power

Leading Regional Power	Dehio Peak	Observed Peak	Dehio Transition	Observed Transition
1 Spain	1585	1560–64 (0.649)	1659–61	1645–49
2 France I	1692	1690–94 (0.484)	N.A.	N.A.
3 France II	1805	1800–1804 (0.537)	Not specified	1870–74
4 Germany	WW I/ WW II	1910–14 1940–44 (0.366/0.486)	N.A.	N.A.

Note: Dehio 1962 is the source of the peak and transition predictions. The numbers in parentheses in the third column represent the highest army proportional share achieved by the leading regional powers during the period indicated.

The regional power series splices together the Spanish series (1490s-1630s), the French series (1640s-1860s), and the German series (1870s-1940s). The global power series splices together naval power proportions controlled by each century's leading maritime power: Portugal (1490s-1575), the Netherlands (1580-1675), Britain (1680-1945), and the United States (1945-).[8]

A Portuguese sea-power wave crested first in the early 1500s and was overlapped by the Spanish continental-power crest of the mid-1500s. The Dutch sea-power peak occurred about 1615, or about six decades after the Spanish continental peak. The Spanish remobilized their troop strength for the Thirty Years' War but failed to alter their essentially downward trajectory. The French regional position peaked in the 1690s, some six or seven decades after the Dutch maritime peak. This was followed by the first British sea-power peak in 1720, certainly a time of trough for regional power concentration. Skipping over the moderate French rally of the mid-eighteenth century as something less than a genuine peak, we find that the next two waves occurred close together.

After a prolonged period of gradual decline in maritime capability concentration, the first German crest of the twentieth century failed to surpass or even meet the declining British position at sea. The World War II peak, however, more closely resembles the Spanish and French peaks observed earlier. A fifth global power concentration peak, based on the U.S. lead after World War II, coincided with the German collapse.

Taken together, then, the navy and army distribution data, however conceptualized, strongly support Dehio's third proposition (hypothesis 2.5):

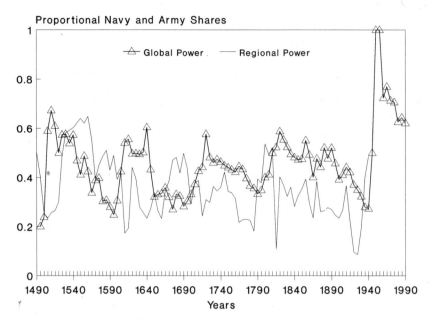

Figure 2.5 Regional and Global Concentration

the rhythms of regional and global power are not in phase with one another. Rather, a general pattern of alternation more or less characterizes the entire period. After the first pair of Iberian waves, global power concentration occurred immediately after the defeat of the hegemonic aspirations of the leading regional power. After a period of global power decay, a new regional source of threat emerged, and the process repeated itself. Hence, while the regional and global power concentration peaks did not coincide, this finding does not mean that the timing of the respective serial peaks is unrelated. A regional threat appears to have encouraged the reconcentration of global power; global power deconcentration, in turn, appears to have encouraged regional power challenges.[9] The only element of Dehio's argument that is not supported is his qualifier about Louis XIV. The data suggest that this alternation pattern preceded the demise of the Sun King by one hundred years.

This chapter has established the first leg of our empirical foundation. We know who led in the global and Western European region, and we know when they were in the lead and when they were in decline. We also have some reasons to believe that global and regional structural dynamics were intertwined at least on an intermittent basis.

If we have the right actors, do we also have the right wars? If either focus is misplaced, there will be room for substantial analytical error. This second foundational leg, why global wars are singled out as especially significant in this story, is established and justified in appendix B. Readers are invited to consider the evidence presented there at this time, particularly if they have doubts about our theoretical emphasis on global wars.

In combination, this chapter and appendix B lay the groundwork for the rest of our explanation of the political economy of ascent, decline, and war in world politics. Chapter 2 has focused on justifying the attention we place on movement in and out of leadership circles. Appendix B examines whether we are right to claim that our list of special wars is more consequential, structurally speaking, than other possible combinations of major bloodletting exercises. Given these justifications of the biases we display openly in giving more attention to some actors and some wars and less to others, it is time to move on to relating structural transition and major power warfare—the principal concerns of chapters 3 and 4.

3.

Global and Regional Transitions

In chapter 2 we argued that alternating concentrations of power at the central regional and global levels have characterized modern world politics. Spain, France, and Germany were regional leaders. Portugal, the Netherlands, Britain, and the United States were successive global leaders. Is it purely a coincidence that these same states tended to fight one another in some of the bloodiest wars of the modern era? We think not. On the contrary, we should be able to use the leadership identifications and transitions discussed previously to anticipate when wars between these leaders are most likely to occur.

One explanation for why transitions should be expected to lead to war is provided by the power transition model (Organski 1958; Organski and Kugler 1980). We propose to co-opt this model, with some modifications, and integrate it within the leadership long cycle framework. The compatibility is quite high in the abstract sense. Power transition arguments emphasize the destabilizing and conflictual implications of a challenger catching up to a declining leader. As the transition is accomplished—that is, when the dissatisfied challenger has caught up to, matched, or balanced its capabilities with those of its once dominant foe—war between a rising challenger and a declining leader is most probable.

In this chapter, we first summarize briefly the power transition model and then discuss how we propose to adapt it to our problem. Much of the chapter, though, is devoted to testing the utility of power transition expectations. Just how helpful is information on ascent and decline in predicting warfare? We find that when we impose our regional and global leadership criteria, the outcome is quite encouraging. Power transitions are not sufficient factors, but they do approach the status of necessary preconditions for the outbreak of war between leaders.

The Power Transition Model

The power transition model described by Organski and Kugler (1980) has two major features. First, systemic stratification is vital to the model. The focus is restricted to major or great powers that are divided into two main groups. One group, the powerful and satisfied, is led by the system's dominant state. This group is the primary beneficiary of the allocation of privileges by the prevailing world order; indeed, it was in all likelihood present at the creation of the order. The dominant state is not only the most powerful great power, but it is also the chief architect and beneficiary of the systemic status quo. Members of the other group, the powerful and dissatisfied, feel that they receive less than their fair or proportional share of the available benefits. One reason for the discrepancy between what is received and what is deserved is that dissatisfied great powers are likely to emerge as major competitors only after the creation of the prevailing world order. The established beneficiaries are reluctant to surrender part of their privileges to newly arrived and arriving powers, despite shifts in the relative positions of the great powers.

The second major feature of the model is its central dynamic of structural change. Position in the system is determined by relative power that hinges on socioeconomic and political development. Uneven rates of domestic growth will enable some great power to overtake and surpass other great powers. The most dangerous situation occurs when a powerful, dissatisfied great power overtakes the leader of the powerful and satisfied group. When the dominant state and its principal challenger have roughly equal power, the structural incentives encourage the outbreak of a major war. Each side can hardly overlook the dramatic narrowing of the gap in respective capabilities. The challenger will be encouraged to attack in order to accelerate the opportunity to change the rules of the game in its own favor. The once dominant state will seek to suppress the challenger's ascent before it is too late. Moreover, the more quickly this dangerous window of equality appears, the more destabilizing is the effect. The less expected it is, the more difficulties decision makers will have in dealing with its implications once it occurs.

Organski and Kugler have summarized their own argument:

The mechanisms that make for major wars can be simply summed up. The fundamental problem that sets the whole system sliding almost irretrievably toward war is the differences in rates of growth among the great powers and, of particular importance, the differences in rates between the dominant nation and the challenger that permit the latter to overtake the former in power. It is the leapfrogging that destabilizes the system. . . . Finally, this destabilization and the ensuing conflict between giants act as a magnet, bringing into war all the major powers in the system, dependent as they are on the order established by their leaders for what they already have, or for what they hope to gain in the future if they upset the existing order. [1980: 61-62]

While this transition model can be sketched succinctly, testing the model is a less straightforward proposition. Organski and Kugler (1980) tested their model for the 1860-1970 era. Others have followed their lead, while often criticizing the 1980 procedures for various reasons. But we need not dwell on the particulars of this debate.[1] Suffice it to say that a leadership long cycle interpretation suggests a distinctively different approach to the question of power transition.

A New Test of the Transition Process

We begin by first establishing which state occupies the peak of the global system's power stratification and which state is the leading challenger among a set of regional powers, predominantly land powers. The principal question is thus whether, or to what extent, conflict becomes more likely as the regional challenger overtakes the declining global power.

Hypotheses and Indicators

The expectations associated with the leadership long cycle interpretation of modern world politics lead to several separate tests of the explanatory and predictive power of the power transition hypothesis. Specifically, the hypotheses are:

HYPOTHESIS 3.1: Wars, especially global wars, are more likely when a regional leader catches up to and passes a declining global leader.

HYPOTHESIS 3.2: Wars are more likely when a new regional leader catches up to and passes a declining regional leader.

HYPOTHESIS 3.3: Wars are more likely when a new global leader catches up to and passes a declining global leader.

The analysis of these hypotheses depends on several assumptions or auxiliary rules of procedure. The temporal unit of analysis is the five-year interval, beginning in 1490-94. The examinations involve ascertaining for each pertinent dyad and each five-year interval whether one state's capability position overtook another's and whether war was initiated.[2] Levy's book *War in the Modern Great Power System, 1495-1975* (1983) is the primary source used to determine the timing of the initiation of wars.

Five-year intervals in which war begun in an earlier interval was ongoing are excluded from the analysis. Following the convention used in the Organ-

Table 3.1 Wars Involving Regional and Global Transitional Dyads

Period of Warfare	Participants
1494–97	Spain vs. France
1501–04	Spain vs. France
1511–14	Spain vs. France
1515	Spain vs. France
1521–26	Spain vs. France
1526–29	Spain vs. France
1536–38	Spain vs. France
1542–44	Spain vs. France
1552–59	Spain vs. France
1580–1608	Spain vs. Portugal (1580), France (1589–98), Netherlands
1625–30	Spain vs. France
1635–48	Spain vs. France
1648–59	Spain vs. France
1652–54	England vs. Netherlands
1665–67	England vs. Netherlands
1667–68	Spain vs. France
1672–78	England (1672–74), France vs. Netherlands
1682–83	Spain vs. France
1688–1713	Netherlands vs. France
1741–48	Britain vs. France
1755–63	Britain vs. France
1778–83	Britain vs. France
1792–1815	Britain vs. France
1870–71	France vs. Germany
1914–18	Britain, France vs. Germany
1939–45	Britain, France (1939–40) vs. Germany

Note: The list of participants is selective. Participants essentially peripheral to the hypotheses are not listed.

ski and Kugler study and in most power transition studies, overtaking requires that one state catch up, within at least 20 percent, to the other state's capability position. Capability positions are measured either by relative army (regional) size or by relative navy (global) size, depending on the primary strategic orientation of the state and the hypothesis involved. Given the nature of the hypotheses, the actor focus is highly selective. Only regional and global leaders are pertinent, even though "leaders" are identified by their proportional share of the pooled army or navy capabilities.

The identity of these global and regional leaders is stipulated in part on the basis of our theoretical interpretation of world politics, rather than a simple determination of which state has the largest capability share at any given moment. To attain the status of global leader (Portugal, 1494-1580; the Netherlands, 1609-1713; Britain, 1714-1945; and the United States, 1945 to the present), a world power is required to emerge as the winner of a global war, in possession of 50 percent or more of global power naval capabilities (Modelski and Thompson 1988). The regional leaders in Western Europe have been Spain (1494-1644), France (1645-1870), and Germany (1871-1945). The end of each period of leadership is determined by the point at which the leader's share of regional army capabilities was eclipsed by that of the next regional leader. Once the leadership pool is identified, it is then possible to select the wars with the pertinent participants. Table 3.1 lists the wars we will examine in this chapter.

The reader will recall that one of our working assumptions is that we can exclude Russian army data from the Western European pool without grossly distorting the subsequent analysis. Changing the nature of the regional share scores could affect some of the transitional calculations. Exempt from this possible threat are the transitions between global powers and the global-regional transitions before 1715, the point at which Russian data would be introduced with a different identification of the Western European region. Transitions between regional powers would not be substantively affected either, at least as long as one did not insist that Russia became the regional leader. The scores of the regional powers at their respective points of transition would simply be lower than they are under the current assumptions. That leaves two global-regional confrontations that might be affected in some way: Britain-France and Britain-Germany. The transitional coding associated with the first dyadic antagonism is not affected by reducing the French capability share. Only one of the twenty-three observations for the British-German dyad is influenced. The one five-year interval affected by the decision on Russia's location will be noted in the section on data analysis.

It is also true that relying exclusively on measures of military clout does constitute some movement away from the initial Organski and Kugler emphasis on "power potential." Unlike economic indices, military indicators are more apt to demonstrate manifested capabilities, as opposed to capabilities that need to be transformed somehow into military capabilities for war purposes. In this respect, the logic of ascending powers' waiting until they had achieved something like battlefield equivalency with their opponents presumably is more likely to be realized in the historical record. But using a five-year interval, rather than the more customary twenty-year interval, restores to the examination a strongly conservative flavor. The army-navy distinction also corresponds well to the types of distinctions being made about land-regional and maritime-global actors and their theaters of operation.

Another way of looking at this question of indicator validity is to ask

Table 3.2 Changes in Major Power Population Size in Western Europe (in millions)

Year	France	Spain	Sweden	Austria	England	Portugal	Netherlands	Prussia/ Germany	Italy	Total
1500	12.0	6.5	0.8	7.0	4.6	1.3				32.2
1550	14.0	20.0	0.9		5.0	1.6				41.5
1600	16.0	10.5	1.0	8.0	5.5		1.5			42.5
1650	18.0	7.5	1.3	7.0	6.8		2.0			42.6
1700	20.0	8.0	1.5	11.0	8.3		2.0	1.8		52.6
1750	22.0	9.5	2.0	15.0	10.3		2.0	3.8		64.6
1800	29.0	11.5	2.5	24.0	16.0		2.0	9.0		94.0
1850	36.0			35.0	27.5			15.5	25.0	139.0
1900	41.0			46.0	42.0			57.0	34.0	220.0

Proportional Shifts among the Main Rivals
(Percentage of Major Power Population)

Year	France	Spain	Prussia/Germany
1500	37.3	20.2	
1550	33.7	48.2	
1600	37.6	24.7	
1650	42.3	17.6	
1700	38.0	15.2	3.4
1750	34.1	14.7	5.9
1800	30.9	12.2	9.6
1850	25.9		11.2
1900	18.6		25.9

Source: McEvedy and Jones 1978.

Note: Population data are given only for periods of major power status.

whether different states would appear to be preeminent in Western Europe if a different index was used. Table 3.2 lists population size information—the one possible alternative index for encompassing so many centuries—for the major Western European states. We should not expect to find exactly the same leadership intervals, since populations need to be mobilized for military purposes and there is no reason to anticipate that all states of the same size are likely to mobilize similar proportions of their populations. Military participation ratios are a function of such variables as the nature of perceived threats, the extent of foreign policy ambitions, and the ability of the economy to sustain armed forces. These factors will vary from country to country and time to time.

Still, we should expect to find some relationship between population and army size. Large populations should be able to produce and sustain large armies. To the extent that soldiers are used for maintaining domestic order, large populations will require large numbers of troops. Also, to the extent

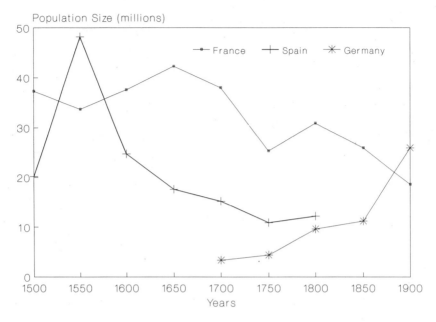

Figure 3.1 Population Shifts among the Main European Rivals

that armed forces are required to expand state boundaries to encompass large numbers of people, a correlation between army and population can be anticipated.

Both table 3.2 and figure 3.1 support these expectations. Spain, because of the temporary unification of the Hapsburg branches, assumed the population lead in the mid-sixteenth century, only to surrender that position once more to the French. France led in Western European population size from the late sixteenth century through the first half or so of the nineteenth century. After 1871 a united Germany assumed the lead. Each of these shifts in population predominance are reflected in roughly similar shifts, subject to varying lags, in army predominance. This finding would seem to suggest that a reliance upon army size as the sole index of regional leadership, while it may greatly oversimplify the nature of regional predominance, does not distort too much the complexities of changing power distributions within Western Europe.

Data Analysis

Table 3.3 and figures 3.2, 3.3, 3.4, and 3.5 portray the outcome for the testing of hypothesis 3.1 by exploring the relationship between global-regional transitions and global wars. Four trials are involved: Spain versus Portugal, France versus the Netherlands, France versus Britain, and Ger-

Table 3.3 Global-Regional Power Transitions

	Equal/Unequal, No Overtaking	Equal and Overtaking			Equal/Unequal, No Overtaking	Equal and Overtaking
No War	48 (90.6%)	8 (66.7%)		No War	42 (91.3%)	2 (33.3%)
War	5 (9.4%)	4 (33.3%)		War	4 (8.7%)	4 (66.7%)

Dyads: Spain-Portugal (1520–80), France-Netherlands (1610–89), France-Britain (1715–94), and Germany-Britain (1820–1939)

Cramer's $\underline{V}$ = 0.262*
($\underline{N}$ = 65)

Dyads: France-Netherlands (1610–89), France-Britain (1715–94), and Germany-Britain (1820–1939)

Cramer's $\underline{V}$ = 0.522*
($\underline{N}$ = 52)

*Statistically significant at the .05 level.

Note: Each five-year interval within the larger dyadic intervals specified above is coded for the occurrence of dyadic transition and the outbreak of war.

many versus Britain. Table 3.3 actually contains two contingency tables. The first table encompasses all four cases; the second table drops the Spanish-Portuguese dyad from consideration. The effect of eliminating the sixteenth-century case is fairly dramatic. The first table reflects a significant but moderate association between war and overtaking behavior. The second indicates a much stronger association.

The Portuguese-Spanish interaction pattern in the early sixteenth century was fairly distinctive. The long history of conflict between Portugal and Castile culminated in some respects in a brief war in the 1470s over the possession of colonial territory. What is most distinctive about the Iberian record was the agreement by the two parties essentially to divide the world between them with papal legitimation. The Portuguese sphere was centered on Brazil, Africa, and most of coastal Asia. The Spanish sphere extended from Latin America to the Philippines. With occasional deviations, the separate sphere arrangement worked reasonably well—no doubt due in part to the different principles on which Portugal and Spain operated. The Portuguese were interested primarily in a crude form of global commerce; the Spanish specialized in territorial control and extractive forms of exploitation.[3] If both states had been genuine maritime powers, the history of their interaction in the sixteenth century might have more closely resembled that of Venice and Genoa in earlier centuries.

A second dimension associated with the Iberian dyad is that there were

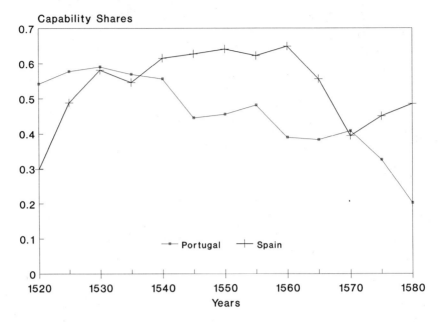

Figure 3.2 Portugal versus Spain, 1520s–1580s

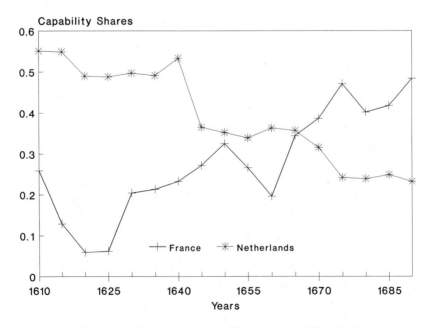

Figure 3.3 France versus the Netherlands, 1610s–1690s

really two Spains in the sixteenth century. The first one was part of the unified Hapsburg drive for European dominance. The second one, most closely identified with Philip II, retained continental aspirations while also posing more direct threats to maritime interests, as represented by the increased value of American gold and silver, the Dutch Revolt, the absorption of Portugal, and the Spanish Armadas sent against England. It may indeed be inaccurate to regard Spain as a single actor between the 1520s and the 1580s, as portrayed in figure 3.2. In any event, it is clear that hypothesis 3.1 mispredicts the initial Spanish overtaking in the 1530s and the conquest of Portugal in 1580.

Hypothesis 3.1 does much better in handling the cases involving France and Germany. Figure 3.3, portraying the relative capability shares of France and the Netherlands, shows a near miss in the 1650s, due in part to the rapid increase in English naval expansion after its civil war (and thus a decline in the Dutch relative share). But the most obvious global-regional transition in figure 3.3 occurs in the 1660s, when France and the Netherlands were at war.

Figure 3.4, depicting Britain versus France, resembles figure 3.3, in that there are two discernible periods of overtaking. In the 1740s the French regional position moved toward the British global position but did not quite succeed in overtaking it. The second event took place in the first half of the 1790s, as the French Revolution evolved into global war. Unlike the French-Dutch outcome, though, both of the French-British overtaking periods were associated with the outbreak of war.

In figure 3.5, we see that the first noticeable movement toward convergence of the German and British positions, in the 1870s, failed to qualify as an overtaking according to the 80 percent threshold rule. The World War I case does qualify, even though the episode fell short of a full transition. Only in the late 1930s did the German regional position finally surpass the declining British global position. Again, both cases of overtaking are linked to bouts of major power warfare centering at least initially on the leading regional and global powers.

Hypothesis 3.1, which matches regional challengers and declining global leaders, fares quite well after the sixteenth century. Yet there is at least one possible threat to the validity of our approach. A skeptic might say that our matching of relative naval and army positions overlooks the possibility that we are simply capitalizing on what regional challengers do when they attempt to overtake global leaders. Not only do they build up their armies, but they also expand their naval fleets. While we saw in chapter 2 that there are limits to the extent of naval expansions, the possibility remains that challengers do not simply overtake declining global leaders. What they do instead is create the decline or its appearance by increasing the size of the

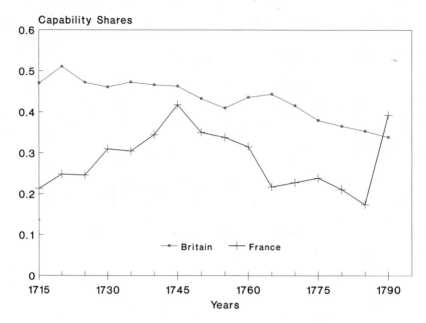

Figure 3.4 Britain versus France, 1710s–1790s

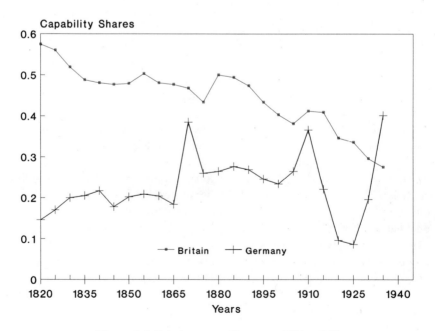

Figure 3.5 Britain versus Germany, 1820s–1940s

Table 3.4 Power Transitions Based on Proportional and Absolute Indices

Proportional Capability Indices	Absolute Capability Indices
Portugal-Spain	
1525–29	
1530–34	1530–34
1535–39	
1540–44	
	1565–69*
1570–74	
1575–79	1575–79
Netherlands-France	
1650–54	1650–54
1665–69	
1670–74	
Britain-France	
	1745–49**
1790–94	1790–94
Britain-Germany	
1910–14	
1935–39	1935–39

*The 1565–69 interval technically represents an "ascending" global leader passing a "declining" regional leader, due to Spain's demobilization from its peak efforts under Charles V. It should not be viewed as a genuine transition interval.

**The 1745–49 interval is coded as an overtaking interval in the proportional indices examination, but it is also a period of war and therefore excluded from the analysis.

naval capability pool. Of course, this still constitutes a relative capability decline for the global leader. But if the challenger's actions alone are primarily responsible for the global leader's decline, then our interpretation of the context of transition struggles and the history of world politics would require considerable adjustment. We could no longer argue, for instance, that global decline seems to encourage regional ascent. The reverse assertion would be more accurate: regional ascent creates global decline.

There are several ways we might test this possible validity threat. The simplest way is to redo our examination using absolute army size and the absolute number of warships possessed respectively by the regional challenger and the global leader.[4] This sort of test introduces major problems of metric comparison (How many troops equal a warship?), yet it removes the possibility that unexamined challenger behavior is creating the appearance of global leadership decline. The question then becomes one of whether we continue to observe the same points of transition after substantially altering the measurement approach.

Figure 3.6 Portugal versus Spain in the Absolute Mode

Table 3.4 summarizes the contrasting outcomes associated with proportional and absolute indices. Figures 3.6, 3.7, 3.8, and 3.9 illustrate each of the four cases employing absolute indices. Ironically, the absolute indices provide even more support for hypothesis 3.1 than do the relative indices. The absolute indices yield six transition points. With the proportional capability indices, it was possible to use an 80 percent equivalency threshold. With the absolute capability indices, the same equivalency criteria cannot be used unless the absolute scores are converted to some common metric. Such a conversion could be attempted, but a visual examination of figures 3.6-3.9 suggest that such a procedure is not really necessary. Most of the transitions are clearly demarcated. The one exception is 1910-14. The German capability line approaches the British line but fails to cross it.[5]

Aside from the World War I exception, which is actually less troublesome than it might otherwise be, since we indicated in chapter 2 that World War I is a special case in our interpretation, and the two other transitions that are ruled as noncountable (the 1565-69 one is a temporary fluke that is not a genuine period of transition, and the other, 1745-49, is an interval of ongoing war), the absolute indices create an analytical outcome in which the ratio between periods of overtaking that break out in war as opposed to those that do not is 3:3 (50 percent versus 50 percent) for all four cases and 1:3 (25 percent versus 75 percent) if the Portuguese-Spanish case is dropped. Since the nonovertaking

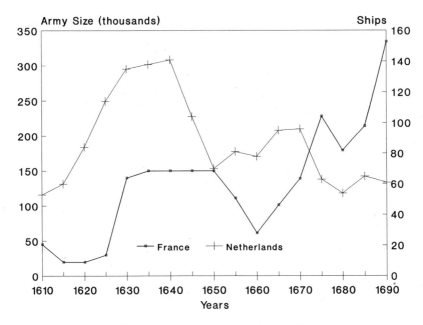

Figure 3.7 France versus Netherlands in the Absolute Mode

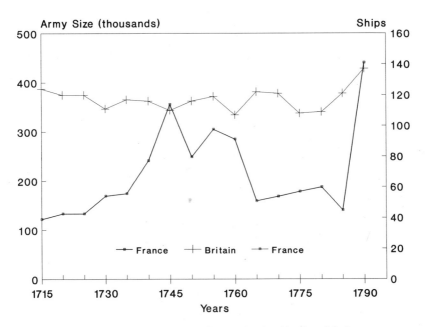

Figure 3.8 Britain versus France in the Absolute Mode

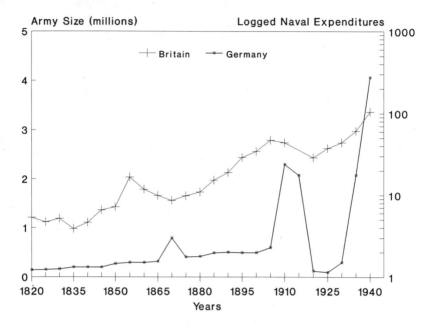

Figure 3.9 Britain versus Germany in the Absolute Mode

war-no war ratios would be virtually the same as those reported in table 3.3 (with one additional period of no overtaking and war), the measures of association would be even higher if we used absolute indices. Thus we can conclude that the support for hypothesis 3.1 is not an artifact of the proportional approach to measuring army and navy capabilities.

The test of hypothesis 3.2 on the relationship between regional transitions and the probability of war is illustrated in figures 3.10 and 3.11. Only two trials are at stake here: Spain versus France and Germany versus France. The second hypothesis also receives some empirical support in table 3.5. About 57 percent of the fourteen overtaking episodes are associated with war outbreaks, while only 19 percent of the forty-seven nonovertaking intervals are linked to war. Nevertheless, the fact that two dyads could generate fourteen periods in which a challenger at least came close to catching up with the regional leader tells us something about European regional transitions. Even though the actors most directly involved were few (only three between 1490 and 1944), they obviously kept trying to improve or maintain their respective positions.

The lion's share of the regional transition attempts are found in the history of the Franco-Spanish dyad, depicted in figure 3.10. The record is not one of regularly spaced, repetitive contests. Rather, the true periods of the most intense contestation were the Italian Wars in the late fifteenth-

Table 3.5 Regional Leader Transitions

	Equal/Unequal, No Overtaking	Equal and Overtaking
No War	38 (80.9%)	6 (42.9%)
War	9 (19.1%)	8 (57.1%)

Dyads: Spain-France (1490–1700) and France-Germany (1820–1944)

Cramer's $\underline{V}$ = .303*

($\underline{N}$ = 61)

*Statistically significant at the .05 level.

Note: Each five-year interval within the larger dyadic intervals specified above is coded for the occurrence of dyadic transition and the outbreak of war.

early sixteenth centuries and the mid-seventeenth century. Spain emerged as the dominant state in the dyad in the former case, and France gained ascendancy in the latter. The numbers in table 3.5 are inflated somewhat by the number of short wars fought in the early period of Spanish ascendance, the protracted nature of regional transitions, and some indicator flaws. An example of a flaw in the indicator system is the apparent overtaking of Spain by France around 1610. This result is entirely a function of relying on an army share index. Spain demobilized rapidly during its truce with the Netherlands, but France did not; therefore it looks as if the French position surpassed the Spanish one early in the seventeenth century. A more accurate reading of the respective positions of this dyad, however, is given two intervals later, when Spain entered the Thirty Years' War.

The Franco-German dyadic record, shown in figure 3.11, is not much cleaner, even if it is shorter. Germany overtook France in the Franco-Prussian War (1870-71) but did not choose, or was not in a position to choose, to establish the type of numerical dominance in its army that the Hapsburgs had enjoyed in the sixteenth century. Franco-German army shares hovered in the same proportional range until Germany moved ahead in World War I. Germany's subsequent defeat and forced demobilization left France briefly in the dominant position by default, but the tables turned again in World War II.

Hypothesis 3.3 is restricted to the leading sea powers of the global system. In view of the circumstances associated with the global transition in the sixteenth century, again only two trials are at stake: Britain versus the Netherlands, and Britain versus the United States. Table 3.6 and figures 3.12 and 3.13 convey the outcome. As indicated by the weak measure of association in table 3.6, hypothesis 3.3 has about the same predictive success as hypothesis 3.2. Part of the problem is that, as in the case of hypothesis 3.2, only two dyadic records are relevant. Britain and the Netherlands fought somewhat inconclusively in a period of potential transition in the

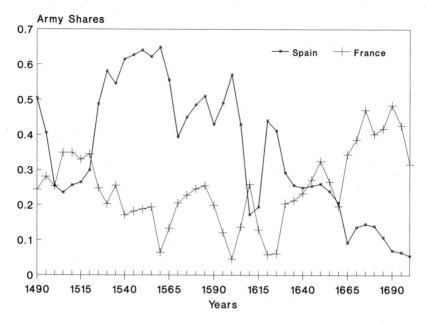

Figure 3.10 Spain versus France, 1490s–1700s

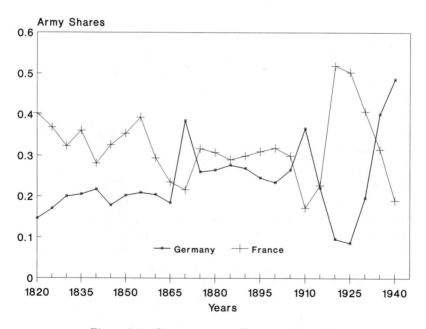

Figure 3.11 Germany versus France, 1820s–1940s

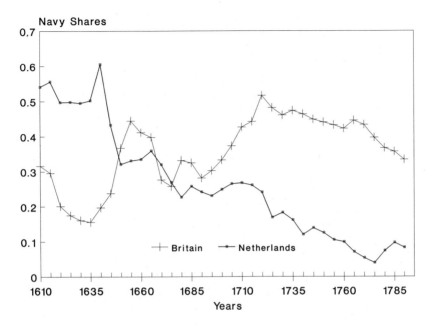

Figure 3.12 Britain versus the Netherlands, 1610s–1790s

Figure 3.13 Britain versus the United States, 1820s–1940s

Table 3.6 Global Leader Transitions

	Equal/Unequal, No Overtaking	Equal and Overtaking
No War	64 (97.0%)	5 (71.4%)
War	2 (3.0%)	2 (28.6%)

Dyads: Britain-Netherlands (1615–1794) and Britain-United States (1820–1939)

Cramer's $\underline{V}$ = .321* ($\underline{N}$ = 73)

*Statistically significant at the .05 level.

Note: Each five-year interval within the larger dyadic intervals specified above is coded for the occurrence of dyadic transition and the outbreak of war.

mid-seventeenth century, as shown in figure 3.12. Britain and the United States fought too, but their military combat ended long before their transitional period, which centered around the years between the onset of World War I and the end of World War II, clearly delineated in figure 3.13. During the period 1820-1945, Britain and the United States were certainly engaged in fighting, but not with one another.

Perhaps the simplest way to deal with this predictive failure is to invoke an *et ceteris paribus* qualification. Both dyads—Britain and the Netherlands, and Britain and the United States—have some common features. As they approached periods of transition, decision makers in the challenging states (from Oliver Cromwell to Woodrow Wilson through Franklin Roosevelt) and defending states were restrained by the perception that greater threats to their security lay elsewhere and that they could better deal with these greater threats in coalition than separately. Even so, these coalitions were slow to develop. Invariably, wartime conditions were necessary to crystallize the nature of the coalitions fully. And while joint attentions were focused on the mutual threat, the intraglobal transition occurred. The new global leader emerged from the war stronger than before. The old global leader emerged from the global war financially exhausted and in no position to contest the transition. The old leaders had worn out their sinews of war in the process of winning the global war.

Thus, despite the variable outcomes associated with the four tests of the hypotheses, the different transitional processes that the hypotheses attempt to isolate remain inherently intertwined. Regional transitions can be protracted affairs. Yet posttransitional dominance, after the sixteenth century, was cut short by the intervention of global leaders. Old and new global leaders became increasingly less likely to fight one another, because of the timely appearance of a mutually perceived regional menace that served as a serious distraction. In the absence of such a threat, as suggested by the extended Dutch-Portuguese combat of the seventeenth century and the first and second Anglo-Dutch Wars, old and aspiring global leaders would fight each other too.

Regional, global, and global-regional transitions, therefore, interact in ways that are difficult to capture readily in two-by-two matrices. Nevertheless, the salience of structural transitions and the intermittent fusion of regional and global structures are graphically and empirically demonstrated. All of the outcomes were correctly anticipated and statistically significant. Without the concept of transition, the major power history of the sixteenth through the twentieth centuries resembles the anarchic and seemingly random conflicts enshrined in realist assumptions about world politics. With the concept, and some theoretical rules about different theaters of operation, the apparent anarchy is reduced to a relatively structured order—or, more exactly, relatively structured regional and global orders.

Examining dyads of rival leadership collisions is one way to systematize the relationship between structural transitions and war. Because we single out certain types of dyads for special attention, we do not regard our analysis in this chapter as simply a dyadic explanation. By focusing only on rival leadership dyads, we view our explanation as fundamentally systemic. It is systemic because our explanation centers on leadership dynamics that represent attributes and processes of the system. But our systemic explanation is firmly grounded in actor motivations. New or aspiring leaders fight to replace old leaders. Old leaders fight to avoid displacement by new leaders.

With this in mind, we can turn in chapter 4 to an even more overtly systemic form of explanation of major power warfare by translating rival leadership collisions into fluctuations in the level of capability concentration—a patently classical systemic attribute of the distribution of power. Leadership dyadic transitions may not always be directly translatable into fluctuations in systemic concentration, but in this case, the translation is quite direct. So too is the relationship of concentration to the onset of the most severe threat to system stability—the global war.

4.
Concentration and Transitional Warfare

The distribution of power has been for some time a predominant focus for analysts examining the environment of conflict, stability, and the effects of ecological changes on the probability of greater or lesser propensities toward instability and war. The study of international relations offers three principal and, in some respects, alternative conceptualizations of structural change: balance of power, concentration, and polarity. One way to distinguish them is to think of *concentration* as an interval way to characterize inequalities in the distributions of power and of *polarity* as an ordinal, or at least a nominal, interpretation. *Balance of power* can mean many things but in this context usually refers to a process involving the coalescing of a group of states against a mutual threat. The coalition can be viewed as a reaction to the development of an imbalanced or overly concentrated distribution of power.

Regardless of the interpretation employed, analysts disagree whether a highly concentrated, unipolar system, or movement toward it, represents a more stable structure than either a bipolar system or a multipolar system, or movements toward these ostensibly less concentrated distributions of power. Similarly, the question of whether balanced or imbalanced power distributions are more or less conducive to conflict remains unresolved. Not only do theories espouse the advantages of each type of system over the others, but conflicting empirical findings also seem to support many of the competing theoretical views.

We contend that one of the fundamental reasons for the continuing analytical controversy on this subject is the persistent tendency of investigators to see only one structure or distribution at work. Historically, we argue, there actually have been two structures—one for global politics and another for politics in the world system's central region—and they have not worked the same way. High concentration and unipolarity have a stabilizing effect at the global level, but the same type of structure is destabilizing at the regional level. Consequently, the most dangerous structural situation has been a deconcentrating global system and a reconcentrating central regional system. Such conjunctures have encouraged the outbreak of a series of global wars over the last five hundred years.

From a different yet related angle, the problem is also one of theoretically specifying the scope and domain of power relations among the major powers (Lasswell and Kaplan 1950; Dahl 1970; Baldwin 1979, 1989). Regional actors have tended to rely on large armies to overwhelm and subdue their opponents. Global actors specialize in the global reach of sea power. Accordingly, the distributions of the types of capability that matter most vary by level of analysis. Analysts, therefore, need different data to analyze regional and global structures.

A third reason for the problems associated with developing systemic explanations has been the failure to make the theories less abstract and more concrete (Lane 1990). Balances of power, degrees of concentration, and types of polarity set the systemic contexts in which actors maneuver. These contexts encourage some types of strategies and discourage others. Thus, the interlocking of regional and global structures that we are emphasizing is so critical because it isolates the highly lethal setting for choices that are likely to be made by aspiring regional hegemons and declining global leaders.

After a brief discussion of earlier work relating concentration to the probability of conflict and instability, we propose to test our double structure interpretation with data encompassing the past five centuries. The results, based on an analysis of the 1490-1990 period, support our argument that system stability depends in part on avoiding a specific and lethal type of interplay between global and regional distributions.

Earlier Work on Power Distributions and War

The literature on the relationships between power distribution and conflict is characterized by an absence of fundamental agreement about appropriate foci, concepts, and indicators. Some analysts prefer to work exclusively with the idea of capability concentration and ignore polarity considerations. The converse is true as well. No standard conventions exist concerning the distinctions between unipolarity, bipolarity, and multipolarity. A number of analysts prefer to conflate the notion of power distribution with polarization or interaction tendencies, while others regard polarity and polarization as two distinct structural attributes. For some, *system stability* means the absence of war, while for others it connotes the absence of fundamental structural change. And since there is no standard indicator for power or capability, the employment of a wide variety of indicators leads to an equally wide variety of empirical findings.

As a consequence, not only have separate literatures on the relationships between concentration and war and polarity and war emerged, but the findings tend to be noncumulative and often confusing. Theories and empirical evidence supporting the stabilizing virtues of hegemony (unipolarity, high concentration), bipolarity, or multipolarity (low concentration) are not difficult to find.[1] Similarly, arguments and supporting evidence suggesting that all of these variables are not as important as is often assumed are also readily available.[2] Reconciling the arguments and findings is a totally different, and most difficult, task.

We see little point in waging further semantic warfare over the multiple definitions that abound. Other terminological reviews are obtainable that more than satisfy the need for this type of evaluation.[3] Nor are we eager to cut the Gordian knot of conflicting theories and findings. The widely varying assumptions upon which these theories and evidence are based would make simply translating the findings into a common language an enormous task. We propose instead to forge ahead with still another interpretation, because we are not satisfied that previous approaches have focused on the processes that we think are most important. One needs, we think, not only to emphasize more than one distribution of power but also to offer an explicit theoretical perspective combined with an interpretation of the central historical dynamics of world politics.[4]

Hypotheses, Variables, Indicators, and Techniques

The literature on capability concentration and warfare suggests that the relationship between these phenomena can be positive, negative, curvilinear, or nonexistent. One obvious reason for such disparate opinions is that different assumptions yield different explanations and findings. It may also be that the relationship is highly unstable and changes as other, more powerful parameters experience change. Our preference, however, is to suggest that one key to the problem is that the multiple interpretations and findings stem from attempting to analyze the contextual influence of one structure on international behavior when more than one type of structure is crucial.

More specifically, we argue that it is the interaction between global and regional structures and their principal actors that provide the context for the system's most significant and serious wars. The relationship between concentration and global warfare differs according to which structure is emphasized. From a regional vantage point, the relationship is positive. As the regional structure becomes more concentrated, more destabilizing violence can be anticipated. But from a global perspective, the relationship is negative. The reason that this is the case, we argue, is that the conjunction of these conditions indicates a situation in which an ascending regional leader is overtaking a declining global leader. Essentially, then, we have one basic hypothesis to examine:

HYPOTHESIS 4.1: The probability of systemic warfare is positively related to the interlocking of global capability deconcentration and regional capability concentration.

In testing this proposition, we are likely to see the emergence of several auxiliary hypotheses concerning research design choices. The nature of these auxiliary hypotheses will become clearer after a discussion of how we intend to measure the meshing of global and regional concentration and systemic warfare.

Concentration

Different levels of analysis warrant different measurement strategies, because the global and regional theaters of competition stress the employment of different types of capabilities. Success in the global political economy has required the ability to mobilize and transport goods and military power over long distances. Success in controlling the European region, historically, has seemed to demand the ability to mobilize and maneuver large armies. Accordingly, global-reach capabilities can be measured by shares of global sea power, while regional land power can be indexed by comparative army size.

We have basically two ways to measure concentration. The simplest approach involves focusing on the leader's share as the principal index. The disadvantage to this procedure is that the analyst must devise auxiliary rules for determining who the leader is at any point in time and then must convince readers that these interventions are appropriate. A more complex approach that involves less analytical intervention indexes simultaneously the relative shares of all the pertinent actors. While results are usually similar regardless of which type of index is employed, we will adopt the same Ray and Singer (1973) concentration algorithm used in Appendix B because it is the most neutral and least controversial index.

Nevertheless, we are most interested in the interlocking of global and regional concentration processes. The most direct way to measure the specific type of structural fusion, we think, is to subtract regional concentration from global concentration. As the global-regional concentration gap narrows, the probability of systemic warfare should increase.

Actors

The major regional and global powers we need to examine were identified previously. As was the case for earlier analyses, the question of how we treat

Russian army data presents a potential problem for measuring concentration and categorizing polarity distributions. Nevertheless, it is not clear that the exclusion of Russian/Soviet data at the regional level is as critical as one might imagine. Figure 4.1 plots two versions of the regional concentration index for Western Europe between 1490 and 1990. One series includes the Russian data in the total after 1715; the other excludes the Russian data. Visually, the two series look very much alike, with two exceptions: immediately after World War I, when the Soviet army was remobilized for civil war and other armies had demobilized, and after World War II, when the Soviet army remained relatively large and the European army sizes shrank considerably. Even so, the series are reasonably correlated: r equals 0.67 for the entire 1490-1990 period but a much higher 0.91 for the pre-World War II period. Excluding the Russian data for theoretical reasons, therefore, should not threaten the validity of any regional concentration-war relationships that we uncover. But it is also possible to ascertain just how much empirical difference this strong assumption makes by comparing the test outcomes associated with both series displayed in figure 4.1.

Five-year periods are the shortest intervals possible for army-based indicators over a several-century span. Accordingly, all of our observations will be based on half decades, beginning with 1490-94.

Systemic War

We will depart from the normal practice of examining various indicators of major power warfare as measures of destabilization. We do this for two reasons. First, we find indicators such as battle deaths difficult to interpret over long periods of time. Occasionally they can be quite misleading. The number of soldiers who die in battle or at least during a war are not fully comparable across centuries, because of expanding armed forces, increasingly lethal military technology, and improving medical services. Second, we take seriously the literature's frequent emphasis on the significance of destabilizing warfare. Most dyadic wars are not particularly destabilizing for the system as a whole. The most destabilizing wars are those conflicts that threaten to change radically the management of regional and global politics. Some wars have strong potential for altering the regional order—for example, the Franco-Prussian War—and we do not mean to slight their significance. Nonetheless, the potentially most destabilizing wars remain the global wars fought between the European regional leader and a coalition headed by the leading global power(s). Global wars were fought in 1494-1516, 1580-1608, 1688-1713, 1792-1815, and 1914-45.[5] Some readers have particular problems with accepting the merging of World Wars I and II as one global war. Consequently, we will analyze the twentieth-century wars both ways—

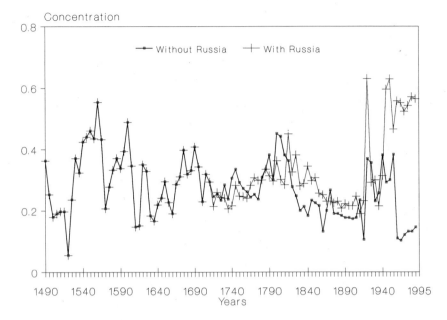

Figure 4.1 Regional Army Concentration in Western Europe

as two wars (1914-18 and 1939-45) and as one war (1914-45)—and report the outcomes separately.

We might code the outbreaks of war in several ways. What we are trying to assess in this chapter is whether a statistically significant pattern of global-regional concentration is associated with the onset of global war. The capability patterns should precede the commencement of war if we are to be able to argue that the capability patterns contributed to the outbreak of war.

To preclude contaminating the test by developments that take place after the beginning of war, we focus on the five- and ten-year intervals immediately preceding the outbreak of war. Any intervals encompassing years of global war are removed from the analysis. For example, the 1688-1713 global war is encompassed by six five-year intervals: 1685-89, 1690-94, 1695-99, 1700-1704, 1705-9, and 1710-14. We have coded the 1680-84 and 1675-84 intervals as prewar periods. Observations for the 1685-1714 period have been dropped from the data analysis. The shortage of prewar data in the fifteenth century forces a slightly different approach. A ten-year prewar interval is not possible. Even the five-year prewar interval is awkward, since the first global war began in the fifth year of the first five-year interval. Faced with a choice of losing the first war observation altogether or fudging slightly on the prewar interval, we have opted for the latter alternative. Nevertheless, the temporal domain considerations associated with Dehio's argument will force us to test whether the inclusion of the first half of the six-teenth century makes some difference.

Temporal Domain

Dehio argued that some important deviations from the general pattern char-acterized the history of European regional politics. First Spain blocked France in Italy, and then France and the Ottoman Empire combined to thwart the united Hapsburg expansion in the early to mid-sixteenth century. The slowness of the emergence of a western sea power balancer suggests we should not expect a global-regional power confrontation until toward the end of the sixteenth century. We could drop a sizable segment of the sixteenth-century data from the analysis as a consequence, but we will leave the early years in, on the premise that the early predominance of regional dynamics is likely to be reflected by our global-regional concentration gap index. That is, regional concentration is likely to be greater than global concentration in the absence of a potent western sea power.

The outbreak of global war in 1914 presents a different sort of problem. Dehio's argument was that German decision makers made a bid for regional hegemony only after the war had started. If this is true, we have less reason to expect a major increase in regional capability concentration before 1914. Global power deconcentration is certainly probable, however, so, other things being equal, there should be some movement toward closing the gap between the two types of concentration. While the pre-1914 onset may rep-resent the weakest link in the six observations of global war, its weakness is not likely to obscure the general relationship between structural change and war.

Technically, our empirical analysis should end with the last World War II interval (1940-44). After 1945 the European regional distribution of power had lost, at least temporarily, its traditional political significance. The Ger-man question, that is, the latest manifestation of regional supremacy aspira-tions in Europe, was resolved primarily by U.S. and Soviet troops during World War II and the ensuing cold war. Only with the recovery of European economies, the demise of the cold war, the withdrawal of Soviet/Russian troops from Eastern Europe, and the reduction of American troops in West-ern Europe is there once again some room for the revival of the European regional leadership question.

It is also debatable whether Europe has retained its claim to being the world system's central region since 1945. East Asia's importance has contin-ued to climb throughout the postwar era. We should also add that our re-liance on the naval and army indicators as instruments for differentiating global and regional actors becomes increasingly problematic in the more complicated twentieth century. Still, the inclusion of a few more years of structural interaction should not pose any serious design threat. Examining a 1490-1990 series should also preempt any concern, despite our theoretical interpretation, that we are manipulating the data in an ad hoc fashion in order to obtain confirmation for our hypothesis.

Of course, if we were to interpret the Soviet Union as the successor to Germany in the *regional* leadership contest, we would be justified in continuing the empirical analysis beyond 1945. We reject this interpretation not because we know that the Soviet Union has subsequently disintegrated but because we continue to maintain that the Soviet Union/Russia is not an indigenous member of the Western European region. It may seem a fine point, but we view the NATO-led containment efforts of the cold war as designed to preclude a Soviet thrust into Western Europe rather than to suppress the ascension of a Soviet hegemony within the European region. But since we will be examining a regional concentration series with Russian/Soviet data included, we can also see whether this interpretation makes some empirical difference.

In sum, we propose to use indicators of concentration to explain and predict the outbreak of global wars. We expect to find that global and European regional structures operate on different principles. When other factors are held constant, high capability concentration in the global political economy makes global war less likely. But high capability concentration in the European region makes global war more likely. Therefore, the narrowing of the global-regional concentration gap should significantly increase the probability of global war. In other words, a negative relationship should exist between the size of the concentration gap and outbreaks of global war.

Given the mixture of types of variables examined in this analysis, we will use a logit regression model, which is especially useful when a dichotomous dependent variable is analyzed, to estimate the pertinent relationships. Our goal is to assess models that will tell us whether the probability of global war increases or decreases depending primarily on the global-regional concentration gap. The logit models will produce coefficients that will tell us the change in the logit (log-odds) for each one-unit increase in the independent variables.

A disadvantage of the application of logit regression on time series data, however, is that it is likely to produce maximum likelihood estimates that are unbiased but inefficient in the presence of serially correlated residuals. Unfortunately, the serial correction problem has proven to be intractable in logit and probit analyses (Aldrich and Nelson 1984: 81). Still, there are two possible ways to approach this problem. The first involves relying on Monte Carlo simulations reported by Aldrich and Nelson (ibid.), who have investigated how large a sample one needs before parameter estimates will converge sufficiently to make use of the asymptotic properties. The answer to this question depends on the number of variables and their degree of covariation, but for the most part, the rule of thumb is that fifty observations per parameter seems to be safe. Since we have met the threshold, we could rely on the simulation findings and report our results with the appropriate caveats.

Another approach is suggested by King's argument that past history should be modeled in the logit equation (1989: 167-76). It may tell us something about the time series process that otherwise would have been neglected; it may also tell us how much the parameter estimates are influenced by the presence of serial correlation. As a consequence, a partial resolution of the autocorrelation problem would involve the inclusion of a lagged dependent variable (war-no war) in the equation with the gap concentration variable. Hence, the structure of the equations that will be used take the following form:

$$\log [\underline{P}_i / (1 - \underline{P}_i)] = \underline{Y} = \underline{B}_0 - \underline{B}_1\underline{X}_1 + \emptyset\underline{Y}_{t-1} + \Sigma_i$$

where $\underline{P}_i$ is the probability that a five- or ten-year interval is a pre-global war interval and $\underline{X}_1$ is the global-regional concentration gap that is hypothesized to be negatively related to the prelude to global war. $\underline{B}_0$ and Σ_i are, respectively, constant and error terms. More details on these procedures can be found in Aldrich and Nelson (1984) and King (1989).

Data Analysis

Six equations are reported in table 4.1. Equations 1 and 4 employ five-year prewar intervals. These equations lack a lagged dependent variable coefficient because there proved to be too few pre-global war observations with which to estimate the coefficients with any degree of confidence. The estimation procedure failed to converge on a stable set of numerical values. The other four equations use ten-year prewar intervals as the dependent variable. In every instance, the concentration gap variable remained statistically significant despite the presence of the lagged dependent variable. This suggests that our main findings are not overly influenced by autocorrelation. Equations 1, 2, and 3 examine the 1490-1990 period, while equations 4, 5, and 6 look at 1565-1990. Finally, equations 1, 2, 4, and 5 treat the two world wars as separate, and equations 3 and 6 merge them as a single 1914-45 global war.

Three findings are most important in table 4.1. First, inasmuch as all six equations contain statistically significant gap coefficients, the five- and ten-year intervals work about equally well in signaling the onset of global wars. The gap coefficients linked with the 1565-1990 equations, however,

Table 4.1 Logistic Regressions of Pre-Global War Intervals on the
Global-Regional Concentration Gap

			Parameter Estimates[a]				
Equation	Time Span	Prewar Interval (years)	Constant	Global-Regional Concentration Gap	Y_{t-1}	Log Likelihood Ratio	N
1	1490–1990	5	-2.10* (-4.79)	-5.52* (-1.74)	—	-19.06	73
2	1490–1990	10	-2.13* (-4.27)	-7.79* (-2.59)	2.88* (3.10)	-20.44	72
3[b]	1490–1990	10	-2.39* (-4.25)	-8.37* (-2.56)	3.13* (2.99)	-16.43	69
4	1565–1990	5	-1.89* (-3.81)	-9.19* (-2.02)	—	-14.97	63
5	1565–1990	10	-1.56* (-2.94)	-12.42* (-2.75)	2.76* (2.73)	-17.34	63
6[b]	1565–1990	10	-1.81* (-3.08)	-13.17* (-2.68)	3.31* (2.63)	-13.61	60

[a] Maximum likelihood estimates.

[b] The 1914–45 period is treated as a single global war. In equations 1, 2, 4, and 5, 1914–18 and 1939–45 are examined separately.

T-statistics are reported below the coefficients.

*p is less than or equal to .05, using a one-tailed test of significance.

are much larger than the coefficients associated with the 1490-1990 equations, suggesting that the concentration gap process is more evident after 1565 than before, just as Dehio would have predicted. Second and most critical to our hypothesis, all of the gap coefficients are negatively signed, as anticipated. Narrowing gaps are more dangerous than widening gaps. Finally, there is little difference in any of these coefficients when the twentieth-century wars are treated as one war or as two.

Figure 4.2 demonstrates why the concentration gap measure works so well in predicting the onset of global wars. Each global war is preceded by a clear decline in the gap between global and regional capability concentration. The years when regional concentration is greater than global concentration tend to be exclusively associated with years of global warfare. Nor is this narrowing gap phenomenon simply a matter of deconcentration in the global system, alone creating a situation of convergence in concentration scores. With the exception of World War I, which is preceded by a less precipitous decline in the concentration gap than the other global wars, one of Dehio's kinks, the global wars broke out in the context of declining global concentration and increasing regional concentration.

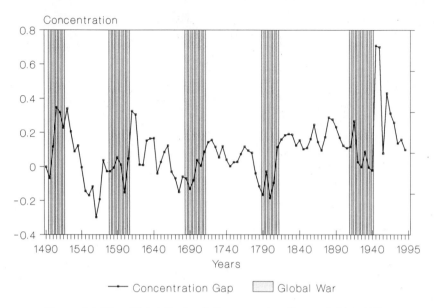

Figure 4.2 The Global-Regional Concentration Gap and Global War

Is this finding an artifact of excluding Russia/USSR from the regional (but not the global) computations? Table 4.2 summarizes six equations designed to duplicate the analysis reported in table 4.1. This time, though, the regional concentration calculations used include Russia/USSR. In every case, the coefficients are roughly the same size and have identical signs. Only four of the six equations (numbers 2, 3, 5, and 6), however, produce statistically significant global-regional gap coefficients. The two exceptions are the equations using five-year prewar intervals. Apparently, the inclusion of the Russian data leads to the need for a longer warning period. Once that is present, though, the outcome of table 4.2 is generally similar to that of table 4.1.

We have reported these outcomes solely to satisfy the curiosity of readers who may not accept our assumption about the location of Russia and the Soviet Union outside Western Europe. We believe that the results of table 4.1 are the more appropriate ones. Yet even if one insists on the regional inclusion of Russia, it is still possible to find statistical support for the basic hypothesis. One must conclude that the findings are fairly robust.

Conclusion

Strong support is forthcoming for the idea that opposing concentration trends are critical to the outbreak of systematically destabilizing violence.

Table 4.2 Logistic Regressions of Pre-Global War Intervals on the Global-Regional
Concentration Gap, with Russia within the Region

				Parameter Estimates[a]			
Equation	Time Span	Prewar Interval (years)	Constant	Global-Regional Concentration Gap	Y_{t-1}	Log Likelihood Ratio	N
1	1490–1990	5	-2.36* (-5.45)	-3.35 (-1.19)	—	-20.02	73
2	1490–1990	10	-2.40* (-4.99)	-4.14* (-1.75)	2.56* (3.04)	-23.25	72
3[b]	1490–1990	10	-2.76* (-4.77)	-6.43* (-2.27)	3.32* (3.10)	-17.99	69
4	1565–1990	5	-2.38* (-4.98)	-4.19* (-1.32)	—	-16.59	63
5	1565–1990	10	-2.18* (-4.54)	-4.39* (-1.73)	2.46* (2.89)	-21.91	63
6[b]	1565–1990	10	-2.51* (-4.38)	-6.91* (-2.28)	3.22* (2.99)	-16.73	60

[a] Maximum likelihood estimates.

[b] The 1914–45 period is treated as a single global war. In equations 1, 2, 4, and 5, 1914–18 and 1939–45 are examined separately.

T-statistics are reported below the coefficients.

*p is less than or equal to .05, using a one-tailed test of significance.

Global war is most probable when regional *and* global structural contexts are most dangerous. The main reason global and regional structures facilitate global war under these circumstances is that they manifest specific actor behavior. The leading continental power was expanding at the regional level. The once leading maritime-commercial-industrial power was declining at the global level. Each actor therefore perceived heightened incentives to hasten the demise or thwart the rise of the other party. The circumstances were structurally explosive and thus highly conducive to intensive conflict a number of times over the past five centuries.

Certainly more was involved in the outbreak of intensive and potentially destabilizing conflict than dangerous structural circumstances. The deviant case of World War I (it was deviant only in the absence of much regional power concentration; global concentration and transition were present) suggests that increasing regional concentration and decreasing global concentration were neither entirely necessary nor sufficient to the outbreak of global war. In some cases, the perception of regional hegemonic expansion may work as an effective substitute for objective regional capability concentration. Nonetheless, the empirical record strongly supports the idea that the combination of the two structural conditions has significantly improved the probability of such an outbreak over the past five hundred years or so.

What of the future? Is this global-regional concentration pattern outdated? Given our assumptions, at least three possibilities exist. First, a future period of intensive global conflict and war is so remote that we need no longer worry about the destabilizing implications of structural change and capability distributions. Second, 1945 demarcated the genuine end of an era when regional capability distributions made some difference. In the post-1945 era, only global capability distributions will matter. Third, the post-1945 absence of a single most significant region and/or the absence of a significant regional capability distribution is only a temporary phenomenon. At some future point, regional capability distribution could matter once again.

Obviously, we have no crystal ball. We can only speculate about what might take place in the future. Of the three possibilities, though, the least likely one is the first, which predicts an end to intensive conflict among the most powerful actors. Global war may or may not have become less likely because of the lethality of available weapon systems, the costs perceived to be associated with a major power war, or changing attitudes toward the practice of war. But the world system's most powerful actors show little in the way of diminished interests in competing for relative prestige, position, influence, and market shares. That sort of behavior is most conducive to intense conflict over systemic leadership. Some probability of the return to a period of increased conflict will persist as long as the requisite underlying motivations persist. The more actors compete and the more their capabilities approach equivalency, the more potentially destabilizing their competition becomes.

Analysts like to emphasize the bipolar uniqueness of the post-1945 era. But what was unique about it was not the bipolar nature of the global system, for earlier periods of global bipolarity have existed. What was unique was the relative absence of concern about European or other regional capability distributions. Regional leadership conflicts did not appear to be much of a threat to global politics. Despite declining concentration at the global level—measured either in sea power or economic wealth—no regional powers were viewed as approaching the exalted status of the two superpowers.

With the disintegration of one of the superpowers—although not necessarily to the point of its losing its global power status—the probability of new rivals' emerging from the regional ranks has increased. Concurrent with the disintegration of the Soviet Union has come a lessened suppression of European leadership aspirations. In Dehioan terms, both the eastern and western balancers have been reducing their European presence, just as their relative resource position vis-à-vis Europe is declining. The possibility of the reemergence of European regional leadership questions as a distinct political problem is enhanced accordingly.

The current leading economic rival to the United States, Japan, hails from the East Asian region, as does one of the last continental behemoths, China. Russia has fought both states more than once in the twentieth century. The United States has fought Japan. Vietnam and India have fought China. The Korean question remains unresolved. If Western European territorial and hierarchical problems appear relatively stable for the present, the same cannot be said of East Asia. In many respects, one could apply a modified form of Dehio's regional dynamics and the global-regional concentration gap model to East Asian developments before the outbreak of World War II.

The question then becomes whether East Asia has the potential to become the world system's most significant region and/or, alternatively, whether it possesses the potential to produce an expanding regional leader that might be viewed as a significant threat to a deconcentrating global system. Neither possibility is easy to reject out of hand.

If forced to choose between two alternative future scenarios—one that involves the absence of much regional leadership competition that matters beyond the region(s) in question and one that sees several regions claiming centrality, or at least high significance—the second scenario seems more attractive. Recent events also seem to support the latter alternative. The 1965-73 Vietnam War was fought in part to discourage the perceived prospects for Chinese expansion in Southeast Asia. The Gulf War was fought in part to discourage the prospects for Iraqi expansion in an oil-rich corner of the Middle East. The Gulf War in turn had been made more probable by the preceding Iran-Iraq War, fought at least in part to prevent Iranian expansion in the Middle East. None of these affairs had much potential for becoming global wars along the lines of the historical pattern. The regions were relatively minor, particularly in the case of Southeast Asia. The expansionary threats turned out to be either more a matter of perception than reality (China) or predicated on less capability than supposed (Iraq, Iran). Global deconcentration, moreover, had not progressed all that much.

Yet the point is that peripheral regions need not remain peripheral forever. Actors once misperceived as expansionary may become genuinely expansionary. For that matter, as we have noted, decision makers have a poor track record in recognizing regional expansion. They have been slow to identify the genuine cases, and they occasionally exaggerate the threat potential of more dubious cases. What may really matter in the future is the likelihood of bringing together the most powerful regional and global actors in a situation of intensive conflict and the appropriate set of perceptions about their relative capabilities (declining global and ascending regional) and respective intentions.

We do not predict that any of these scenarios must take place in the near future. At the same time, the world does not seem to have changed sufficiently to exclude either variation as a future possibility and perhaps even a future probability. To the extent that this remains the case, the global-regional concentration pattern that we have identified for the 1490-1990 and 1565-1990 eras is likely to retain its theoretical significance into the twenty-first century.

Up to this point, we have focused on relating the rise and fall of regional and global leaders to the onset of major power warfare. The conjunction of decline at the global level and reconcentration at the regional level creates a context highly conducive to systemic violence. But if structural change produces war, what produces structural change?

At the European regional level, the roots of structural change historically have been relatively simple and slow moving. Idiosyncratic ambitions, decades of territorial expansion and population aggregation, and occasional abilities to mobilize the resources of the largest states in Western Europe go a long way in explaining the emergence of Spanish, French, and German problems in Western Europe. The roots of structural change at the global level, however, are a bit more complex. Specifying and validating what we think are and are not the roots of change constitute our next task.

5.

Innovation, Decline, and War

Critical to the type of analysis in the first four chapters is the idea that levels of power concentration in global and regional systems oscillate between high and low. Moreover, the periods of high concentration are associated closely with the lead position of a single state. Global leaders, with which we will be most concerned in this chapter, rise to singular prominence for a period. At their peak position of influence, they have an opportunity to structure trans-oceanic transactions and the rules that govern these long-distance interactions in their own favor. In the process of doing so, global leaders help create some semblance of order and management in world politics and the world economy. They are able to achieve this outcome in part because they have developed a resource base, specializing in global-reach commercial and military capabilities and economic innovation, that is vastly superior to the resources controlled by allies and rivals alike.

Ultimately, the capability edge of the leaders of the global system erodes. As the resource foundation deteriorates vis-à-vis the competition, so too does the ability to generate order and policy in global affairs. As power concentration ebbs, the system moves into a more multipolar and more generally competitive mode. The level of conflict increases, and the level of order decays, until systemic warfare facilitates the emergence of a new round of global leadership.

In this chapter we focus on the role of economic innovation as the key to the rise and relative decline of global leaders. After discussing the nature of long waves of economic innovation, lead economies, and leading sectors, we demonstrate empirically the linkages that exist among technological innovation, economic leadership, naval leadership, and war.

Interpretations of Long Waves of Economic Growth

If one extracts the half dozen or so variables from the discussions of why long economic waves (the fifty-year variety) occur, the general pattern suggests that many different analysts are talking about pretty much the same phenomena. Different clusters of interpretation emphasize some variables over others. Analysts operating within these interpretative clusters may also disagree over which way the causal arrows connecting the variables should be pointed. Nevertheless, the various groups increasingly seem to be discussing the interconnections between many of the same variables.[1]

Distilling the common denominators and interconnections requires putting aside the idiosyncratic concepts such as organic capital, heroic entrepreneurs, and stages of growth. Some risk of oversimplification must also be assumed. These caveats aside, however, a set of core propositions on the dynamics of long waves can be reduced to the following statements concerning technological innovation:

1. Major technological innovations are discontinuous in time and space.

2. Economies are characterized by uneven growth rates across different sectors of activity. Some sectors lead the aggregate or average rate of growth, while other, more stagnant sectors retard the overall rate of growth.

3. Major technological innovations give rise to new commercial and industrial sectors (leading sectors) and ways of doing things that are highly significant in propelling industrial and economic growth.

4. New industrial sectors and ways of doing things require considerable investment and the development of extensive infrastructure.

5. The development of new industrial sectors and ways of doing things may be facilitated by war, but the benefits are not necessarily shared equally by all participants in the war.

6. New industrial sectors and ways of doing things are subject to variable mixes of diffusion and imitation, increasing competition and protectionism, market saturation, and overcapacity. They are also subject to increasing costs, diminishing marginal returns, and various types of institutional rigidities that constrain further growth and innovation.

With the possible exception of the rarely discussed war facilitation proposition (number 5), these statements are accepted implicitly or explicitly by the extended circle of analysts exploring long waves. What they disagree about is whether or to what extent technological innovation is the prime mover of the multiple factors thought to be bound up in long-wave phenomena. Figure 5.1 helps illustrate the multiple interpretations and emphases. Many of the same variables receive attention despite different starting points. What varies are the directions of the causal arrows and the different accents placed on the primary movers in the ensemble.

While most long-wave analyses reserve a prominent role for technological innovation, only one group argues that the timing of the innovations themselves generates the long-wave fluctuations.[2] Radical innovations increase profits and employment, require new investment on a large scale, and

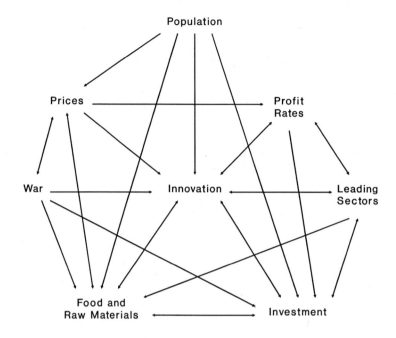

Figure 5.1 Potential Core Long-Wave Relationships

stimulate overall economic growth. A second school of thought emphasizes rates of profit as the principal source of long waves.[3] A variety of exogenous triggers—for instance, new markets or changes in productivity or raw material prices—may influence rates of return. But once profits are tending upward, capital will become available for investment in new production techniques. At some point, though, the cumulative impacts of the triggering factors begin to erode. Profits and investment decline as a consequence.

Still another group stresses the reinvestment process.[4] New investment comes in spurts because it is focused on major technological innovations, associated infrastructural requirements, and the finite potential for expansion in any given time period. In one version, new investment leads to economic expansion, which tends to undercut the factors that facilitated the investment in the first place (low prices and interest rates and high propensities to save). An alternative interpretation emphasizes that the root of the problem has to do with overexpansions in capital equipment. Downswings and declining investment serve the dual function of using up the overcapacity and the old technology. Eventually, conditions are again ripe for a new technological and investment buildup.

A fourth cluster of arguments draws attention to cyclical fluctuations in the prices of primary commodities: food and raw materials, especially energy materials.[5] Prices and interest rate increases reflect the interaction of disruptive warfare and the pressures of population growth and migration, with constraints on agricultural production and energy consumption. When prices rise, investment flows toward increased production in the primary commodities. When prices decline, funds are available for the expansion of leading sectors and technological change.

Finally, some analysts stress the impact of war in shaping long price waves and stimulating industrial innovation.[6] Alternatively, it is also argued that economic upswings increase competitive tensions and the probability of war among the major producers, who, not coincidentally, have also become more capable of financing armed conflict.[7]

Figure 5.1 brings these multiple interpretations together uncritically by linking the core variables as the various authors have suggested.[8] Other variables certainly could be introduced to expand the basic long-wave model. For example, war, prices, profit rates, and leading sectors are thought to be linked to wages, labor unrest, and domestic political change and realignments (Cronin 1979; Berry 1991). Leading sectors also have some systematic connection to aggregate industrial production, productivity, and export volumes. Figure 5.1, therefore, is an underdeveloped portrayal of the set of possible long-wave relationships. Much more theoretical and empirical investigation needs to be done before we will really know which variables are most influential and which ways the causal arrows actually point.

In the interim, we will proceed on the assumption that whatever the causal order of the variables involved in long waves of economic expansion and contraction, technological innovation plays a central role. Even if it is not the prime mover of the process, it is quite likely to be one of the most important process drivers. One substantial reason for thinking this is the case is tied to the conceptualization of leading sectors and their role in the economic growth process.

Leading Sectors

Rostow's extensive argument on leading sectors begins with the assumption that economic growth consists of successive, marginal augmentations to some existing base that is predicated on the progressive generation and diffusion of new technologies (1978: 106-7, 365-72). Some of these technologies represent small, incremental improvements to prevailing practices. Others constitute major, often radical, technological breakthroughs. These two basic types of innovation obviously are not of equal significance. Consequently, they should not be lumped together indiscriminately.

The radical breakthroughs are most likely to create leading sectors or new industries that expand at a rate in excess of the expansion of overall industrial production. Initially, leading-sector growth is explosive. While the initial technology will experience continual refinement, the rate of growth decays as the sector matures and as the technology diffuses throughout the economy.

A point that needs particular emphasis is that this technological expansion is not a straightforward matter of a newly created and ultimately large industry expanding the size of the economy in direct proportion to the industry's size. A leading sector may not be all that large. What is of interest is whether the sector's impact on growth tends to be disproportionate in its early stages of development. When a new major industry is beginning to develop, its claim on investment and entrepreneurial resources is greater than one might expect given the industry's scale of activities. Once initiated, the new leading sector requires a variety of activities and economic infrastructure to sustain its efficient operation. The novel technology can be expected to spill over into other sectors. Leading sectors, Rostow emphasizes, often accelerate urbanization, with its collateral impacts on patterns of demand.

Hence, the greatest marginal stimulation to growth may come early in the sector's development, at the time when the sector itself is expanding rapidly. As the sector continues to exploit its particular contribution to efficiency and productivity, its linkage to overall economic growth should stabilize. The sector gradually becomes a more routine component of the economy, even though its size may continue to grow. Interestingly, however, should the one-time leading sector enter a phase of decline or stagnation, it is argued, the impact on overall growth may once again become strong, but this time in a negative direction.[9]

No one is suggesting that leading sectors are the exclusive source of economic growth. Much economic growth is incremental and can be traced directly to activities that are not normally associated with leading sectors, such as food processing, construction, and services in general. These same activities are likely to engage the lion's share of an economy's total resources. Whatever the proportional division of labor and capital, though, not all growth is incremental. The attention given to leading sectors thus is an explicit attempt to focus on the discontinuous sources of technological change and economic growth.

Any economy can have leading sectors of some sort. From a global perspective, however, the most important leading sectors, the ones that periodically alter the world system's growth trajectories, are pioneered in one economy.

Lead Economies

One of the most important discontinuities in the unevenness of growth across time and space is that the lead in the development of radical innovations tends to be confined to a single national economy, the global system's lead economy. In fact, the leading national economy operates in the world economy in a manner very much akin to leading sectors within national economies. It is the system's most active economic zone. Modelski wrote: "To operationalize the concept of 'lead economy' we emphasize not size (as it might be indexed by area, population, or GNP) but those indicators that bear on status as 'active zone': the creation of leading sectors and the relative size of the industrial economy, and participation in world trade, both qualitatively (in goods of the leading sectors) and quantitatively (in shares of world trade or of foreign investment)" (1982: 104).[10]

Britain in the nineteenth century and the United States in the twentieth century have operated as the world economy's most recent active zones. Britain accounted for 50 percent or more of leading-sector production between the 1790s and 1870s. The leading-sector output of the United States outpaced Britain's by the 1890s. Within two decades, the American proportion had itself climbed to 50 percent or more.

Lead economies do not emerge upon the politico-economic landscape abruptly. Rather, they develop gradually, even though their preeminence, greatly facilitated as it is by successful warfare, may seem quite sudden. Moreover, all of the attributes of a lead economy are unlikely to materialize simultaneously. At some point, a single economy may lead all of its competitors in agro-industrial productivity, commercial supremacy, and financial centrality—as Wallerstein would have it—but it will have taken some time to put all of these components together in one place. The pace of integrating preeminence in these spheres will also vary from century to century.

The distinctiveness of each lead economy can usually be summarized in a few words. The Portuguese developed the appropriate armed vessels and navigational information necessary to circumnavigate Africa and then the world. The initial reward was West African gold and silver. In the early sixteenth century, the Portuguese were able to capture the Indian Ocean spice trade. Seventeenth-century Dutch economic preeminence was based primarily on dominance in the North Sea fisheries, control of the Baltic grain trade, and technological innovations in shipbuilding and textile production, as well as Amsterdam's pivotal role as Europe's leading entrepôt. The Dutch also supplanted the Portuguese in Asian waters.

The eighteenth-century British lead centered initially on Britain's increasingly commanding position in the Atlantic economy. British shipbuilding skills are thought to have caught up with those of the Dutch by about 1700 (Wilson 1965: 171). Britain, too, gradually became the leading European commercial power in Asian trade. Only toward the end of the eighteenth century did it begin to become clear that the economic foundation upon which the British lead was to be based would fixate on revolutionary approaches to industrialization. The Industrial Revolution of the late eighteenth century transformed Britain into the world's center for industrial innovation. The initial foci were textiles and iron. Railroads and steam engines predominated as the central concern of the next phase. By the late nineteenth century the locus of innovation had shifted once more, this time to the United States. Steel and electricity fueled the first American burst of innovation. Automobiles and semiconductors became critical foci for the mid-twentieth century.

The pattern of two innovational waves per lead economy is quite pronounced. Modelski and Thompson (1992, forthcoming) are able to show that each of the four global leaders was associated with two specific waves of innovation. The first one peaks immediately before the outbreak of global war. The second one peaks shortly after the conclusion of the war. The first wave is critical to the emergence of a new global leader, for it provides the surplus that underwrites the development of a commanding position in global-reach capabilities. Victory in the ensuing global war is also critical. A war victory, moreover, is crucial to the timing and probability of the second burst of innovation and growth. In this fashion, economic innovation, economic leadership, naval leadership, and war are closely and often reciprocally intertwined.

The concept of lead economy, we should note, does not carry with it some specific threshold of lead. There are at least two implications of this observation worth elaborating. First, unlike the alternative concept of hegemony, the concept of lead economy does not need to emphasize the extent of economic dominance of one group over others. The extent to which a lead economy or a hegemon dominates other actors' economic activities is variable. While we are likely to dismiss the Portuguese or even the Dutch and certainly the eighteenth-century British as good candidates for hegemons because they do not seem to measure up to some unspecified standard of control, it is quite another matter to dismiss these actors as not possessing more dynamic economies than their contemporary rivals. It is also much easier to capture emphatically the dynamic rhythm of their leads than it is to systematically plumb the extent of their influence.

Second, while it is possible to advance a single abstract definition of what a lead economy represents, the real-world manifestations of this phenomenon need not all look alike. There are weak leads and strong leads. The scope of the lead may also be relatively narrow or fairly wide in the number or variety of commercial and industrial activities encompassed. The American lead in the twentieth century has been stronger and wider than the British lead in the nineteenth century. Both leads were more impressive than any that preceded them. The Dutch seventeenth-century lead is the next most comparable case. In contrast, the leads established in the sixteenth and eighteenth centuries were substantially weaker and/or more narrow.

Relative Decline

Rising and falling system leaders are intimately related to long-wave fluctuations. Lead economies help establish a commanding position in the pace of commercial-industrial growth. This growth facilitates the development of the lead economy's commercial and financial centrality in the global system. The movement toward increasing productive, commercial, and financial centrality encourages the development of two other essential ingredients: the gradual ascendancy of a globally oriented, domestic ruling coalition and the creation of a politico-military infrastructure of global-reach capabilities. Victory in global war is of course still another facilitator, and a historically crucial one, in the promotion of many of these processes.[11]

The precise rate at which this leadership cycle plays itself out is variable and dependent on several factors. The number and nature of the competition make some difference, although this may be a partly spurious consideration. The competitive field increases in number and ambition in interaction with the pace of the lead economy's relative decline. Competitors hasten the tempo just as they are encouraged by the perception of its existence.

The frequency and scope of warfare matters, particularly to fluctuations in commerce and prices, but these factors are also double-edged. Wars can be diversionary drains, as manifested in the damage done to the Dutch commercial position by Spain, England, and France in the seventeenth century. The Anglo-French wars of the eighteenth century, by way of contrast, facilitated the British lead in that century and the next. In the sixteenth century, major power warfare in Italy, as well as even earlier Mongol and Ottoman combat, facilitated the Portuguese opportunity to seize control of maritime trade in the Indian Ocean. We should also keep in mind that the Dutch position in the Baltic grain trade had been taken away from Hanseatic towns by force.

The location of the lead economy also makes some difference. The Portuguese certainly were well situated for exploration in the South Atlantic. The Dutch were nicely located in a variety of ways for playing the role of a commercial intermediary in Europe. The English found themselves ideally situated for harassing Dutch maritime traffic and taking over some of Amsterdam's functions. Furthermore, geographic location implies something concerning resource endowments as well. The rise of Britain as an industrial leader, for instance, was linked closely with the relative ease with which it was able to exploit its ample coal deposits.

Yet there is also a negative side to the role of location. An advantage at the beginning of a century may turn out to be a disadvantage a number of years later. Portugal's location, no doubt, encouraged its diversionary preoccupation with Moroccan expansion and its eventual conquest by neighboring Spain. The easiest, although not the most comprehensive, way to explain Dutch decline is that the Dutch found themselves physically trapped in a squeeze play between globally ascending England and regionally rising France, after its long duel with Spain. The British dependence on coal, like the Dutch reliance on peat, eventually proved to be a disadvantage when the time came to shift to new sources of energy.

Ultimately, though, the shape, if not the sources, of long-term growth rhythms can be reduced to the technological innovations that fuel growth and the conditions that encourage or discourage continued technological innovation. Competition, warfare, and location must be counted among these conditions. Also noteworthy is the diffusion that facilitates the catch-up efforts of rivals. At the heart of the matter, though, is the tendency for innovation to encounter diminishing marginal returns at some juncture. In addition, the development of complacency and institutional rigidities helps ensure that experimentation with new ways of doing things are more apt to be tried somewhere other than in the economy that pioneered the currently conventional methods. Resource exhaustion or scarcities, of both the human and the nonhuman variety, may also play some role in discouraging the prospects for the renewal of economic growth.

It is difficult to maintain a national monopoly in leading-sector innovation for long. The technology diffuses too easily to other economies. International competition increases accordingly, as does protectionism, when newly emerging competitors seek to insulate their own infant leading sectors. The lead economy begins to find its access to markets abroad more restricted. At roughly the same time, older leading sectors in the lead economy are confronting increasing costs and diminishing marginal returns in the once innovative technology. Ubiquitous institutional rigidities—complacency, the conservative avoidance of risks, and vested interests rank among the most important forms—only compound the difficulties of maintaining a technological lead.[12]

It is impossible to summarize the complex processes of relative decline in a paragraph or two. Nor do the processes come together exactly the same way every time. Brief summaries, therefore, cannot do justice to the nuances of the sixteenth-century Portuguese, the seventeenth-century Dutch, the eighteenth- and nineteenth-century British, and the twentieth-century American cases. Nevertheless, it is possible to use the long waves in leading-sector growth rates to illuminate quickly some key aspects of the relative decline of global leaders.

As Polybius noted many centuries ago, there are two different, basic

Table 5.1 Leading-Sector Growth Rates, 1830s–1900s

Decade	Cotton Textiles	Iron	Railroads	Chemicals	Steel	Mean Growth Rate
Britain						
1830s	0.076	0.051	0.357	—	—	0.161
1840s	0.064	0.064	0.198	—	—	0.109
1850s	0.047	0.056	0.047	—	—	0.050
1860s	0.030	0.041	0.040	0.097	—	0.042
1870s	0.023	0.011	0.018	0.047	0.156	0.048
1880s	0.034	0.038	0.011	0.001	0.145	0.046
1890s	0.014	0.015	0.008	0.010	0.036	0.043
1900s	0.005	0.038	0.007	0.010	0.024	0.080
United States						
1830s	0.112	0.070	0.952	—	—	0.350
1840s	0.108	0.115	0.127	—	—	0.117
1850s	0.073	0.022	0.144	—	—	0.051
1860s	0.070	0.101	0.047	0.276	—	0.081
1870s	0.060	0.061	0.074	0.132	0.367	0.133
1880s	0.053	0.119	0.063	0.112	0.153	0.100
1890s	0.057	0.088	0.024	0.052	0.140	0.072
1900s	0.039	0.096	0.027	0.068	0.137	0.140
Germany						
1830s	0.000	0.046	2.042	—	—	0.305
1840s	0.608	0.006	0.383	—	—	0.152
1850s	0.136	0.097	0.069	—	—	0.101
1860s	0.062	0.112	0.050	—	—	0.075
1870s	0.079	0.048	0.069	0.083	0.174	0.089
1880s	0.069	0.076	0.023	0.144	0.152	0.093
1890s	0.031	0.062	0.020	0.059	0.115	0.058
1900s	0.046	0.048	0.018	0.061	0.073	0.103

Source: Based on Thompson 1990a: 228–29.

Note: For each sector, data were first averaged on an annual basis. Annual averages were then summed for each decade. Mean growth rates represent the means of the annual averages summed for each decade. They are not the means of averages reported in the columns on average growth rate. For that matter, averages for all sectors examined to calculate the mean growth rate are not reported in this table.

economic manifestations of relative decline. One type involves international comparison. A state's relative share of the world's total in some aspect of economic activity (such as production, trade, financial services, and technological innovation) declines relative to the shares held by its competitors. Such an occurrence need not really imply faltering economic performance on the part of the state falling behind. It may simply be that the competition is doing better.

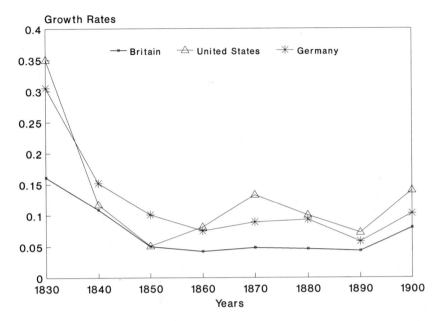

Figure 5.2 Leading-Sector Growth Rates in Britain, the
United States, and Germany

The second type of relative decline does entail faltering performance.
An economy experiences relative decline if it no longer performs as well as it
once did. Hence, declining rates of growth in production, productivity, and
employment indicate an economy declining relative to its own past record of
achievement. This type of relative decline, however, need not imply any
loss of relative shares. Everyone else in the system may be doing equally
poorly or even worse.

The relative economic decline of global leaders combines both types of
decline. The global leader surrenders its preponderant leads in various
spheres of activity primarily because rivals catch up and surpass the faltering
leader. A focus on technological innovation and leading-sector production af-
fords an unusually good vantage point from which to observe these processes.

Concentrating on the period between the 1830s and World War I, we
show in table 5.1 and figure 5.2 what took place in the leading sectors of the
nineteenth-century system leader and its two important contenders. In the
second half of the century, the growth potential of the old sectors—textiles,
iron, and railroads—began to erode in Britain much more than in the United
States or Germany. The new sectors—chemicals and steel—yielded high
growth rates initially, but they were not as high as those in the two contending states. British growth rates in chemicals and steel also decayed quite

rapidly, especially in comparison with American and German rates. Electrification was comparatively slow to catch on in Britain. Automobile production looked promising at first, but the promise was never fully realized in what became, for a long while, the preeminent American specialty.[13]

Leading-sector growth did not disappear altogether in late nineteenth-century Britain. The aggregated growth rates, however, did go flat from the 1860s through the 1890s. The same thing cannot be said about American and German growth rates, as we see in figure 5.2. Of course, knowing this does not tell us exactly why the British lead faltered and was overtaken. But it does help narrow our field of inquiry. The relative decline of Britain was not simply a matter of the rise of competitors with superior resource endowments. The rise of competitors is an important part of the explanation, but so too are the factors that account for the slowdown in growth within the leader's lead sectors.[14] The focus on leading sectors also supports the argument that World War I did not bring the British leadership down. It only capped a process of competitive decline that was first discernible in the mid-nineteenth century and perhaps even a little earlier.

More might be said about the processes of relative decline, both about how they have played themselves out in the past and how they proceed in general. Now, though, we propose moving on to this chapter's last task—testing the relationships among innovation, economic leadership, naval leadership, and war. For if these alleged relationships are absent, it will become evident that we are barking up the wrong tree. If the relationships are present in the anticipated form, we will have additional reason to believe that the rise and fall of leading sectors and lead economies are central to the etiology of systemic warfare.

Modeling Innovation and War

The Hypotheses

Our expectations include the following seven hypotheses:

HYPOTHESIS 5.1: Innovation increases the probability of leading-sector share concentration and naval capability share concentration.

HYPOTHESIS 5.2: Leading-sector share concentration increases the probability of naval capability share concentration.

HYPOTHESIS 5.3: An increase in innovation, in the first wave of a two-wave set, increases the probability of global war.

HYPOTHESIS 5.4: Leading-sector share deconcentration increases the probability of global war.

HYPOTHESIS 5.5: Global war increases the probability of innovation within the economy of the global leader.

HYPOTHESIS 5.6: Global war increases leading-sector share concentration favoring the global leader.

HYPOTHESIS 5.7: Global war increases naval capability share concentration favoring the global leader.

In hypothesis 5.1, we expect the fluctuations in innovation to influence leading-sector share concentration (economic leadership) and naval capability share concentration (naval leadership). The link between innovation and leading-sector production should be quite direct. Innovation in commercial activities is also likely to lead to an expansion of the naval resource base for protecting new trade networks. As the emphasis shifts to industrial exports, the need for naval protection continues.

Hypothesis 5.2 connects leading-sector share concentration to naval capability share. The hypothesized relationship that is consistent across time is that economic leadership paid for a commensurate naval capability. Earlier in the modern system's history, naval capability was probably a major causal influence on leading-sector share. Before the mid-eighteenth century, naval power was essential to a state that wished to acquire control over a commercial leading sector, whether it was Baltic grain, Indonesian spices, Indian cloth, Caribbean sugar, or Chinese tea. In every case, sea power proved critical to breaking into these trades—or taking them away from someone else—as well as subsequently protecting the market shares that had been captured. By the late eighteenth century, the emphasis had begun to shift to industrial developments that depended more on technological innovations at home than on control of long-distance markets. Hence we do not expect the relationship between these two variables to be fully reciprocal in the nineteenth and twentieth centuries.

Relating innovation and global war in a bivariate statement, as in hypothesis 5.3, requires qualification because of our argument that radical innovation comes in paired spurts and only the first spurt is destabilizing. The second spurt further consolidates the pecking order established after the first spurt and the global war. Because the second spurt follows a period of global war, its potentially destabilizing consequences are absorbed by an environment not yet ready for major challenges to the status quo. The hierarchical destabilization inherent to the first spurt might suggest a positive relationship between leading-sector share concentration and warfare, but we suspect that the stronger effect is registered in the global leader's decline phase. Decreasing concentration should make global war more likely, as specified in hypothesis 5.4. We do not expect a corresponding link from naval capability share concentration to war because of the intervening variable of

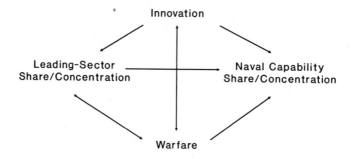

Figure 5.3 Four Variables and Their Interrelationships at the Core of the Structural Transition Model

regional concentration, which is not present in this abbreviated version of our larger model. It is possible that such a relationship might be found. Theoretically, however, we have little reason to expect it.

Hypotheses 5.5, 5.6, and 5.7 reverse the usual emphasis on war as the object of explanation. We have argued that global war facilitates a global leader's second innovational spurt (hypothesis 5.5). Waging global war in the first innovational spurt, in addition to the effects of the postwar spurt, should be expected to increase the leader's sectoral share (hypothesis 5.6). Global war is also a period of crisis in which one expects to find a significant expansion of naval capability (Thompson 1988). The nature of global war additionally works to reduce the naval capabilities of the leader's opposition. Thus we anticipate a positive link from global war to naval capability share concentration (hypothesis 5.7). In sum, eight relationships, sketched in figure 5.3, are expected.

The Variables

The naval capability share variable is indexed primarily by the relative proportion of capital ships possessed by the global leader. Two of the four indicators employed are based on a leading-sector data set described by Thompson (1988). Following the arguments of Schumpeter (1939) and Rostow (1978), thirteen production indicators for twelve leading-sector commodities—raw cotton consumption, pig iron, railroad track, crude steel, sulfuric acid, electrical energy, motor vehicles, nitrogen fertilizer, plastics/resins, synthetic fibers, semiconductors, and civilian jet airframes—were aggregated for the periods during which a significant sector is thought to have been leading in the sense that its rate of growth exceeded the general rate of growth of industrial production. These data, collected for Britain, France, the United States, Germany, and Japan, were used to calculate relative shares of leading-sector production.[15] The leading-sector growth rate measures the pace of innovation.

While data on leading-sector growth rates are currently available back to the fourteenth century (Modelski and Thompson forthcoming), the ability to calculate relative shares is restricted largely to the Industrial Age, or the late eighteenth century on. This restriction limits the empirical analysis to the two most recent global system leaders, Britain and the United States. Analysis of the British data begins in 1780 and concludes in the year before World War I began. The U.S. relationships are examined between 1870 and 1980.

We do not assume that these cases are identical in every respect. Most important, Britain completed two cycles, whereas the United States has yet to finish its current cycle. But the nineteenth- and twentieth-century leaderships should have more in common with each other than with earlier cases, because the latest global regimes have been predicated on industrial innovation and prowess, as opposed to the earlier emphasis on the dominance of key commercial networks. As a consequence, we expect these two cases to manifest similar basic relationships among the selected variables.

One indicator remains to be justified. Battle deaths have become the most conventional index for measuring the amount of warfare in models requiring continuous data (as opposed to the type of analysis conducted in chapters 3 and 4). The modeling we propose does make this requirement, but, as noted earlier, we have a number of reservations about the practice of examining battle deaths. The number of military personnel killed is not always a consistent indicator of the political significance of a war to the functioning of the global system. This distinction is critical to our theoretical approach. Some local and regional wars have managed to kill as many soldiers as some of the earlier global wars.

Other problems include historical changes in the size of military forces (the more troops mobilized, presumably, the more that are likely to be at risk in combat), the medical support for troops in the field, and the lethality of weapon systems. The longer the time series, the more difficult it is to ignore the impact of these types of change on the interpretation of military casualties. There are also severe technical problems associated with attempting to analyze a series that fluctuates a great deal from year to year in the early modern phase, only to register infrequent but incredibly violent activity in the late modern period (after 1815). Even if one eliminates the earlier centuries, as we are doing, a series with a large number of zero observations, while desirable given the subject matter, is awkward to analyze. At least, the quantitative outcome must be viewed with more than the normal degree of caution.

There is an alternative measure of the significance of war that avoids many of the problems associated with battle-death indices. Indeed, we find it surprising that this measure is so rarely employed. The indicator that we

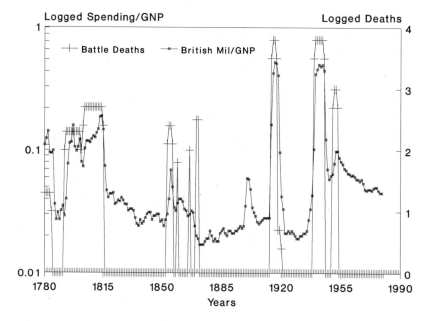

Figure 5.4 Great Power Battle Deaths and British Military Spending/GNP

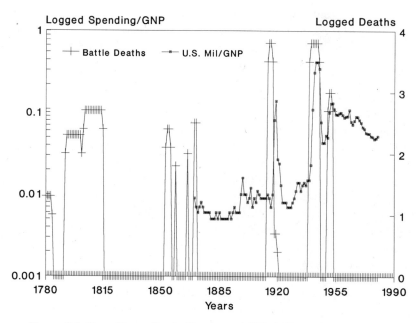

Figure 5.5 Great Power Battle Deaths and U.S. Military Spending/GNP

have in mind is military expenditures as a proportion of gross national product. The main drawback is that it is difficult to project this indicator much farther back than the late eighteenth century, because of the paucity of national income data. This is not a problem for our two global leader cases, though. Moreover, the indicator, which taps directly into the level of resources mobilized for the purpose of warfare, works quite well in differentiating between wars of global and less than global significance.

In figures 5.4 and 5.5 we demonstrate this by comparing British and American military expenditures as a proportion of GNP with great power battle deaths (see Goldstein 1988).[16] The highest peaks in the two resource mobilization indices are reserved for the global warfare in the 1792-1815 and 1914-45 periods. The less than globally significant combat in the middle of the nineteenth century and during the Korean War is not given as much weight by the resource mobilization approach as it is by the battle-death index.

We do not claim that the resource mobilization approach provides a perfectly valid instrument, only that it is less handicapped than the battle-death approach. For instance, we can see in figure 5.4 that the American Revolution appears to approximate the effort expended during the French Revolution. If we were examining the earlier portion of the eighteenth century, we would certainly have more difficulty distinguishing between the Anglo-French fighting of the 1739-83 era and the 1792-1815 period. There is also the problem of the late nineteenth-century Boer War expenditures, which are more prominent in the figure than that war's general political significance probably warrants.

The liabilities are a little different in the U.S. series. The late entry of the United States in World War I is noticeable in figure 5.5's serial comparison. One might also point to the United States's relatively high, cold war resource mobilization rate after 1950 as a source of a potential interpretation problem. Are we measuring global war, preparations for war in general, or both? *Both* seems most accurate. Yet it is possible to view this attribute of the indicator as a plus. Battle deaths, particularly after 1815, resemble a series of spikes that rise abruptly and disappear equally abruptly. The major wartime spikes in military spending as a proportion of GNP are often preceded by more gradual preparations for an impending conflict. Following war, the mobilization effort frequently takes some time to revert to peacetime norms. Which image of warfare seems more appropriate? We prefer the more graduated portrayal, especially since we are trying to determine how economic and military decline are related to warfare. Certainly in this context, the high cost of preparing for global war after 1950 may be just as germane as the resources expended in fighting the last global war.

A related issue is raised by Bremer (1992), among others. If we are interested in explaining the occurrence of wars, should we not isolate out-breaks from what happens after the war begins—including duration, battle deaths, and resources expended? While we are sympathetic to this argu-ment, a nominal index of war is restrictive in the type of modeling that can be explained. More important, in this segment of the model we are inter-ested in processes that lead to war *and* the postwar consequences for these processes. That is to say, we are less concerned with precisely how low the pace of innovation or the shares of leading-sector production and naval capa-bility are the year before the outbreak of global war than with the reciprocal pattern of economic and military activities. Thus we prefer the approach of measuring resources expended for this set of questions. Obviously, this is not an absolute preference. In chapters 3 and 4, we used the nominal ap-proach to global warfare (the presence or absence of an outbreak) to examine the questions pertaining to transitions and the contextual interaction of global and regional concentration.

Despite the various interpretation liabilities, we should note that the battle-death and resources expended approaches to measuring war are re-lated. The 1780-1980 correlation between British proportional military spending and great power battle deaths is 0.715. The correlation is even higher (0.766) for the 1780-1913 period. In the case of the United States, the correlation between the two indices is more moderate (0.492 for the 1870-1980 period), in part owing to the spending levels of the cold war. The 1870-1945 correlation is a bit higher (0.584). Nevertheless, since our posi-tion is that the military spending indicator has fewer interpretation liabilities than the battle-death index, it is not incumbent upon us to demonstrate that the two war indicators measure precisely the same behavior. As we have noted, they do not. They do, however, definitely overlap.

Methodology

We use three methodological techniques to explore the causal linkages among the variables: cross-correlational analysis, Granger causality, and—for the appropriate cases—time series regression estimation.[17] But to sim-plify the presentation, we have placed the cross-correlational analysis and time series regression findings and discussions in appendix C. Cross-correla-tional analysis is a preliminary technique for assessing the direction and tim-ing of relationships among our four variables. The preliminary correlational findings are then subjected to the more demanding tests associated with Granger causality analysis. In Granger causality examinations, the goal is to determine which variable antecedes another. *Antecedence* is not a synonym for causality but a minimal expectation related to the claim that one variable "causes" another: the variable being influenced must be preceded in time

Table 5.2 Quasi F-statistics for Granger Tests of Antecedence:
United States, 1870–1980

| | | Dependent Variable | | |
Independent Variable	War	Naval Capability Share	Leading-Sector Share	Leading-Sector Growth Rate
Granger Tests of Antecedence:				
War	—	4.39*	2.32*	6.73*
Naval Capability Share	1.10	—	0.89	2.50
Leading-Sector Share	2.70*	4.45*	—	1.50
Leading-Sector Growth Rate	6.83*	1.28	0.89	—
Instantaneous Tests of Antecedence:				
War	—	—	—	—
Naval Capability Share	—	—	—	—
Leading-Sector Share	—	—	—	—
Leading-Sector Growth Rate	—	3.13*	3.25*	—

*p is less than or equal to .05

Note: Lag structure for war and naval capability share, naval capability share and leading-sector share, naval capability share and leading-sector growth rate, and leading-sector share and leading-sector growth rate is 4 lags on the endogenous and exogenous variables; war and leading-sector share is 5 lags on the endogenous and exogenous variables, plus lag 12 on the exogenous variable; and, war and leading-sector growth is 4 lags on the endogenous and exogenous variables.

Coefficients for statistically insignificant, instantaneous tests of antecedence are not reported.

by the influencing variable. While the Granger analyses are rigorous, they do not produce estimates of the varying strengths of the relationships. Time series regression can provide such estimates as long as the relationships are unidirectional. Since our hypotheses do not speak directly to the question of relationship strength and since we will also encounter some reciprocal relationships, our estimates of the strengths of the unidirectional relationships are reported in appendix C.

Data Analysis

A rigorous appraisal of the causal relationships among the variables may be obtained by calculating quasi F-statistics so that reductions of sums of squared errors with the addition of causally prior variables can be assessed according to statistical tests of significance. The results for the United States and Britain can be found in tables 5.2 and 5.3 respectively. Starting with the U.S. case, the statistical tests of antecedence show that, among the nonwar variables, only leading-sector share is statistically significant and antecedent to the naval capability share series. The remaining relationships show weak connections. These are not unexpected results. The cross-correlations (appendix C) show that the strongest relationship between leading-sector share and naval capability share occurs in the first three time lags and only when leading-sector share lags behind naval capability share. The relationships between leading-sector growth rate and leading-sector share, and leading-sector growth rate and naval capability share, are strongest at the zero time lag. Therefore, $\underline{F}$-statistics for tests of instantaneous causality are conducted for these relationships. They appear in the second half of table 5.2. Interestingly, the results indicate that the current and past values of leading-sector growth rate predict significantly to the current values of naval capability share and leading-sector share but not the other way around.

The tests relating the naval and leading-sector variables to war confirm the cross-correlational findings. There are indeed two-way relationships between war and leading-sector share and war and leading-sector growth rate. A one-way relationship between war and naval capability share is disclosed, with war as the exogenous variable. The signs of the coefficients also match the signs of the cross-correlational values in appendix C.

Turning to the British case, the initial results in the top half of table 5.3 indicate that leading-sector share and leading-sector growth rate are statistically antecedent to naval capability share. The cross-correlations between the series tend to support these results. The highest correlations occur between leading-sector share and naval capability share at the ninth and tenth time lags when leading-sector share is lagged behind naval capability share. Although the correlations between leading-sector growth rate and naval capability share are small at the earlier time lags, a 0.2 correlation occurs at the seventh time lag when leading-sector growth rate is lagged behind naval capability share.

Similarly, the lack of any strong association between leading-sector growth rate and leading-sector share beyond the zero time lag is reaffirmed by the inconclusive antecedent tests. Nevertheless, the instantaneous statistical tests in the second half of table 5.3 indicate that there is a two-way or feedback relationship between leading-sector share and leading-sector growth rate. In this instance, both the current and previous values of leading-sector share predict to the current values of leading-sector growth rate and vice versa.

The inferential tests for the relationships involving war suggest that, as in the U.S. case, in the British case there is a one-way directional relationship between war and naval capability share, with war as the exogenous variable. The sign of the lag 5 coefficient matches that of the correlation (see appendix C) with a positive and statistically significant value.

We again find two-way relationships between war and the two leading-

Table 5.3 Quasi $\underline{F}$-statistics for Granger Tests of Antecedence:
Britain, 1780–1870

	Dependent Variable			
Independent Variable	War	Naval Capability Share	Leading-Sector Share	Leading-Sector Growth Rate
Granger Tests of Antecedence:				
War	—	2.22*	5.83*	2.53*
Naval Capability Share	0.60	—	1.48	0.63
Leading-Sector Share	10.37*	2.22	—	1.00
Leading-Sector Growth Rate	5.34*	2.14	0.96	—
Instantaneous Tests of Antecedence:				
War	—	—	—	—
Naval Capability Share	—	—	—	—
Leading-Sector Share	—	—	—	8.11*
Leading-Sector Growth Rate	—	—	7.47*	—

*$\underline{p}$ is less than or equal to .05

Note: Lag structure for war and naval capability share is 6 lags on the endogenous and exogeneous variables; war and leading-sector share is 4 lags on the endogenous and exogenous variables, plus lag 16 on the exogenous variable; war and leading-sector growth rate is 4 lags on the endogenous and exogenous variables, plus lags 5 and 11 for the exogenous variable; naval capability share and leading-sector share is 10 lags on the endogenous and exogenous variables; naval capability share and leading-sector growth rate is 7 lags on the endogenous and exogenous variables; and leading-sector share and leading-sector growth rate is 11 lags on the endogenous and exogenous variables.

Coefficients for statistically insignificant, instantaneous tests of antecedence are not reported.

sector variables. When leading-sector share is causally prior to war, we obtain not only a significant $\underline{F}$-statistic but also only one statistically significant coefficient, which happens to be negative at lag 16. Likewise, the $\underline{F}$-statistic is significant when war is causally prior to leading-sector share and there is one statistically significant coefficient at lag 16, which in this case is positive.

Unlike the cross-correlational results, there is indeed a bidirectional association between war and leading-sector growth rate. When leading-sector growth rate is lagged behind war, we obtain a statistically significant $\underline{F}$-test and a significant positive coefficient at lag 5. When war is causally prior to leading-sector growth rate, the $\underline{F}$-test is also significant, along with a statistically significant positive coefficient at lag 5.

Interpreting the Findings

The essence of our research problem has involved searching for evidence to support or reject the anticipated ways in which the four variables in figure

5.3 are related. Through seven hypotheses, we hypothesized eight relationships: innovation to leading-sector share concentration, to naval capability share concentration, and to global war; leading-sector share concentration to naval capability share concentration and to global war; and global war to innovation, to leading-sector share concentration, and to naval capability share concentration.

As depicted in figure 5.6, all of the hypothesized relationships proved to be significant for both the British and U.S. cases. Reciprocal relationships were found linking innovation and global war (hypotheses 5.3 and 5.5) and global war and leading-sector share concentration (hypotheses 5.4 and 5.6). A positive, one-way relationship between war and naval capability share concentration was also found (hypothesis 5.7). We view this outcome as striking support for our interpretation of the lethality of structural transition.

Technological innovation thus has important implications for economic leadership, naval leadership, and the likelihood of global war. In the absence of radical innovation, economic and military leadership are most unlikely. But naval leadership also depends upon economic leadership. Relative economic decline ultimately will lead to the decay of naval leadership. Both types of decline, in conjunction with threatening regional capability concentration, increase the probability of global war. Winning a global war then has further important implications for innovation, leading-sector concentration, and sea power.

Each of the three methodological approaches has yielded consistent empirical results. In the U.S. case, the causal linkages show that leading-sector share and leading-sector growth rate influence the naval capability share series and that leading-sector growth rate influences the leading-sector share series. In the British case, leading-sector share and leading-sector growth rate influence the naval capability share series at ten- and seven-year lags respectively. Less anticipated, but hardly a devastating deviation from the prediction, leading-sector growth rate and leading-sector share have a two-way relationship.

The processes examined appear to work similarly in the two leadership cases. The major exception to this observation is found in the different lag structures and some reciprocal linkages. Perhaps the processes linking innovation to relative capability have accelerated in the twentieth century. This may help to explain why the "American century," in comparison with the Pax Britannica, has seemed so brief to some observers.

Acceleration is one explanation. Another avenue to consider is the ways in which the two leadership cases differ. They differ in both the rise and the decline dimensions. Britain enjoyed two terms of global or transoceanic leadership. Our British data analysis begins toward the end of the first term (1780) and concludes at or near the end of the second term (1913). Through-

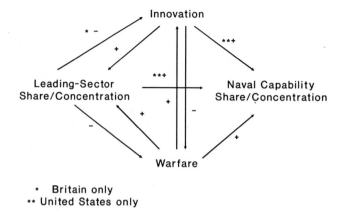

Figure 5.6 Four Variables and the Tests of Antecedence Findings

out this period, Britain maintained a lead in naval capabilities that nevertheless demonstrated some degree of fluctuation. Relative decline was manifested toward the ends of the eighteenth and nineteenth centuries. A major improvement in relative naval position occurred toward the end of the Napoleonic Wars.

The relative decline of Britain's leading-sector share, in contrast, was precipitous after 1870. Earlier, Britain's leading-sector share had climbed most rapidly between 1780 and 1810. Hence, the general pattern is one of abrupt rises and declines in leading-sector activity (encompassing the cyclicity of leading-sector growth as well) and much more gradual and belated adjustments in naval capability shares. The main exceptions are the nineteenth-century postwar spike and the more gradual twentieth-century postwar erosion (not included in the data analysis) in naval capabilities. But these exceptions deviate only from the gradual movement tendency of naval capability shares and not from the notion of a roughly decadal lag between leading-sector activity and naval share adjustments.

The U.S. case is not complicated by an earlier rise that predates the data analysis. Leading-sector and naval capability position climbed roughly together to peaks around world wars I and II, with positional erosion characterizing the postwar eras. Leading-sector growth took place most prominently before World War I, when the two positional series were trending upward, and during the 1940s, when the positional series were peaking.

Of course, we do not mean to suggest that a description of how the series fluctuate in correspondence to one another should also serve as an explanation of those fluctuations. The verbal description reinforces the finding of a lag in one case and its absence in the second one. The explanation, however, has to do with history and timing. If Britain had replaced some other state as the leader of the world's transoceanic political economy in the Napoleonic Wars, as opposed to reinvigorating its own economic foundation, the lag between economic and naval activity at the rise might have been less. Similarly, if we had an American series projecting well into the twenty-first century, it might be possible to discern more of a lag developing between the erosion of economic position and the diminishment of global-reach capabilities. In some respects, the 1990 Kuwait crisis offers an illustrative metaphor, with an American system leader capable of projecting military force into the Arabian Peninsula but initially finding it somewhat more awkward to finance the undertaking.

In situations of relative decline, we therefore should expect to find some lag in the comparative pace of erosion in economic and military capability positions. Less of a lag should be anticipated in situations of ascent, unless the circumstances are biased somehow by previous history. In particular, two types of bias come to mind. The first is the reimposition of a leadership regime, as in the British case, in which a substantial amount of naval capability is already present when a state's economic fortunes begin to improve once again. The other type of situation involves economic leaders who are constrained by internal and external pressures from developing corresponding capabilities of global military reach. Contemporary Japan and Germany are good examples.

The reciprocal relationship between leading-sector growth rate and share—observed in the British case but not in the American one—may also be traceable to the "fuller" history associated with the British case. The British began their rapid slide from technological leadership and leading-sector production share in a period of slow sectoral growth. It was also a period of slower sectoral growth for the British than for the Americans or the Germans, Britain's ostensible successors. Because Britain was sliding or relatively declining away from the leadership position in the late nineteenth century, should not that have had some effect on the state's continued ability to innovate?

The statement may sound tautological, but the historical pattern seems to be that declining leaders find it difficult to extricate themselves from a descending trajectory. The one exception to date has been eighteenth-century Britain, and that turnaround required an industrial revolution. More often than not, however, people find it extremely difficult to abandon ways of doing things that have proved successful in the past. Old leaders miss, or catch too late, new waves of innovation because they are still focused, like generals prepared to refight the last war, on exploiting earlier technological and commercial waves. If the British case is the norm, then innovation and decline interact to create a vicious circle, with more decline leading to even less innovation, or at least slower innovation.

Whether or not one finds these post hoc explanations of lagged and reciprocal relationships plausible, it is equally important to stress that the uncovered relationships are sufficiently robust that they can survive unusually demanding statistical tests designed to challenge assertions of causality as much as is methodologically feasible. In other words, the findings encourage us to continue probing the validity of the overall model.

Combining these current findings with our earlier findings on the impact of global war on phases of naval capability concentration (appendix B), we can also further our understanding of how the processes of the central global political economy operate. The relative economic and military positions of the system leader clearly depend on the pace of technological innovation or the extent to which system leaders maintain their dynamic growth and lead economy status. Paraphrasing Modelski (1987: 229), we might say that the profits of innovation pay for the system leader's enterprises and commitments on the world stage. If the profits decay and are not renewed, the material foundation of systemic leadership will decay as well. To the extent that this positional decay goes unchecked, the probability of global war is enhanced accordingly, because deconcentration in the global system is one of the prerequisites for systemic war. Completing the circle, global wars have important consequences for the subsequent likelihood and pace of innovation, leading-sector concentration, and sea power.

We do not regard our emphasis on technological innovation as the key to global leadership ascent and relative decline as deterministic. Others no doubt will insist on seeing it that way, but we view it as more closely approximating a necessary but not sufficient factor in attaining and maintaining leadership status. In the absence of the right type of innovational edge at the right time, global leadership is highly unlikely. For that matter, leadership on the part of anyone is not inevitable. A discontinuous pattern of economic growth, subject to bursts of radical change in the way things are done, helps lay the groundwork for the probability of inequality. The tendency toward innovative monopoly on a national basis further accentuates the types of bias in system structure that promote periods of clear national leads, if not leadership.

Innovation increases the probability of economic and naval leadership. All three variables are related directly and indirectly to warfare. Yet surely other factors intervene in this simplistic formulation of the cyclical road to war. We certainly do not preclude significance for all other variables left outside the quartet examined in this chapter. Our own model (see figure 1.3) explicitly incorporates other variables. We can also conceive richer, more detailed maps of the connection(s) between innovation and economic leadership. In chapter 6 we will review the history of one of the more often asserted connections that comes in a variety of guises—namely, that leaders undermine their own leads by overspending their limited resources. The point of chapter 6 is to establish a basis for empirically testing this idea; the actual execution is left to chapter 7.

6.

Perspectives on Overconsumption and Decline

We are certainly not the first, nor will we be the last, to raise the question of why major political organizations rise and decline. For at least twenty-five hundred years and no doubt more, observers have speculated on the rise and fall of dynasties, states, and empires. Their efforts are worth reviewing. Not only do they suggest plausible hypotheses to examine, but their explanations of decline also exhibit strong elements of continuity.

One such element is the development of some type of capability edge as the main avenue of ascent. Our interpretation of the roots of global leaders' capability edges was discussed in chapter 5. A second element of continuity is an emphasis on "excessive" consumption as a principal root cause of decline. Overconsumption dissipates the capability edge. While this is an enduring theme of decline arguments, we suspect its applicability to the global leaders is limited. Overconsumption, we believe, is something of a red herring. We will explore this problem empirically in chapter 7. But first we need to understand where and how these ideas originated.

Focusing primarily on the historical development of the overconsumption theme, we first review the perspectives of the ancient Greeks and Romans and the medieval theories of Ibn Khaldun. Next we examine two more contemporary and highly synthetic models of decline: Cipolla's (1970) imperial decline model and Gilpin's (1981) hegemonic decline model. A third model, constructed by Sprout and Sprout (1968), is less ambitious. Whereas Cipolla and Gilpin sought to model generic imperial behavior, the Sprouts were interested primarily in processes associated with the decline of industrialized and democratizing major powers. Britain in the late nineteenth and the twentieth centuries was their principal reference point. We conclude our review with discussion of the ongoing policy debate about the slowdown in U.S. economic growth and productivity. We combine these literatures because we think they have much in common and because they point the way toward basic tests of overconsumption arguments—tests that we actively pursue in chapter 7.

The Greco-Roman View of Rise-and-Fall Dynamics

According to de Romilly's (1977) useful interpretative overview of ancient Greek ideas about decline, several generalizations describe Greek theories of the rise and fall of states or empires. First, states could be discussed as if they were individuals. No meaningful differences were felt to distinguish how a person behaved from how collective political organizations functioned. In part for this reason, the most obvious metaphor for an imperial rise-and-fall process was the biological cycle of birth, maturity, and the deterioration of old age. The defeat of an old state by a young and rising state was an outcome foreordained by nature. A second implication of this perception was the lack of explanatory emphasis placed on contextual factors such as socioeconomic considerations or population movements. Instead, the Greeks preferred to explain individual and state behavior in psychological terms.

Two seemingly conflictual approaches to explaining the rise of empires thus prevailed. When describing the ascent of an empire, ancient Greeks devoted little attention to discussing why some states became more powerful than their neighbors. Evidently, the assumption of greater power was also viewed as a natural process that raised few interesting questions. States expanded their power when and if they could. It therefore sufficed to describe the activities that marked successive mileposts in the successful expansion.

More interesting was the question of decline. Then as now, authors were drawn to contemporary policy problems. The decline of Persia, Athens, Sparta, Carthage, and Rome, not surprisingly, constitutes an important theme in many of the ancient writings that have survived. Yet, somewhat contrary to the lack of explicit interest in questions concerning rise, the Greeks thought that rise-and-decline phenomena were closely related. Decline was basically a corruption of the principles responsible for the initial ascent. Thus, general factors underlying the rise of states or empires were identified, but usually only in retrospect when an author was discussing their fall from power.

No single detailed decline scenario or model emerges from de Romilly's survey of Greek authors. A highly generalized model, however, can encompass the various extant arguments. Success breeds hubris, which is defined in this respect as "ambition and the wish to have more than one's share." Hubris or excess in turn leads to doom and disaster.

There are three basic variations on this general model. The oldest form explains the problem by describing gods who are angered by human excesses. A metaphor employed by Herodotus (1972) in a Persian context is the tendency for lightning—a visible manifestation of the wrath of the gods—to strike tall buildings and spare more modest structures. Imperial decline, therefore, is a consequence of supernatural punishment for mortals who have exceeded the boundaries of appropriate behavior.[1]

A more sophisticated explanation of the downfall of Athens is found in Thucydides (1954). De Romilly interprets Thucydides as stressing two or three routes to the demonstration of hubris. One avenue is associated with sudden success, which encourages overconfidence. A second and more complicated route concerns the need for powerful states to seek more power continually and to exercise it intermittently, as in displays of force. As this imperial dynamic is played out, the probability of deviating from prudent courses of action and of making errors increases. De Romilly views moral decline as Thucydides' causal agent underlying the arrogance of great power. Alternatively, we might see the decay of civic virtues as a third source of policy errors. Whereas an earlier generation followed the dictates of state interests— the Periclean policies—successors abandoned the superior strategies because of personal greed and ambition. The concomitant erosion of communal cohesion was simply a collective manifestation of the decay of individual morality.

For the third variation to appear, some time had to elapse. Since the Greeks prided themselves on their relative poverty—in comparison with the Persians, Phoenicians, and Egyptians—the fall of Athens was more likely to be explained by reference to the excesses of political power, especially the excesses of imperial political power. Power remained a source of corruption in the next epochal imperial fall, that of Rome, but a "new" factor emerged as the most important causal agent of decline.

Whether one chooses to view the success of the long Pax Romana as a function of prudent imperial policy or something that occurred despite major errors of imperial decision making, the Roman Empire, unlike Athens, defeated its opponents for an appreciable period. It stands to reason that something other than political hubris was at fault. The most evident form of excess associated with Rome was linked readily to its impressive concentration and consumption of wealth. Two quotations from historians of Rome capture the basic argument. The first comes from Sallust:

Power is easily preserved by the same qualities which it was first obtained with; but when idleness seizes the place of toil, passion and arrogance the place of self-control and equity, then fortune undergoes the same change as do the habits of life. [de Romilly 1977: 70]

The second commentary on Rome, taken from the *Histories* of Polybius, is more detailed but exhibits the same spirit:

Now there are two ways in which any type of state may die. One is the ruin which comes from outside; the other, in contrast, is the internal crisis. The first is difficult to foresee, the second is determined from within. . . . When in fact a community has overcome many and serious dangers and has reached unquestioned power and leadership, new factors come into play. Prosperity takes its seat in that community and life turns towards luxury. Men become ambitious in their rivalries to achieve magistracies and other distinctions. As this goes on, the aspiration to magistracies or the protest of those who see themselves rejected, the pride and the luxury, will give rise to decadence. . . . The masses of the people will be responsible for the crisis. They feel themselves abused by those who wish to pile up wealth; and by others, ambitious for office, they will be puffed up and flattered with demagogic wiles. Excited and stirred up, they will not wish to continue in obedience or to remain within the limits of law laid down by the patricians. They will want to have all the power, or the greatest power. After that the constitution will have the finest name there is: liberty and democracy. In reality, on the other hand, it will be the worst possible, the rule of the masses. [Mazzarino 1966: 23]

The root of imperial decline had taken on a strong economic flavor. Prosperity facilitated luxury and idleness. The civic virtues that had enabled Rome to rise to Mediterranean imperium once again gave way to private ambitions. Political energies increasingly focused on internal rivalries. Successful expansion had meant the incorporation of non-Romans into the empire as well as into the army. This last development was also fueled by the increasing reluctance of prosperous Romans to serve in the legions as they once had. The decay of military effectiveness presumably was closely linked to the "barbarianization" of Roman military recruitment.

The expanding nature of excess thus evolved in the ancient world from some form of supernatural provocation through the arrogance of imperious power to the corrupting influences of economic prosperity.[2] Too much of a good thing inevitably meant the ultimate decline and fall of the offending party. Subsequently, a leading philosophical question emerged, attempting to determine how best to enjoy the fruits of power without paying the ultimate costs assumed by Athens and Rome.

Models of decline continued to evolve as well. Yet the Greek emphasis on the corrupting influences of excess persists to this day. The next three models we will review, one medieval and two modern, illustrate this point. They also highlight more recent variations on the excess-decline linkage.

Ibn Khaldun's Model of Dynastic Decline

Ibn Khaldun, a fourteenth-century Arab historian and the only one to produce a sociological interpretation of societal decline during the Middle Ages (see Mazzarino 1966), developed a theory of dynastic rise and decline that begins by categorizing people in one of two groups.[3] On the one hand, there

Table 6.1 Ibn Khaldun's Cycle of Dynastic Rise and Decline

Stage	Description
Success	Opposition defeated and public authority appropriated
Power Concentration	Power, resources, and rewards reserved for ruler and immediate household, clients, and followers
Leisure and Tranquillity	Concentration of wealth and conspicuous public consumption from a position of maximum strength
Contentment and Peacefulness	Complacency and avoidance of departures from tradition
Waste and Squandering	Destruction of dynastic foundation through waste, poor leadership, corruption, and alienation of military and popular support

Source: Based on Ibn Khaldun 1967: 141–42.

are the bedouin desert-dwelling nomads. Since bedouins are the group closest to nature, they are described as brave, energetic, and independent. They also possess the vital assets of toughness, savagery, and tribal solidarity. In vivid contrast, sedentary city dwellers are characterized as soft, cowardly, meek, and dependent. Bringing the two groups together is not unlike causing "beasts of prey" to descend upon "dumb animals." Ibn Khaldun wrote: "Superiority comes to nations through enterprise and courage. The more firmly rooted in desert habits and the wilder a group is, the closer does it come to achieving superiority over others, if both [parties] are approximately equal in number, strength, and group feeling" (1967: 107).

New dynasties emerge when tough nomads conquer and dominate soft urban populations. Once this event takes place, a dynastic cycle with five stages, lasting roughly 120 years, is set in motion (see table 6.1). In the first stage, the local opposition is eliminated, and the defeated dynasty assumes royal authority. The second stage involves the concentration of political power and authority around the ruler and his family and entourage. In the third stage the ruler increases control over the distribution of wealth and the enjoyment of "the fruits of royal authority": property acquisition, monument construction, and fame.

All the ability [of the ruler] is expended on collecting taxes; regulating income and expenses, bookkeeping and planning expenditure; erecting large buildings, big constructions, spacious cities, and lofty monuments; presenting gifts to embassies of nobles from [foreign] nations and tribal dignitaries; and dispensing bounty to his own people. In addition, he supports the demands of his followers and retinue with money and positions. He inspects his soldiers, pays them well and distributes fairly their allowances every month. Eventually, the result of this [liberality] shows itself in their dress, their fine equipment, and their armor on parade days. The ruler, thus, can impress friendly dynasties and frighten hostile ones with [his soldiers]. [Ibn Khaldun 1967: 141-42]

After the third stage, the situation begins to deteriorate. A fourth stage is marked by complacency and the absence of any significant reforms. To depart from tradition, it is felt, would signify straying from a successful, proven path. This lull before the storm ushers in a final stage of dynastic senility. Rulers squander their resources on pleasures. Unqualified state managers are appointed. Opposition and conspiratorial activities spread. Soldiers defect when they are not paid. Foreign mercenaries may be brought in, but they either prolong the dynasty's tenure only momentarily or establish new dynasties of their own.

The root of this decline explanation can be traced to the twin principles that luxury corrupts those who enjoy it and that new conquerors are apt to assimilate themselves into the dominated culture. However spartan the dynastic origins, sooner or later the rulers begin to resemble their predecessors by overconsuming. Their sedentary corruption vastly increases their vulnerability to attack from within and without.

Describing corrupted rulers who have abandoned the pure ways of their desert forebears may seem a too simplistic explanation for the generic phenomenon of decline. In another section of his discourse, however, Ibn Khaldun touches upon the subject of taxation and its implications. Here his decline explanation begins to take on a more modern cast—even to the extent of developing a fourteenth-century Laffer Curve. Bedouin dynasts, Ibn Khaldun argues, commence their rules with limited needs, small expenses, and restricted expenditures. Indeed, tax revenues bring in more money than is required: "When tax assessments and imposts upon the subjects are low, the latter have the energy and desire to do things. . . . enterprises grow and increase, because the low taxes bring satisfaction. When . . . enterprises grow, the number of individual imposts and assessments mounts. In consequence, the tax revenue . . . increases" (Ibn Khaldun 1967: 230).

Luxuries for a sedentary lifestyle raise the costs of rule. The expenses of the ruler's entourage increase. So too do the expenses of the military. Expenditures soon surpass revenues, necessitating tax increases. Yet at the same time, the ruler's ability to collect taxes, especially from outlying provinces, has declined. New taxes are imposed. As taxes increase, business incentives are affected, to the detriment of expanded possibilities for tax collection.

The assessments increase beyond the limits of equity.

The result is that the interest of the subjects in . . . enterprises disappears since when they compare expenditures and taxes with their income and gain and see the little profit they make they lose all hope. Therefore, many of them refrain from all . . . activity. The result is that the total tax revenue goes down. Often, when the decrease is noticed, the amounts of individual imposts are increased. This is considered a means of compensating for the decrease. Finally, individual imposts and assessments reach their limit. . . . The costs of all . . . enterprise are now too high, the taxes are too heavy, and the profits anticipated fail to materialize. Finally civilization is destroyed, because the incentive for . . . activity is gone. [Ibn Khaldun 1967: 231]

In these passages, Ibn Khaldun's decline explanation is transformed from a moralistic tract on the corruptions of sedentary city dwellers and their rulers to a more sophisticated consideration of the impact of rising public consumption on business incentives. As agricultural and commercial activities decline, owing to excessive taxation, the dynastic regime undercuts its own financial foundation in a vicious circle of escalating spending and diminishing revenues.

Decline along this pattern is inevitable, according to Ibn Khaldun. Even if rulers recognize the nature of their dilemma, they are unable to turn things around. How long the decline lasts depends largely on how extensive the dynasty's territorial control is at the peak of its powers. Attackers, rebels, and secessionists will pressure the center from peripheral territory. The larger the periphery, the more time the center has to postpone its disintegration and defeat.

Modern Variations on Ancient Themes

At least since the fall of Rome, a number of decline arguments have stressed the squandering of resources by elites and societies as a, if not the, key to understanding the degeneration of once powerful states. These arguments are interesting from a historical point of view. But there is more to be gained from their review than mere historical perspective, for many of the arguments are still with us in one form or another. This point can be driven home by considering three contemporary models dealing with decline and one ongoing policy debate that also involves decline. They do not all say the same thing. Yet they frequently focus on the same variables—especially consumption-investment tradeoffs. Societies are thought to pay for too much consumption by experiencing investment shortfalls and future productivity losses. The fundamental question that observers fail to resolve, however, is whether these tradeoffs are primary causes of decline, derivative effects of decline, or some combination.

Modern Variation I: Cipolla's Imperial Decline Model

Carlo Cipolla, a modern Italian economic historian, has sketched a complex and comprehensive model of the economic reasons for imperial decline. He begins his discussion by first delineating what he means by *decline* and *empire*. Decline occurs when an imperial unit suffers a loss of preeminence. The notion of empire, however, is not restricted to the customary connotation of political-territorial control. It may also encompass economic and cultural predominance. As a consequence, Cipolla's examples are wide-ranging. The Italian city-states of the late Middle Ages, the seventeenth-century Netherlands, and twentieth-century Britain are mentioned. So too are Greece, Carthage, Rome, the Mayan civilization, Byzantium, Ming and Ch'ing China, sixteenth-century Spain, and the Ottoman Empire.

The best way to describe Cipolla's model is to focus on successive phases of the decline process, although Cipolla is less than explicit on this point. The early stage of decline is characterized by increasing consumption, which results from three types of influence. Political expansion and development increase the organizational complexity and costs of empire. This pressure toward expanded public consumption is aggravated further by the tendency for imperial prosperity to diffuse outward. Hostile or potentially hostile neighbors develop. External threats and, in response, military expenditures increase. Obsolete military equipment sparks technological change; the need to replace it with more sophisticated matériel constitutes another path to increased public consumption.[4]

Even more critical to Cipolla's presentation, however, is the role of private consumption. Economic growth improves income levels and standards of living in a trickle-down fashion. Private consumption inevitably rises: "Instinctively and irresistibly people strive towards greater consumption, incessantly creating new needs no matter how artificial, desultory, or even pernicious, as soon as the old needs are satisfied" (Cipolla 1970: 5). Other spin-offs of enhanced living standards include stronger preferences for leisure, extravagance, a disinclination to perform society's least attractive tasks, and more expensive military personnel.

Rising public and private consumption are critical factors in creating situations conducive to decline. Another significant component in the equation is the way in which an empire responds to competition. Increasing competition could be offset by increased productivity. Foreign competition could be met by innovation and by adopting new techniques and principles introduced by the most successful competitors. Yet these reactions do not tend to occur. Instead, more commonly, change in any form is resisted.

This response is attributed to attitudes and emotions. The behaviors that most need changing once worked well. Why abandon techniques that are known to work for new and riskier approaches? Ironically, this proclivity to resist change may be all the more likely to surface if the empire was founded on innovative successes. Conceit, complacence, and pride hamper the ability of people to embrace change. People even have difficulty in rec-

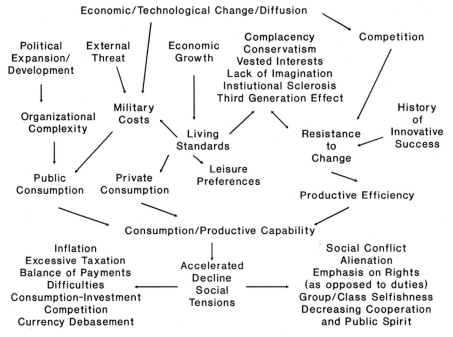

Figure 6.1 Cipolla's Model of Imperial Decline

ognizing decline, despite numerous previous examples, and this problem contributes to their inertia.

In addition to the psychological barriers, time and improved living standards make it less likely that people will be as inclined to compete as their grandparents were. Cipolla's "third generation effect," he acknowledges, is a vague amalgam of cultural, biological, social, psychological, and economic influences. Interactively, these influences produce an effect that suggests that the third generation is less likely to build empires—or to maintain them—than was the first generation.

Reinforcing the sources of psychological resistance, finally, are the vested interests who will be harmed by change and the institutions that prove difficult to transform for new types of activities. Cipolla nicely describes the situation: "Institutional rigidities reflect cultural rigidities. Conservative people and vested interests cluster around obsolete institutions, and each element supports the other powerfully" (1970: 11).

Economic problems are brought on initially by rising consumption and increased competition. If the ways of doing things are not altered, relative productive efficiency and the capability to produce dwindle. At this stage of the decline process, consumption begins to exceed productive capability. For a variety of reasons only hinted at in figure 6.1, the situation becomes increasingly critical. "Ways of doing things are strategically important in determining the performance of a society. If the necessary change does not take place and economic difficulties are allowed to grow, then a cumulative process is bound to be set into motion that makes things progressively worse. Decline enters then in its final, dramatic stage" (Cipolla 1970: 13).

Symptoms of economic difficulties emerge. States attempt to pump more and more wealth from the economy through taxation, currency debasement, and inflationary policies. Imports exceed exports. Consumption squeezes out investment and vice versa. Economic problems are accompanied as well by a cluster of sociopolitical and psychological difficulties. Group conflict increases as the available pie shrinks. Alienation increases collectively, and public spirit declines. Individuals, groups, and classes adopt more zero-sum perspectives.

In such an environment, the probability of constructing and executing a successful program for renewal is low. People will have to be forced by the state to do things they are unwilling to do on their own. To the extent that compulsion and taxation lead to corruption, evasion, and income redistribution in favor of the powerful, Cipolla adds, the psychological atmosphere will only display increased frustration and pessimism. Innovation in such circumstances becomes less rather than more likely.

Modern Variation II: Gilpin's Model of Hegemonic Decline

Robert Gilpin (1981) has developed a cost-benefit model of post-1815 hegemonic expansion and decline that nevertheless relies heavily on pre-1815 imperial history. Dividing national income into three broad sectors—protection, the costs of national security and safeguarding property rights of citizens; consumption, the private and public (nonmilitary) consumption of goods and services; and investment, the savings returned to the productive sector of the economy in order to improve efficiency and productivity— Gilpin argues that protection and consumption shares rise over time at the expense of the investment share and subsequent economic growth. As shown in figure 6.2, protection costs depend in part on the number and strength of military rivals. They are also influenced by two other tendencies. Effective military techniques rise in cost over time. Moreover, as societies grow more affluent, the cost of military personnel, reflecting resource competition from other sectors of the economy, rises as well.

The threats posed by military rivals and the escalatory expenses associated with maintaining armed forces are not unique to hegemons. Other states have protection costs. Yet the hegemonic problem vis-à-vis protection costs is twofold. Because the hegemon dominates the system, the protection costs necessary to maintain the preeminent position are apt to be large—

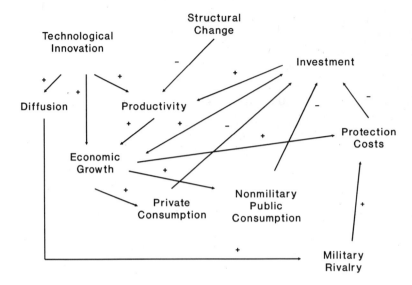

Figure 6.2 Gilpin's Model of Hegemonic Decline

quite probably larger than the costs incurred by other states in the system. Military expenditures constitute a major proportion of these costs, but the costs also include various forms of subsidies for allies and clients. The liquidity costs linked to maintaining the world economy, though difficult to measure, constitute another component of protection costs.

Thus hegemons are burdened with protection costs for the entire system over which they preside. One might argue, of course, that hegemons derive obvious benefits from their positions of dominance. Protection costs are therefore a form of quid pro quo. The problem for Gilpin is that over time the benefits erode and the costs continue to climb. In this sense, protection costs "are not productive investments; they constitute an economic drain on the economy of the dominant state" (Gilpin 1981: 157).

Underlying this emphasis on the burden of protection costs is an essentially imperial dynamic. Gilpin assumes that states will seek to expand in territorial, political, and economic terms if the benefits of expansion are perceived to exceed the costs. Some type of relative advantage is critical to the process. An edge in relative power facilitates expansion, which in turn permits the development of greater relative power and economic surplus. Occasionally a state will accumulate enough of an advantage or surplus to be in a position to dominate the international system.

Eventually, the expanding hegemon will reach a point beyond which further expansion is discouraged by diminishing returns and escalating costs. Many factors contribute to this return-cost balance. The opposition generated by successful expansion and the gradual diffusion of power are among the important factors. But so is the principle that expansion will reach a threshold of optimum size—variable across historical eras—beyond which overhead (protection) costs tend to increase more rapidly than the revenues derived from political dominance.

Increases in private and nonmilitary public consumption are also to be expected with the passage of time. Affluence gradually increases the demand for goods and services throughout the society in Gilpin's model, as in Cipolla's trickle-down process. Roughly matching this trend is the tendency for nonmilitary public consumption to expand at a rate faster than the economy is growing, "whether in the form of bread and circuses in the ancient world or medical care for the lower classes and social security for the aged in the modern world" (Gilpin 1981: 164).

If all the forms of consumption—private, nonmilitary public, and protection costs—are increasing, then investment must suffer. Gilpin writes: "As a consequence, the efficiency and productivity of the productive sector of the economy on which all else rests will decline. If the productive base of the economy erodes, it becomes more difficult to meet the rising demands of protection and consumption without further cutbacks in productive investment, thus further weakening the future health of the society" (1981: 158). In other words, the tendency for consumption to rise saps the hegemon's productivity.

Gilpin acknowledges Cipolla's emphasis on ways of doing things by noting that conservatism and the disinclination to take risks are attitudinal restraints on expansion that characterize societies experiencing relative decline. Rather than focus on these attitudinal correlates, though, Gilpin emphasizes, in addition to the consumption thesis, the fluctuations in leading-sector technological innovations. As noted earlier, the hegemonic position is initially predicated on an edge created through technological innovation. Yet the benefits from a specific innovation are finite. So too are its contributions to economic growth. Without repetitive bursts of innovation or technological borrowing, growth is apt to proceed at a slower rate.

Innovation and wealth are also subject to considerable international diffusion. New competitive centers emerge as a consequence. Still another element of importance is the propensity for economies to mature. Agrarian economies are transformed first by industrial manufacturing and then by the growth of a relatively less productive service sector. All of these elements combine to create an S-shaped growth curve. The pace of growth slows and may become negative. Less surplus is available for consumption and investment. Protection costs nevertheless continue to rise, thanks to technological diffusion and the development of new competitors-rivals.

Diminishing productive efficiency and rates of growth, combined with the draining effect of consumption increases, bring a halt to hegemonic expansion. Relative decline sets in.

Once a society reaches the limits of its expansion, it has great difficulty in maintaining its position and arresting its eventual decline. Further, it begins to encounter marginal returns in agricultural or industrial production. Both internal and external changes increase consumption and the costs of protection and production; it begins to experience a severe fiscal crisis. The diffusion of its economic, technological, or organizational skills undercuts its comparative advantage over other societies, especially those in the periphery of the system. These rising states, on the other hand, enjoy lower costs, rising rates of return on their resources, and the advantages of backwardness (Gilpin 1981: 185).

Gilpin is not alone in adopting this perspective on decline. Calleo (1982, 1987) stresses the point of view that military commitments made at a time when system leaders are in unusually strong resource positions prove difficult to support when the relative resource positions erode. Supporting this view in general, Huntington (1988) has referred to the foreign policy situation as a Lippmann Gap problem, after Walter Lippmann (1943), who argued that imbalances between national commitments and national resources result in political insolvency and domestic dissension. Still, the precise causal implications of overcommitment in protection costs are not always straightforward in the analyses of foreign policy insolvency.[5] Kennedy's (1987b) and Rosecrance's (1990) positions are exceptions. As Kennedy put it: "Yet achieving the first two feats [providing military security and satisfying socioeconomic needs of the citizenry]—or either one of them—with the third [ensuring sustained growth] will inevitably lead to relative eclipse over the longer term, which has of course been the fate of all slower-growing societies that failed to adjust to the dynamics of world power. . . . the basic argument remains: without a rough balance between these competing demands of defense, consumption, and investment, a Great Power is unlikely to preserve its status for long" (1987b: 447).

Modern Variation III: The Sprout and Sprout Model of the Demands/Resources Ratio

One of the more interesting models in the tradeoff literature is the rising demands-insufficient resources model developed by Harold Sprout and Margaret Sprout (1968). We give the model special attention for three reasons. It deserves more notice than it has received. It was developed specifically for one former system leader's politico-economic problems (those of Britain), even though it does possess wider applicability. Most important, the model offers some intriguing contrasts with other tradeoff models.

At the heart of the rising demands-insufficient resources model are three statements about trends in political systems. First, some variable ensemble of goods and services exists. The amount of goods and services actually available at any given time will fluctuate. The amount available is also likely to increase over time, even though the rate of growth may not be rapid.

A second tendency describes the likely behavior of a system's set of commitments. The flavor or the biases of these commitments will vary from system to system, but in all systems, authorities will choose to allocate resources to meet the perceived needs of the system and some proportion of its membership. Once the allocations are decided upon, they do not tend to fluctuate. Nor are they likely to remain constant over time. Instead, they are most likely to expand in scale and in the proportion of the population encompassed.

A leading reason for the proliferation of commitments involves a third tendency. The demands placed upon the political system by its members are likely to escalate. Old demands may or may not be translated into ongoing commitments, but new demands are sure to be made. Changes in environment create new problems. Expectations rise. New groups emerge as politically significant actors. All these factors work together to guarantee the escalation of political demands.

The political dilemma implicit to the three trends is clear. The odds are that ongoing commitments plus new demands will tend to surpass the aggregate resources available for meeting commitments and demands. Something has to give. Either more resources must be generated, or commitments and demands must be suppressed or altered. Neither option is particularly attractive to politicians who must seek reelection.

Precisely how this process is played out will vary from system to system, depending in part on the types of political economies involved, the degree of consensus on collective goods, and the quality of the prevailing public order. In the case of Britain, the pertinent facts include its lengthy history as a major power and the associated extensive and expensive commitments to foreign policy objectives and military security. Concurrently, and especially since the late nineteenth and early twentieth centuries, Britain has been a relatively open political system with an expanding electorate. Electoral victories have increasingly depended on what the Sprouts quaintly refer to as government paying more attention to the demands of less privileged constituents.

In addition, Britain became an increasingly import-dependent society. Paying for a large number of imports required a large number of competitive exports. To generate these competitive goods, a steady flow of new fixed capital investment was essential to maintain the efficiency of British production equipment and methods. Investment funds, however, must compete with propensities for societal consumption. Private consumption, military consumption, and nonmilitary governmental consumption have the potential to reduce the availability of investment funds. Moreover, all of the various types of consumption compound the problem by leading directly or indirectly to greater import consumption, which in turn raises the need for more exports. And since many exports require imported ingredients, the import-export spiral is made all the more vicious.

Post-World War II British decision makers have experienced an acute form of this dilemma of rising demands and insufficient resources. According to the Sprouts, domestic capital formation and exports earned the highest political priority in order to keep the economy functioning. Private consumption and social services (nonmilitary governmental spending) also received high priority to ensure governmental tenures. Much lower priorities were assigned to foreign commitments and military spending. In sum, to maintain fixed capital investment, private consumption, and nonmilitary public spending, the proportion of resources allocated to military consumption was reduced. Reducing the other components of gross national product simply would not have been politically expedient.

The Sprouts' model is parsimonious and straightforward. Note, however, that it is not so much a generic model of decline but rather an explanation for political expedience and, in the case of Britain, a diminishing international profile. Given finite resources and rising demands, decision makers will opt for the choices that are more rewarding politically. Proportional cuts in investment, private consumption, or social services, therefore, are more likely to be avoided than are proportional cuts in defense and foreign policy commitments. As a consequence of actions such as these, Britain has been priced out of the great power league.

The end result is, of course, a relative decline in Britain's international politico-military standing. In that respect, the Sprouts do offer an explanation for decline but envision it to be a second-order form. The original sources of British decline, according to the Sprouts, are four in number. Nineteenth-century technological innovations brought about reduced changes in naval engineering that had the general effect of reducing the politico-military significance of naval power and, derivatively, the significance of the world's leading naval power.

A second change is labeled change in geopolitical structure and scale. *Structure* in this case refers to the number of important competitors. The late nineteenth-century emergence of Germany, the United States, and Japan crowded the great power playing field. Some of the new players also enjoyed access to more impressive resource bases (scale) in raw materials, population, and domestic market size. Unless Britain could somehow bring about a political-territorial amalgamation of its far-flung empire, it would find itself gradually eclipsed by the emergence of these new powers.

Presumably both a cause and an effect of this process of eclipse was the erosion of Britain's industrial, commercial, and financial primacy, the Sprouts' third factor. While it seems rather awkward to try to explain decline by decline, one should remember that the Sprouts were attempting to describe the contextual antecedents for subsequent foreign-domestic commitment trade-offs. The erosion of primacy suggests a major qualitative change in the aggregate resources available to competing political claimants.

The fourth factor emphasized by the Sprouts is the development of lower-class political mobilization at home and abroad. At home, political mobilization meant increased demands for governmental services. Abroad, political mobilization made it increasingly unlikely that the metropole could continue to dominate the imperial periphery as it had in the past. In other words, domestic political demands were rising while access to external resources was increasingly challenged.

Modern Variation IV: The American Productivity Slowdown Debate

Some scholars, such as Huntington (1988) and Nye (1990a), insist that the deterioration of U.S. productivity growth—measured in U.S. shares of world manufacturing output—is mainly the consequence of the postwar recovery of Western Europe and Japan. The problem is not so much that management and labor in the American economy are doing something wrong but that management and labor elsewhere are doing things better than they did when they were struggling in the aftermath of World War II.

More generally, Baumol, Blackman, and Wolff (1989: 86-87) support the "convergence" hypothesis. Technological transfer allows a small number of countries to catch up to, but not necessarily surpass, the economic leader. The leader's absolute productivity growth may give no cause for alarm. This is the Baumol, Blackman, and Wolff position on the U.S. productivity situation. It is its relative performance vis-à-vis the countries in the process of catching up that causes concern. Comparatively speaking, the leader eventually will lag behind its followers' performance as the lead is reduced.

Others are not as willing to dismiss what Baumol, Blackman, and Wolff observe as simply a matter of the rest of the world catching up to American standards. According to Baily and Chakrabarti (1988), had U.S. productivity growth continued at its pre-1965 rate, American output would have been 45 percent higher than it actually was, with no additional labor used in production. Although the growth rate from 1948 to 1965 was unusually high by historical standards, Baily and Chakrabarti calculate that had the growth in output per hour after 1965 simply equaled the average rate from 1870 to 1965, output would still have been more than 20 percent higher in 1985 than

Table 6.2 Growth Acceleration and Slowdown
(differences in average annual compound growth rate)

	1913–50 to 1950–73 Acceleration		1950–73 to 1973–89 Slowdown	
	GDP Per Capita	Labor Productivity	GDP Per Capita	Labor Productivity
Australia	1.7	1.2	-0.7	-0.9
Austria	4.7	5.0	-2.5	-2.2
Belgium	2.8	3.0	-1.5	-1.4
Canada	1.4	0.5	-0.4	-1.1
Denmark	1.6	2.5	-1.5	-2.5
Finland	2.4	2.9	-1.6	-3.0
France	2.9	3.1	-2.2	-1.8
Germany	4.2	4.9	-2.9	-3.3
Italy	4.2	3.8	-2.4	-3.2
Japan	7.1	5.8	-4.9	-4.5
Netherlands	2.3	3.5	-2.0	-2.4
Norway	1.1	1.7	0.4	-0.7
Sweden	1.2	1.6	-1.5	-2.8
Switzerland	1.0	0.6	-2.1	-2.1
United Kingdom	1.7	1.6	-0.7	-0.9
United States	0.6	0.1	-0.6	-1.5
Average	2.6	2.6	-1.7	-2.1

Source: Based on Maddison 1991: 129.

Note: Labor productivity is measured as GDP per worker hour. The labor productivity calculations for the most recent period are restricted to the 1973–87 era.

it actually was (1988: 1-9). Moreover, the U.S. economic downturn shows no clear signs of abatement: in the aggregate, productivity performance has continued to fall since 1979. From 1973-79 to 1979-82, the growth rate of actual national income fell from 2.6 to -.54 percent, while that of actual national income per person employed declined from .36 percent to -.83 percent (Denison 1985).

Maddison (1991) has improved our understanding of this problem by examining the historical productivity records of a number of member states of the Organization for Economic Cooperation and Development. As table 6.2 shows, there can be little question about the U.S. economic slowdown in the 1973-89 period, especially in comparison with the 1950-73 period. Yet it is also clear that all of the other economies listed in the table have also experienced the post-1973 slowdown. Some states have slowed less than the United States, while others have experienced even greater slowdowns.

During roughly the same periods, Maddison's data (1991: 130) indicate that all of the economies listed in table 6.2 also converged toward the U.S. position in labor productivity. The rate of convergence, however, was generally less in the most recent period (1973-87) than in the earlier period (1950-73). Thus, while some convergence definitely has occurred among the most sophisticated economies, a general slowdown has also transpired. After developing and estimating empirical models to explain growth, growth acceleration-slowdown, and rates of divergence-convergence, Maddison concluded that "the real mystery of the post-1973 slowdown is the sharp deceleration of productivity growth in the lead country, the USA. In the follower countries there is no mystery, and their slowdown had some elements of inevitability. As the productivity gap between the followers and the lead country narrowed, the scope for easy growth by replicating lead country technology was reduced. A greater burden of innovation fell on the followers, the profitability of high levels of investment faltered. Capital stock ceased to grow as fast" (1991: 131-32).

So what accounts for the U.S. slowdown? A significant body of theoretical literature has recently emerged, linking increases in national spending—particularly social welfare expenditures—with declining capital investment as an underlying cause of the downturn in productivity growth. This literature has come from communities that are relatively isolated from one another. Nevertheless, it reflects three major orientations—capital shortage and profit squeeze hypotheses, the crisis of advanced industrialism, and the dilemma of world leadership decline. The arguments within these perspectives not only cross the ideological spectrum but also, surprisingly, converge in placing a large proportion of the blame for declining levels of investment and the subsequent economic downturn on the macroeconomic policies of the national government.

There is little consensus on the nature and the underlying reasons for the downturn in the U.S. economy. Despite a number of economic analyses on the productivity dilemma, the causes of the slowdown remain controversial (Brainard and Perry 1981). Familiar refrains have focused on management style, technology, education, overregulated industries, and labor-management cooperation for potential explanations. One of the most widely perceived characteristics of this decline, however, has been the relatively slow growth of capital investment (Clark 1979). The sluggishness of nonresidential fixed investment has generated pronouncements from both the Left and the Right about the declining incentive to invest and warnings that investment performance must be improved in order to maintain the growth of national income (Thurow 1985; Peterson 1987).

Yet the economic arguments reflect disagreement about the exact nature of the role played by capital investment. Some theorists argue that the concentration on capital investment has been exaggerated at the expense of

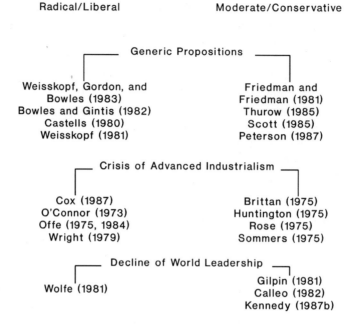

Radical/Liberal   Moderate/Conservative

Generic Propositions

Weisskopf, Gordon, and   Friedman and
Bowles (1983)   Friedman (1981)
Bowles and Gintis (1982)   Thurow (1985)
Castells (1980)   Scott (1985)
Weisskopf (1981)   Peterson (1987)

Crisis of Advanced Industrialism

Cox (1987)   Brittan (1975)
O'Connor (1973)   Huntington (1975)
Offe (1975, 1984)   Rose (1975)
Wright (1979)   Sommers (1975)

Decline of World Leadership

Wolfe (1981)   Gilpin (1981)
                                   Calleo (1982)
                                   Kennedy (1987b)

Figure 6.3 Investment Squeeze Arguments

understanding nontangible factors associated with productivity decline, such as declining work intensity and lagging business innovation (Magaziner and Reich 1982; Weisskopf, Bowles, and Gordon 1983). Baily (1981) suggests that part or all of the slowdown might be attributable not to a deterioration in the amount of capital but rather to a declining and inefficient use of capital in the 1970s. Denison (1980: 220) maintains that increased capital is not the only source of output growth but one among many, despite the contrary view held by financial and government analysts. He asserts that 15 percent of the growth in total potential national income from 1948 to 1973 resulted from more capital, in particular more nonresidential structures and equipment and more inventories. Nonetheless, Denison (1980: 220-23) says that it is wrong to blame investment for the recent reductions in the growth of American output and productivity or to suppose that merely raising investment would go far toward restoring the old growth rate of productivity.[6]

Regardless of Denison's qualifications about overgeneralizing the links between investment and productivity decline, a large body of new theoretical literature presumes that the accumulation of fixed capital is an important determinant of growth and that government policies play a critical role in shaping the share of output devoted to business investment. In particular, it pinpoints the expansion of the welfare state as the main culprit for declining investment and argues that further spending in this area is a luxury the American economy can ill afford in a period of growing deficits in the federal budget and foreign trade.[7]

In figure 6.3 we situate the theoretical positions of the major arguments and their contributors. Horizontally, the arguments are arranged on an ideological axis, although the distinctions are not all that clear in some instances. The ideological nature of the arguments, though, is not a crucial issue in the analysis. Vertically, the arguments are organized into three competing perspectives, which in turn are ordinally arrayed on the basis of explanatory specificity. The first level on the vertical axis represents generic propositions generally made by economists without much regard for the applicability of their comments to certain types of political and economic systems. Since most of these economists are American, their statements refer to the U.S. experience, but in large measure their positions would be appropriate for any economy that has both a large welfare commitment and a burgeoning budget deficit. Second-level explanations restrict the sample considerably by describing the welfare-investment tradeoff in the context of larger economic problems endemic to advanced industrialized democratic states. Finally, the explanations at the third level restrict the sample still more by placing the issue of welfare expenditures within the economic domain of a declining world power, such as the United States or Britain.

Capital shortage and profit squeeze hypotheses. Not unlike the classical "guns versus butter" debaters, the capital shortage theorists view welfare expenditures within the context of a "consumption versus investment" tradeoff; that is to say, as a significant portion of the national budget, welfare allocations increase public consumption and accelerate federal deficits. By keeping interest rates high, deficit financing in turn crowds out or absorbs savings in the private sector, reduces the availability of capital investment, and ultimately chokes off economic growth. The difficulty multiplies in the presence of a low personal savings rate and a high level of personal consumption.[8]

Radical variants of this theme, the profit squeeze theories, stress the historical expansion of the welfare state as an important factor in redistributing a greater proportion of the national income from capital to labor. As the growth in real income available to U.S. citizens slowed down in the 1970s, private wages, government transfer payments (e.g., social security), and public services (e.g., health and educational programs) were not similarly restrained, thereby reducing the share of the national income going to profits after taxes. The growth of state measures for social welfare and income maintenance (unemployment compensation), however, have cushioned the impact of unemployment and made it difficult for business leaders to suppress wages during recessions. Therefore, the inability of business to pass the burden of regenerating the economy to labor through wage reductions has decreased not only the rate of profit but also the expectations about future profitability—both of which contribute to reductions in new investments (Castells 1980; Bowles and Gintis 1982; Weisskopf 1981).[9]

The political crisis of advanced industrialism. Neoliberal and neo-Marxist views on the relationship between public consumption and investment begin with the premise that democratic political structures are the historical by-products of advanced capitalism. Industrialism ultimately generated the pressure for and the subsequent growth of public participation in the political arena via urbanization, secularization, and social mobilization. The result of that expansion has been a more democratic society. After World War II, the United States and Western European states extended their commitments to a democratic agenda by adopting Keynesian economic principles in order to ensure full employment, steady growth, and greater welfare security for the poor. Ironically, a consequence of these policies is the current crisis in economic stagnation (Martin 1977: 342-49).

According to neoliberals, democracy encourages consumption at the expense of investment and therefore endangers growth. National strategies aimed at economic security and a redistribution of income—through progressive taxation, transfer payments, unemployment compensation, education, and health and consumer services—have contributed to a society in which citizens continually expect more from government. Hence, the public sector steadily assumes new roles and becomes responsible for a greater share of aggregate demand. At the same time, labor expects more and more wage increases, which absorb a larger share of the national income. These developments elevate the consumption share relative to the investment share by discouraging the propensity for personal savings and reducing the availability of funds for investment (Sommers 1975).

Thus, the crisis of democracy, from this standpoint, is that government is overloaded by the demands of citizens who have excessive expectations about what government can do for them without their incurring costs to their own interests. The outcome of this process is that the capacity of the economy is exceeded and long-term growth and international competitiveness are jeopardized (Brittan 1975; Huntington 1975; Rose 1975).

Neo-Marxists also observe a crisis that in their view stems from the increasing inability of advanced capitalist states to meet two primary responsibilities: accumulation and legitimation. While "accumulation" refers to the state's role in mobilizing the resources necessary for sustaining economic growth—such as investments in infrastructure, research and development, education, public housing, mass transit, and medical care and social insurance—"legitimation" pertains to the state's interest in preserving social harmony by co-opting sources of popular discontent through the provision of full employment and social welfare services. After World War II, capitalist states were able to fulfill these responsibilities for a while through demand management policies, but eventually full employment policies and welfare expenditures undermined national growth by squeezing profits, generating inflation, and impairing the capital formation process. In an effort to regenerate economic growth, a state increases its expenditures more rapidly than it has the means to finance them, producing a "fiscal" crisis. This situation is exacerbated by the presence of special interest groups whose power over the national budget creates waste, duplication, and bias toward military and welfare spending. The final result is a political crisis: the inability of the state to finance new policies designed to reverse declining productivity in the face of constant pressure from political interest groups.[10]

The decline of world leadership thesis. After all is said and done, the economic explanations discussed above are based on the premise that America's current economic situation is not unlike that of Western Europe and Japan, where governments are also faced with difficult political choices in a contracting world economy. Some scholars, however, reject this view as too simple, maintaining that the United States is not directly comparable to its First World counterparts because its troubles are intimately tied to its global role as a world power. The toll of America's expanding welfare budget must be discussed in the context of its political and military commitments abroad— burdens that far exceed those of Japan and NATO allies. In that respect, the United States represents a special case, where the gap between rising demands and insufficient resources has reached a crucial threshold.

Although the dilemma between demands and resources is not a new phenomenon by any means, governments face it in many variations and degrees of severity. According to Sprout and Sprout (1968: 688-89), several variants are likely to appear within developing societies, other forms within mature industrial societies (including former great powers priced out of the international power market), and still different forms within societies that are highly involved in the maintenance of the international system, such as the United States.

For scholars such as Gilpin (1981, 1987), Wolfe (1981), Calleo (1982, 1984, 1987), and Kennedy (1987a, 1987b), what makes the United States stand out is its particular brand of variation: the dilemma between domestic demands and external commitments in the context of "relative" economic decline. When the United States sponsored the formation of institutions such as the International Monetary Fund, the General Agreement on Tariffs and Trade, the World Bank, the United Nations, and the North Atlantic Treaty Organization as the linchpins of a new international political and economic order, the American economy dominated the world system. In 1948 the United States produced 41 percent of the world's goods and services, and by 1949 it possessed nearly 60 percent of the world's financial reserves (Pollard and Wells 1984: 333; Rupert and Rapkin 1985: 170-71). Those figures dwindled to 30 and 16 percent respectively by 1970, but America's military commitments had escalated. By 1970 the United States had "more than 1,000,000 soldiers in 30 countries, [was] a member of 4 regional defense alliances and an active participant in a fifth, [had] mutual defense treaties with 42 nations, [was] a member of 53 international organizations, and [provided] military or economic aid to nearly 100 nations across the face of the globe" (Ronald Steele, quoted in Kennedy 1987a: 29).

During the same period, the U.S. government invested enormous resources in efforts to land an American on the moon, alleviate poverty in the country, abolish urban and rural ghettos, refurbish and protect the natural environment, secure the future of the elderly, and support an equal opportunity agenda for minorities and women. Unfortunately, the juggling between competing domestic and international claims, it is argued, has fueled the declining productivity of the American economy relative to its First World partners and has ended the economic foundations of the international order.

Tradeoffs: Primary or Secondary Decline Phenomena?

It is certainly possible to quarrel with aspects of these alleged sources of decline. But that is not the purpose of this chapter. Instead, we set out to trace the intellectual history of arguments about consumption-investment tradeoffs. The question that remains open is what role(s) these tradeoffs play in processes of relative decline. Are they cause or effect?

In the Sprouts' model of rising demands and insufficient resources, general background conditions and environmental changes are seen as setting up a situation in which demands are more likely to be escalating while the available set of resources is more likely to be found less than optimally satisfactory. Choices have to be made. The central question is which set of preferences is most likely to predominate.

Contrast this approach with the generic decline model for hegemons designed by Gilpin. Most of the ingredients are the same. Gilpin divides gross national product into four principal components: investment, protection costs (spending on defense and foreign commitments), nonmilitary public consumption, and private consumption. He asserts that the three types of consumption tend to rise proportionally over time. To the extent that one or more consumption types increase proportionally without an equivalent reduction in another type of consumption, the proportion of GNP allocated to investment must diminish. Diminished investment leads to future erosion in efficiency, productivity, and international competitiveness. Equally eroded are the prospects for underwriting hegemonic politico-military activities.

Which way do decline processes work? Do processes of decline lead to tradeoffs between consumption and investment, as Cipolla's and the Sprouts' models suggest? Or is decline basically caused by choices, implicit or explicit, made among types of consumption and investment à la Gilpin's model and the ideological spectrum involved in the ongoing American policy debate on the productivity slowdown? Of course, this theoretical question need not be an either/or proposition. First-order tradeoffs could easily lead to consequent second-order tradeoffs. Nor is it clear that all preeminent powers must experience the same processes of decline. What is a first-order response for one case may be a second-order consideration in another setting. Then again, just because people have been talking about tradeoffs for centuries does not mean that their roles must be significant.

The overconsumption arguments used to explain how leading states pull themselves down by their own bootstraps are multiple in form and often intuitively appealing. They are also testable. Nonetheless, their apparent applicability to global system leaders leaves something to be desired. In chapter 7 we will explore these questions concerning the applicability and testability of consumption-investment tradeoffs more fully.

7.

The Case against Tradeoffs as a Primary Cause of Decline

According to Samuel Huntington (1989b), the United States has experienced five waves of decline. Each wave has generated arguments forewarning the imminent loss of American power, and more often than not the waves have emerged at the ends of American presidential administrations.[1] Huntington believes that the most recent wave of declinist arguments, like the previous ones, will turn out to be largely unfulfilled. Huntington remains unconvinced by these arguments, because "with some exceptions, declinist writings do not elaborate testable propositions involving independent and dependent variables. With a rather broad brush, they tend to paint an impressionistic picture of economic decline, mixing references to economic trends and performance (economic growth, productivity), educational data (test scores, length of school year), fiscal matters (deficits), science and technology (R&D expenditures, output of engineers), international trade and capital flows, savings and investment, and other matters" (1989b: 77).

There is much merit to Huntington's position. A good portion of the declinist literature has not carefully specified causal relationships, linked appropriate variables, and systematically examined the evidence. And unless it begins to do so, the theoretical significance of decline will continue to be undervalued. This chapter, however, represents a departure from the pattern described by Huntington. In chapter 6 we set up the arguments that we propose to test. We have some other observations to make about why we think the interpretations based on overconsumption are unlikely to withstand rigorous scrutiny. Our dependent and independent variables will be specified clearly. As a result, there should be little ambiguity about the pattern of causation at work—or the lack thereof.

The Grounds for Suspecting the Applicability of the Overconsumption Thesis

The models reviewed in the previous chapter illustrate a number of points. Developing models of decline obviously is an analytical preoccupation with an ancient lineage. The models that observers have developed possess certain elements of diversity and continuity. One conspicuous element of continuity in the models described earlier is the notion of excess. We do not mean to suggest, of course, that models have not evolved and become more complex with the passing of time and more cases of decline. Personal hubris, for instance, has given way to macroeconomic concepts of overconsumption. An emphasis on idleness and sedentary luxuries has given way to the interplay between private and public forms of consumption and their hypothesized squeeze on investment.

As the models have developed, they have become more plausible for modern tastes. Conceivably, they have also become more applicable to the problems of the system leaders who have risen to preeminence in the past few centuries. The wrath of the gods and the savage nobility of the desert nomad appear to have limited utility when it comes time to account for the decline of the first beneficiary of the Industrial Revolution, Britain, or its successor, the United States. Lavish spending on warfare and welfare seems a far more fitting form of modern excess.

Despite the appeal, the ancient lineage, the apparent plausibility, or the conceivable appropriateness, there are reasons to suspect the accuracy of the overconsumption arguments. We will leave the explanation of the fall of Athens, Rome, and northwest African dynasties to other analysts who are better equipped to deal with their intricacies. The Cipolla and Gilpin models, on the other hand, have been developed at least in part to explain the decline of those states in which we are most interested—the leaders of the modern world system.

Therein lies the first clue to why we might doubt the full utility of these models. The Cipolla and Gilpin models were explicitly developed with imperial experiences in mind. Yet empires come in a great variety of shapes and hues. Most important, all empires have not been system leaders. A few empires so dominated their respective regional systems that it would be more accurate to say that the systemic and imperial boundaries, for all practical purposes, were coterminous. Phases of the Roman, Incan, Aztec, and Chinese experiences come readily to mind as good examples.

In marked contrast, a number of other empires were never strong enough to seize the lead position in their international systems. The Ottoman and French empires offer illustrations. Yet invoking these examples raises a corollary problem. Whether an organization is deemed to have been the lead unit in its system depends on how the system is defined. Both the Ottomans and the French certainly dominated their home regions at various times. But the system we have in mind when we speak of modern system leaders is not regional in scope. Rather, it is that extraregional, transoceanic system that began to emerge or, at least, underwent substantial transformation only after the Europeans stumbled their way into the Indian Ocean that interests us. That this new global system remained interlocked with the European region is a fact of post-1500 international politics that probably was inescapable. Until the nineteenth century, the principal rivals in this global, transoceanic system were based in Europe. As a consequence, the local politics of the region were mixed with extraregional transoceanic politics. Analysts have had considerable theoretical problems in separating these different activities ever since.

Nonetheless, the point is not merely that some empires are omnipotent while others are relatively less powerful. Nor do we wish to dwell too long on the abstractions of levels of analysis per se. The point that we wish to make is that modern system leaders constitute a special category of actor in international relations. They are special because their leadership was predicated on naval power, long-distance trade networks, economic innovation, and industrialization. They are special because their strategic orientations were more global—or transoceanic—than those of their rivals, who were more likely to become bogged down in local or regional problems. They are also special because their lead position in transoceanic affairs was accomplished and maintained in competitive, multiple-actor systems that never succumbed to the systemwide type of unicentric domination suggested by the concept of empire.[2]

These capabilities and orientations differentiated Portugal from Spain in the sixteenth century, the Dutch from the French in the seventeenth century, and the British from the Russians and Germans in the nineteenth century. The same characteristics and orientations differentiated the United States from the Soviet Union in the late twentieth century as well. The differences also suggest that during their systemic leadership phases, Portugal, the Netherlands, Britain, and the United States were not simply the most recent inheritors of the roles played by the ancient, territorially based imperiums.

Even so, the idea that system leaders are special in some sense is a theoretical observation that, understandably, not all readers will embrace eagerly. We believe that to the extent we are right about the distinctive status of modern system leaders, we have some reason to be cautious about models based on generic experiences of imperial decline.

In detailing these contrasts, we do not mean to imply that system leaders have had no imperial tendencies. The Portuguese, the Dutch, and the British certainly developed empires. Whether the United States is imperial remains a subject of debate (see Liska 1978; Mead 1987). An important difference, however, is that the long-distance trade-oriented system leaders went to some lengths to avoid the acquisition of territorial empire. To the variable extent that they yielded to the temptation of territorial acquisitions, they were behaving more like their more traditional rivals and less like global leaders (Thompson and Zuk 1986).

Large territories that necessitate the infrastructure of intensive control represent excessive burdens for states preoccupied with nonterritorially based political problems of order and rule creation and maintenance. Exclusive empires were not necessarily beneficial to trade. Nor were they necessary. Moreover, the global leaders share extensive histories of attempts at breaking down the trade monopolies of their opponents. We should also acknowledge that before the nineteenth century, extensive empires in Africa and Asia were not technologically or military feasible.

The emphasis on managing long-distance transactions historically has also gone hand in hand with political systems that, not coincidentally, placed significant restrictions on the scale of governmental operations and public consumption. Wars constituted exceptions to this domestic political rule. Immediately after a war concluded, however, governmental activities and budgets were usually reduced.[3] This facet of domestic political culture in system leaders works against excessive public consumption's being a major culprit causing decline. It also means that gaining extensive territorial empires to police was not the highest priority on the governmental agenda.

In the context of twenty-five hundred years of speculations about overconsumption and decline, then, it is imperative that the excesses of system leaders, if that is where the problem lies, be related carefully to the type of actors they represent. If system leaders behave differently than the typical empire, the erosion of their preeminence may work differently also. One model may not fit all cases of relative decline.

A second reason for expressing reservations about the overconsumption thesis is linked to the related problems of dating the onset of decline and distinguishing cause from effect. Where should one begin in dating decline? The answers vary and range from Wallerstein's (1984) insistence that hegemons begin to decline as soon as they first achieve agro-industrial, commercial, and financial supremacy to explanations that pinpoint some last-minute, unanticipated catastrophic destruction as the primary causal agent of downfall. A useful illustration of the general problem is provided by the case of the Roman Empire. Rome, or at least the western half of the empire, is thought to have "fallen" in the late fifth century A.D. Yet in the literature on Roman decline, portents and processes of decay have been traced as far back as the second century B.C. Does this suggest that the Roman Empire declined for some six hundred years before falling to the attacks of the Visigoths and Huns?

Designating a specific year as the beginning of a period of decline is frequently an arbitrary exercise. One advantage that we have with system leaders over the imperial cases is that the system leaders are displaced during times of global warfare. Portugal was incorporated into the Spanish Empire during the global power warfare of the 1580-1608 period. The Dutch were clearly supplanted by the British during the 1688-1713 warfare. The British in turn were replaced by the United States sometime between the ends of World Wars I and II. However one interprets this most recent transition, Britain was no longer able to function as the global leader after 1918. Consequently, we can say that a state was no longer a global leader after a certain point. This facility is helpful in evaluating arguments about the reasons for the loss of preeminence. If, for example, the explanations rely on processes that took place after the loss of leadership status, or only toward the very end of ascendancy, then we again have some reason to doubt whether we are in fact dealing with putative causes or the possible effects of decline.

Rome again provides a useful illustration. The sacking of Rome in 410 took place shortly after Theodosius I had banned the worship of the pre-Christian gods. One analyst described the non-Christian attitudes on the causes of decline: "It was plain that the ancient gods by whose favour Rome had climbed to universal power had withdrawn their protection and were chastising the faithless Romans who had abandoned their worship" (Jones 1964: 1025). We may not find this explanation intellectually appealing in the late twentieth century, but this accusation required responses by several contemporary authors, including St. Augustine (1957).

This form of religious explanation for Rome's fall admittedly is an extreme case.[4] Another example, much of interest to our inquiry, is suggested by contrasting the consumption arguments of Cipolla (1970) and the Sprouts (1968) with those of Gilpin (1981). Cipolla (see figure 6.1) argues that consumption tends to rise. If consumption exceeds productive capability, a consequence one should anticipate is competition between consumption and investment. The Sprouts argued that societies in decline are likely to pick and choose among different consumption-investment priorities. Increasing demands in democratic systems beset by diminishing resources should lead to a lower priority for spending on military and foreign policy commitments. Gilpin (see figure 6.2) also argues that consumption tends to rise. In his model, however, increases in consumption come at the expense of investment, which leads to future erosion in productivity and economic growth.

For Cipolla and the Sprouts, then, the consumption-investment tradeoff is a possible effect of rising consumption and declining productivity. For Gilpin, the tradeoff is an important cause of the decline in productivity. It is possible that both views are at least partially correct, as far as a general

Table 7.1 British and American Proportional Consumption Patterns

	Consumption as a Proportion of GNP					
	Britain			United States		
	Nonmilitary		Military	Nonmilitary		Military
Year	Private	Public		Private	Public	
1830	0.897	0.040	0.032	—	—	—
1840	0.878	0.040	0.028	—	—	—
1850	0.854	0.047	0.027	—	—	—
1860	0.853	0.030	0.040	—	—	—
1870	0.826	0.028	0.020	—	—	—
1880	0.826	0.032	0.018	0.751	0.045	0.005
1890	0.808	0.033	0.022	0.724	0.045	0.005
1900	0.797	0.030	0.059	0.730	0.050	0.010
1910	0.781	0.048	0.028	0.763	0.052	0.009
1913	0.762	0.047	0.028	0.752	0.055	0.009
1920	0.806	0.034	0.042	0.704	0.040	0.027
1930	0.802	0.071	0.019	0.773	0.092	0.009
1938	0.762	0.087	0.043	0.754	0.139	0.015
1950	0.710	0.091	0.064	0.671	0.085	0.050
1960	0.662	0.101	0.064	0.646	0.107	0.088
1970	0.619	0.130	0.047	0.632	0.139	0.076
1980	0.596	0.213	0.040	0.634	0.142	0.052
1985	—	—	—	0.650	0.139	0.065

Sources: For Britain, Mitchell 1988; for the United States, calculated from data in Berry 1978 and U.S. Office of the President 1988.

model of systemic leadership decline goes. This might be the case if Gilpin has a different phase of decline in mind than do Cipolla and the Sprouts. A sequence of consumption problems leading to decline and more consumption problems is not implausible. It is also possible, nevertheless, that one or both of these consumption interpretations are incorrect.

A third reason for being skeptical about the overconsumption argument stems from some familiarity with the history of consumption behavior among the modern system leaders. In table 7.1 we list nineteenth- and twentieth-century proportional consumption data for Britain and the United States. Absolute consumption certainly increases over time. Consumption increases calculated as a proportion of gross national product have been less than inevitable.

Private consumption basically has declined proportionally since the nineteenth century. Nonmilitary public consumption has increased, but the increases have come primarily in the twentieth century—too late to have been a causal factor in Britain's decline as a system leader.[5] British nonmilitary public consumption actually declined in the nineteenth century. Similarly, British and American military consumption is greater in the twentieth century than it was in the nineteenth. What is particularly missing from the military series, however, are positive, monotonic increases. British and American military consumption, especially before World War I for Britain and after World War II for the United States, simply fluctuates.

If the imperial overconsumption theses applied to the modern system leaders, we would expect consumption patterns that spiraled upward. Table 7.1 does not provide much support. British consumption increases (in the proportional mode) occur after World War I. The best case for American consumption is found in the nonmilitary public consumption column for the period after the depression and World War II. Even here, however, the rate of increase is less than breathtaking. A number of advanced industrial societies allocate much more of their resources to nonmilitary public consumption.

In addition, elsewhere we report no statistically significant tradeoff between British military spending and investment in the 1870-1913 period (Rasler and Thompson 1988). While a significant tradeoff is found in the post-World War II American case, the findings of Rasler (1990) cast doubt on the role of this tradeoff in modern U.S. relative decline. Analysts of all ideological stripes who discuss American decline usually identify some year between 1966 and 1973 as the turning point for U.S. prosperity and leadership. If the military spending-investment tradeoff data are divided into two subperiods (1948-70 and 1971-86) and the relationship is recalculated, the statistical significance of the tradeoff disappears in the pre-1970 period but remains in the post-1971 period.

We believe that this finding suggests that the squeeze of military expenditures on investment may at best be a derivative phenomenon of decline processes. By *derivative phenomenon*, we mean that the problem develops only after relative decline sets in. The tradeoff should show up in the erstwhile "predecline" phase if we are to have confidence that military spending is a root cause of the loss of preeminence.

These findings and table 7.1 prove discouraging for the applicability of the explanations for decline based on overconsumption. Yet they reinforce our suspicions that the roots of system leadership decline lie elsewhere. Economic and technological innovation, diffusion, and the resistance to change, all of which also play prominent roles in the Cipolla and Gilpin models, seem much more promising avenues for explanation. Visual scrutiny of data series, always a useful preliminary procedure, nevertheless rarely yields conclusive results. We are in a position to do better. Not only can we measure the statistical relationships between consumption, investment, productivity, and economic growth, but we can also delineate the sequence in which these variables influence other variables of interest. Do consumption increases lead to productivity declines and a slowdown in economic growth? Or do productivity declines and growth slowdowns lead to consumption problems? Are both sequences correct but at different phases of decline? Or is it possible that the causal linkages between excessive consumption by the system leader and decline are simply spurious?

Questions, Cases, and Variables

The contemporary version of the overconsumption-underinvestment hypothesis is predicated on a macroeconomic accounting identity. If gross national product equals consumption plus investment or savings, then, other things being equal, any proportional increase in consumption requires a proportional decrease in investment and savings and vice versa. Of course, other things are not always equal. The assertion of a zero-sum tradeoff assumes full employment and ignores the possibility of foreign lending. Both of these qualifications are of some interest to the ongoing American case. But we have no interest in challenging the basic macroeconomic equation. That is, we accept it as true by definition. We are also not interested in developing a comprehensive model of economic growth—a task best left to analysts who specialize in these matters.

What we are curious about is whether specific types of consumption can be pinpointed as the systematic villains of relative decline. In particular, Gilpin's general model and the work of others of the "solvency" school tend to highlight the roles of various forms of public consumption. But it is equally possible that investment tradeoffs driven by public consumption are secondary effects of ongoing decline processes. We interpret Cipolla and the Sprouts as suggesting something on this order. Either the absence of a negative relationship or the secondary effect is the outcome most compatible with our own speculations on the nature of system leaders' standard operating procedures. Our central question, therefore, is whether or to what extent various forms of consumption antecede investment, economic growth, and productivity. If consumption does antecede investment, we must also ask whether the relationships are appropriately signed. A significant negative relationship would be minimally required for evidence supporting a macroeconomic tradeoff.[6] In general, however, we assert

HYPOTHESIS 7.1: Consumption-investment tradeoffs are more likely to be the consequences than the antecedents of the relative decline of global leaders.

To analyze these questions, we propose to examine initially two cases: Britain in 1831-1913 and the United States in 1950-86.[7] We wish to look at the three specific types of consumption highlighted in both Cipolla's and

Gilpin's models. These consumption variables are expressed annually as proportions of GNP and are based on information supplied by Mitchell (1988) and the U.S. Office of the President (1988). In response to Gilpin's (1987) interpretation of the U.S. case, we have added budgetary deficits as a proportion of GNP to the American consumption set.[8]

Since it is awkward to model capability diffusion and catch-up efforts without also modeling the entire field of competitors, we opt to focus on the second type of relative decline (the historical performance variant as opposed to the international comparison). Economic growth is measured as gross domestic product per capita (Maddison 1979, 1982, 1987; Organization for Economic Cooperation and Development, 1980-87). For the American case, productivity is measured as manufacturing output per worker hour (U.S. Office of the President 1988). Investment is measured as gross domestic fixed capital formation in the British case (Mitchell 1988) and as net nonresidential, nonfinancial, fixed domestic investment as a proportion of net domestic product of nonfinancial corporate business in the American case (U.S. Office of the President 1988).[9]

Data Analysis

The structure of our test is simple. If consumption-driven tradeoffs are basic to the processes of relative decline, then we should expect to find that consumption in some form is a strong, negatively signed antecedent of investment, productivity, and/or economic growth. If the tradeoffs are derivative effects, then antecedence, as discussed in chapter 5, should flow from the opposite direction, that is, from productivity and growth to consumption. Of course, the tradeoffs could be both basic and derivative, in which case we should observe a two-way or reciprocal relationship. Finally, if the tradeoffs are neither basic nor derivative or if there are no tradeoffs, independence should be registered. Hence, the test basically asks which way, if any, the arrows of antecedence point.

To ascertain the direction of antecedence, each of the variables is logged and first differenced.[10] For convenience, the data analysis is separated into two stages. We first search for significant noninstantaneous patterns of antecedence, and then we reexamine the data for the possibility of instantaneous causality relationships.[11]

In table 7.2 and figure 7.1 we indicate two clusters of interrelationships and two antecedent paths for the British case. Investment and economic growth are related reciprocally, as are military spending and nonmilitary public consumption. Public consumption is in turn antecedent to private consumption, and investment also precedes private consumption. The critical

Table 7.2 Quasi F-statistics for Bivariate Vector Autoregressions, Britain, 1831–1913: A Test for Antecedence (annual data)

Independent Variable	Dependent Variable				
	EG	I	PC	GC	M
Economic Growth	—	9.6*	1.4	1.4	1.2
Investment	5.1*	—	4.0*	0.98	1.3
Private Consumption	0.88	1.0	—	1.2	1.4
Nonmilitary Public Consumption	0.46	1.0	2.3*	—	3.1*
Military Spending	0.96	0.9	0.65	3.7*	—

Lag structure = 2, 6.

*p is less than or equal to .05

EG = Economic Growth, I = Investment, PC = Private Consumption, GC = Nonmilitary Public Consumption, M = Military Spending

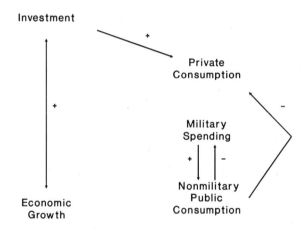

Figure 7.1 The Paths of Antecedence: Britain, 1831–1913

outcome is the absence of exogenous linkages from the consumption variables to investment and economic growth. The coefficients derived from the bivariate tests of Granger causality are available in appendix C, table C.4. The results indicate that all three of the consumption variables with lags 1-6 are not statistically related to economic growth or investment. The signs of these relationships are also mixed, indicating an absence of clear evidence concerning whether they are solely positive or negative relationships.[12]

In the American case, investment is antecedent to manufacturing productivity, which in turn is antecedent to economic growth (see table 7.3 and figure 7.2). Investment and economic growth share a reciprocal relationship as well. We also find that nonmilitary public consumption precedes military

Table 7.3 Quasi $\underline{F}$-statistics for Bivariate Vector Autoregressions, United States, 1950–1986: A Test for Antecedence

Independent Variable	Dependent Variable						
	EG	P	I	PC	GC	M	D
Economic Growth	—	2.6	9.2**	3.0*	3.5**	0.89	2.5
Productivity	3.3*	—	1.1	0.4	2.3	2.3	0.9
Investment	6.8**	3.3*	—	0.25	1.1	0.52	2.1
Private Consumption	3.3*	2.0	0.36	—	1.8	1.4	1.5
Nonmilitary Public Consumption	1.3	1.6	0.25	0.87	—	4.7**	4.6**
Military Spending	0.5	1.1	0.15	0.31	2.4	—	2.5
Governmental Deficits	0.69	2.0	1.2	0.31	5.1**	1.6	—

Lag structure = 4, 4.

*p is less than or equal to .05

**p is less than or equal to .01

EG = Economic Growth, P = Productivity, I = Investment, PC = Private Consumption, GC = Nonmilitary Public Consumption, M = Military Spending, D = Governmental Deficits

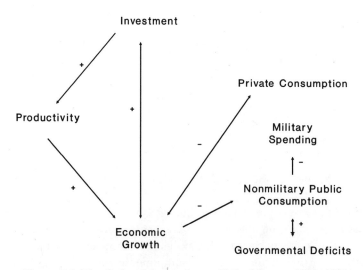

Figure 7.2 The Paths of Antecedence: United States, 1950–1980

spending and is related reciprocally to deficit spending. As for any relationships between consumption and economic performance, we find that there is a two-way linkage between economic growth and private consumption and that economic growth antecedes nonmilitary public consumption. These last findings represent a departure from the nineteenth-century British case. The

Table 7.4 Quasi $\underline{F}$-statistics for Bivariate Vector Autoregressions, United States, 1950–1986: A Test for Instantaneous Antecedence (annual data)

Independent Variable	Dependent Variable						
	EG	P	I	PC	GC	M	D
Economic Growth	—	0.50	1.2	2.3	0.11	0.33	0.01
Productivity	0.42	—	0.02	0.22	0.05	0.02	0.43
Investment	1.2	0.03	—	8.4*	0.46	0.56	0.14
Private Consumption	2.2	0.21	8.2*	—	—	—	—
Nonmilitary Public Consumption	0.15	0.26	0.43	—	—	—	—
Military Spending	0.35	0.05	0.53	—	—	—	—
Governmental Deficits	0.00	0.41	0.12	—	—	—	—

Lag structure = 4, 4.

*p is less than or equal to .01

EG = Economic Growth, P = Productivity, I = Investment, PC = Private Consumption, GC = Nonmilitary Public Consumption, M = Military Spending, D = Governmental Deficits

findings also reflect relationships that are different from the investment-oriented tradeoff predicted by Gilpin's hegemonic decline model.

Unlike the British case, the test for instantaneous linkages in the American case does yield additional significant relationships that help clarify the problem of interpretation. As expressed in table 7.4, private consumption and investment are linked reciprocally on an instantaneous basis. Thus, the combined outcome supports the idea of one kind of a consumption-investment growth linkage. The evidence of a tradeoff is restricted to the impact of private consumption alone.

An examination of the bivariate coefficients in appendix C, table C.5, shows that private consumption is both statistically significant and negatively related to economic growth and investment. There are also statistically significant, negative lags between nonmilitary public consumption and economic growth and investment. Yet the current and past values of public consumption do not together predict significantly to these latter variables as does private consumption. The same holds true for the linkages between military spending and economic growth and investment.

As a check on the credibility of the bivariate tests of antecedence, a multivariate vector autoregression approach was used for U.S. quarterly data on investment and the three basic forms of consumption.[13] Simple tests of antecedence in table 7.5 indicate that there is only one directional relationship—from private consumption to investment.[14] Instantaneous tests of antecedence reported in table 7.6 do not reveal any significant linkages. In short, the

Table 7.5 Quasi F-statistics for Multivariate Vector Autoregressions, United States, 1954–1986: A Test for Antecedence (quarterly data)

Independent Variable	Dependent Variable			
	I	PC	GC	M
Investment	—	3.4*	2.1	0.57
Private Consumption	2.3	—	0.53	0.58
Nonmilitary Public Consumption	1.7	0.48	—	1.5
Military Spending	2.2	0.98	1.1	—

Note: The quarterly series begins in the second quarter of 1954 primarily as a consequence of data availability.
Lag structure = 4, 4.
*p is less than or equal to .05
I = Investment, PC = Private Consumption, GC = Nonmilitary Public Consumption, M = Military Spending

multivariate tests for the available quarterly data substantiate the basic findings of the bivariate tests. The coefficients derived from this estimation can be found in appendix C, table C.6. They indicate that the relationship between private consumption and investment remains negative.

Our findings do not support the argument that consumption-driven investment tradeoffs are critical to an understanding of the relative decline of system leaders. The evidence suggests that they are derivative phenomena of decline. What is still not clear, however, is the extent to which these tradeoffs act as second-order influences on continuing decline. There is some suggestion of this in the Rasler (1990) findings based on dividing the U.S. case into two temporal segments—before and after the onset of productivity decline. But the U.S. decline is still under way and therefore awkward to analyze. It may be too soon to develop reliable findings on the relative decline of the United States.[15] Alternatively, future developments could conceivably reverse the U.S. decline. What we need is a case with a longer history and one in which the question of relative decline is no longer controversial. A third requirement is that we be able to model the relationships among the kinds of variables that we have been discussing. Only the British case satisfies all of these criteria.

A Longer Look at the British Case

Earlier in this chapter we examined the relationships between consumption, investment, and economic growth in Britain from 1831 to 1913. We assumed that the era of British systemic leadership had ended by the onset of World War I, if not earlier. To explain the erosion of British preeminence, as op-

Table 7.6 Quasi $\underline{F}$-statistics for Multivariate Vector Autoregressions, United States, 1954–1986: A Test for Instantaneous Antecedence (quarterly data)

Independent Variable	Dependent Variable			
	I	PC	GC	M
Investment	—	1.2	0.43	0.23
Private Consumption	0.95	—	—	—
Nonmilitary Public Consumption	0.54	—	—	—
Military Spending	0.27	—	—	—

Note: The quarterly series begins in the second quarter of 1954 primarily as a consequence of data availability.

Lag structure = 4, 4.

*p is less than or equal to .05

I = Investment, PC = Private Consumption, GC = Nonmilitary Public Consumption, M = Military Spending

posed to its consequences, we needed to focus on the period preceding World War I. But what happened after World War I? More specifically, did the Granger relationships observed to describe the 1831-1913 period continue to characterize the British political economy after 1918? If consumption-investment tradeoffs are indeed second-order influences on decline, we should expect to find more evidence for tradeoffs in the later period, even though, or especially since, we found no evidence of tradeoffs in the nineteenth century.[16] In the interests of minimizing the nature of the modeling problems involved, we will avoid the increasingly chaotic behavior in the interwar years and concentrate on the period after World War II.

We predict that we will find the relationships observed in 1831-1913 at work in the 1950-80 period as well. In addition, we expect to see the emergence of some consumption-driven investment tradeoffs in the 1950-80 period that did not exist in the 1831-1913 period. If the Sprouts were right in 1968, however, we may find causal arrows pointing from investment growth to military consumption, but we should not expect to find any reciprocal relationships or causal arrows pointing from military consumption to investment growth.

Whether we should anticipate nonmilitary public consumption-driven tradeoffs with economic performance variables is less clear. The Sprouts argued only that investment and social service spending enjoyed a higher priority than military spending. They did not discuss which of the two enjoyed the more politically significant constituency. At the same time, there is no compelling reason to suppose that these particular priorities or the significance of their constituencies have remained constant across Labour and Conservative regimes. This observation alone would suggest, at least,

Table 7.7 Quasi F-statistics for Bivariate Vector Autoregressions, Britain, 1831–1913 and 1950–1980: Tests for Antecedence (annual data)

Independent Variable	Dependent Variable				
	M	GC	PC	I	EG
1831–1913					
Military Spending	—	3.7*	0.65	0.90	0.96
Nonmilitary Public Consumption	3.1*	—	2.3*	1.0	0.46
Private Consumption	1.4	1.2	—	1.0	0.88
Investment	1.3	0.98	4.0*	—	5.1*
Economic Growth	1.2	1.4	1.4	9.6*	—
1950–1980[a]					
Military Spending	—	1.8	1.9	0.01	1.0
Nonmilitary Public Consumption	3.3*	—	1.8	1.5	0.97
Private Consumption	1.1	3.1*	—	2.7*	2.3
Investment	8.1*	2.9*	2.4	—	4.0*[b]
Economic Growth	6.0*	6.9*	2.8*	3.5*[b]	—

[a] The 1950–80 relationships were estimated from 1953–80 data to outliers in military spending from 1950 to 1952.

[b] The reported quasi-F test outcomes are based on instantaneous tests of antecedence.

Lag structure = 2, 6.

*p is less than or equal to .05

M = Military Spending, GC = Nonmilitary Public Consumption, PC = Private Consumption, I = Investment, EG = Economic Growth

the potential for the development of reciprocal relations among nonmilitary public consumption and investment-economic growth in the post-World War II era. Moreover, to the extent that nonmilitary forms of consumption receive higher priority, we should also expect their economic impact or significance to expand.

Table 7.7 and figure 7.3 display the outcome of our analysis of central relationships in Britain's political economy. Our principal interest concerns whether the forms of consumption, and which forms of consumption, antecede investment and economic growth. We also ask whether this relationship changes over time, particularly after relative decline has been experienced for a lengthy period.

In table 7.7 we report which of the twenty possible paths of antecedence are statistically significant in the 1831-1913 and 1950-80 eras.[17] Six significant paths are demarcated for the first period. Ten paths are disclosed in the more recent period. Figure 7.3 helps clarify which variables are predictors and in which direction they predict. Tables C.4 and C.7 in appendix C list the respective coefficients and their relationship signs, although this information is less critical to questions of antecedence than to those of tradeoffs.

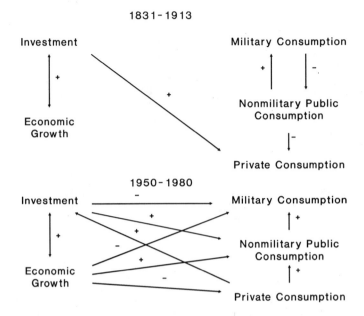

Figure 7.3 British Paths of Antecedence, 1831–1913 and 1950–1980

In both cases, investment and economic growth are related reciprocally and positively. The two forms of public consumption also are related in both time periods, as are nonmilitary public and private consumption. The signs of the intraconsumption relationships, however, appear to have changed over time. Before 1913 nonmilitary public consumption negatively anteceded private consumption. After 1950 the direction of antecedence reversed, and the sign changed as well. Before 1913 military spending and nonmilitary public consumption were related reciprocally, but the relationship signs were curiously dissimilar. The nonmilitary consumption-to-military spending relationship was positive, while the military spending-to-nonmilitary consumption relationship was negative. After 1950 the complexity of the relationship was reduced considerably, with nonmilitary public consumption positively anteceding military spending.

In retrospect, these findings do seem to match their respective centuries. In the nineteenth century, military spending increased when nonmilitary public consumption increased, and military spending decreased when nonmilitary public consumption decreased. Major changes in military spending, though, had a negative impact on nonmilitary public consumption. In late twentieth-century Britain, however, nonmilitary public consumption positively antecedes military spending. Evidence for a tradeoff relationship is no longer apparent.

Table 7.8 Proportional Central Government Expenditure by Function, 1890–1975

Year	Defense	Administration/ Justice	Economics/ Environment	Social Services	Other
1890	43.4	15.5	1.2	9.8	30.1
1900	74.2	6.3	0.8	7.4	11.3
1910	52.4	10.9	1.3	20.4	15.0
1920	40.8	4.9	10.0	18.7	25.7
1930	16.4	4.9	2.4	35.9	40.3
1938	44.4	4.1	3.4	27.6	20.4
1950	24.0	4.0	12.7	39.6	19.7
1960	24.1	3.5	9.3	36.3	26.8
1970	17.3	3.8	9.2	44.9	24.8
1975	14.7	4.7	11.2	44.2	25.2

Source: Flora et al. 1983: 444–45.

Note: Some rows do not total 100.0 because of roundings.

Nevertheless, the most interesting relationships for our inquiry into relative decline are those that connect investment and economic growth to consumption. The one significant path between the consumption categories and the two economic variables in the 1831-1913 examination points from investment to private consumption. This finding fundamentally contradicts the expectations one would derive from the Gilpin model, in which proportional consumption increases reduce investment and growth opportunities. Before World War I in Britain, the process seems to have worked primarily the other way around. Investment influenced consumption opportunities.

After World War II, the picture becomes more complicated. The one path linking investment to consumption in the 1831-1913 period disappears in the 1950-80 period. It is replaced instead by six new arrows. Five of the six point from investment or economic growth to the consumption categories. After 1950 economic growth negatively antecedes military spending and private consumption and positively antecedes nonmilitary public consumption. Similarly, investment negatively antecedes military spending and positively antecedes nonmilitary public consumption. The one arrow from the consumption side of the 1950-80 portion of figure 7.3 links private consumption to investment. The relationship, though, is positively signed.

What do these findings mean for the alternative models discussed earlier? First, we find no evidence for military spending crowding out investment in either period. All the arrows point the wrong way. Next, Gilpin's model is not very helpful in the 1831-1913 period. Again, all of the important arrows point the wrong way. No consumption variables predict to investment or economic growth. This is not quite the case in the 1950-80 period. But the sign of the solitary exception is mispredicted. No consumption-driven tradeoffs emerge between the five variables after 1950.

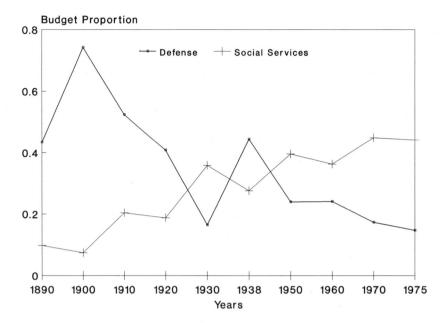

Figure 7.4 British Allocations to Defense and Social Services

The Sprout and Sprout model never argued that protection costs had undermined British hegemony. Nor did the Sprouts discuss consumption as a first- or second-order cause of relative decline. What they did say was that the nature of British political economy had evolved in a direction that gave highest priority to investment and growth, private consumption, and non-military public consumption. From this we deduced that military spending was more likely to be influenced by changes in the allocations to the high-priority agenda items than the other way around. For the most part, this approximates what we found. Investment and economic growth predict to military spending after 1950. The "only" influence military consumption projects in our simple five-variable model is to nonmilitary public consumption. The degree to which this intrapublic consumption tradeoff has become simplified with the passage of time and political economy developments presumably supports the Sprouts' argument.

The degree to which the outcome matches the Sprouts' prediction—or, more accurately, our interpretation of what that prediction might have been—is less than perfect in at least one sense. The Sprouts' arguments were predicated to a great extent on assumptions about the effects of an expanding electorate and their rising demands for social services. Other things being equal, as social services expanded, military spending would have to be curtailed. We know that proportional allocations to social services have indeed expanded and military spending has declined in Britain. We certainly do not wish to contest this fact. The information in table 7.8 provides ample support for this observation. Yet the phenomenon is largely a twentieth-century one (see figure 7.4).

Our reservation at this juncture is that the evidence is mixed concerning major changes, vis-à-vis the implications of the Sprouts' arguments, in how the British political economy influence map works from one time period to the next. The electorate expanded, demands rose, and governmental services grew between the pre-World War I and post-World War II eras. Priorities clearly changed. Yet even though military spending once had a higher priority in the British policy preference schedule, there is no evidence that it once had a greater impact on the political economy.[18] Partly as a consequence, the influence of military spending does not become less visible in 1950-80; it stays about the same. The two other types of consumption, on the other hand, have become more influential, and this development is certainly in accord with these categories' improved priorities. Perhaps we should simply be content with two out of three predictions, a record that is not all that bad by social science criteria.

Implications and Conclusions

Clearly, every case of systemic leadership decline need not represent the interaction of identical processes. Evidently private consumption plays a significant role in the American case but not in the earlier British case. This observation needs to be counterbalanced by the uniform absence of any support for public consumption—either military or civilian—acting as an antecedent of investment, productivity, or growth in either case. Moreover, in the American case the economic performance variables more often precede the consumption variables than the other way around. Our findings are therefore only partially mixed.

We certainly cannot reject the idea that some forms of consumption deserve further consideration in the etiology of leadership decline. Yet it would also appear to be the case that neither public nor private propensities for consumption are either necessary or sufficient factors in the relative decline of modern lead economies. Support is also quite evident for the proposition that relative decline influences the ability to consume. Such a conclusion is hardly startling. But if we had to choose between viewing consumption as a primary or a secondary factor in bringing about leadership decline, the evidence in our two cases is tilted considerably in favor of the secondary emphasis.

Of course, we are not forced to make a final choice between the two interpretations at this time. There are, after all, potential threats to the validity of our findings that suggest analytical caution. On the technical side, there is the potential problem of spurious relationships. A more ambitious modeling effort with many more variables might reveal different findings. Much more subtle, indirect relationships between public consumption and investment might be uncovered.

In our research design, we have what might be termed a historical problem. Confined as we are to the two most recent cases (encompassing, however, the last century and a half), we encounter some awkwardness in the fact that only one of the subjects has completely lost its once preeminent position. We cannot dismiss the possibility that American relative decline has simply not progressed far enough to make it a good case for analysis. We may be jumping the analytical gun to compare the late twentieth-century United States with nineteenth-century Britain.

This possibility must remain open. Yet we should not exaggerate its potential threat to the validity of our findings. The evidence for the erosion of the relative economic foundation of American preeminence is plentiful. While the passage of more time and the availability of longer data series may produce different findings, it is difficult to ignore the temptation to try improving our understanding of what is presumably an ongoing process. For example, the optimistic, mainstream position is that faltering U.S. economic performance remains a temporary problem that can be fixed by reducing something, such as imports, interest rates, entitlements, taxation, the value of the dollar, the size of the national debt, military spending, and the size of the budget deficit. We have not examined all of these variables. Yet the cases for some of these quick-fix candidates, especially those pertaining to public spending, have not been strengthened by our present analysis.

Budgetary and trade deficits and consumption-investment tradeoffs are not to be taken lightly. They are, if nothing else, genuine policy problems. The point remains that should they somehow be addressed successfully, their resolution would not necessarily serve to halt the process of systemic leadership decline. Despite the ancient lineage of overconsumption arguments—or, indeed, because of the lineage—we need to be wary of mistaking secondary manifestations of decline for the roots of the problem.

The principal root of the problem, we believe, is found readily enough in the nonconsumption portions of the Cipolla and Gilpin models: the diffusion of innovation, the rise of competition, the resistance to change, and the consequent failure to lead forever in technological innovation and production.[19] There may not be much that can be done to stem the diffusion of the system leader's technological edge. The eventual increase in competition is no doubt the most inevitable part of relative decline. The resistances to change, however, can be attacked. Institutions and ways of doing things can be reformed—at least in theory.

Technological innovation can be promoted and facilitated. Nonetheless, measures taken along these lines may not suffice to reverse the processes of relative decline. Nor do we know all that we need to know about the connections between innovation, productivity, and growth. Also, the invention and development of dynamic growth sectors have not proved to be an easily manipulated process. Industrial policies and their authors can guess wrong as well as they can guess right the sources of the innovations that will count most tomorrow. Still, we can advance one statement on the issue of decline without fear of immediate contradiction. The losses of the lead systemic positions experienced by Portugal, the Netherlands, and Britain are irreversible. As far as we know, the same statement cannot yet be made about the current system leader, the United States.

The analysis of "overconsumption" in this chapter has concentrated largely upon internal sources of resource diversion. There is of course an external dimension to resource diversion that deserves some discussion, especially in light of the attention attracted by the 1987 publication of Paul Kennedy's book *The Rise and Fall of the Great Powers*. In the next chapter we will continue the examination of overconsumption by focusing on a different type of tradeoff conceptualization—the ideas of overextension and territorial traps.

8.

Observations on Overextension and Territorial Traps

Much of Paul Kennedy's (1987b) argument is similar to Robert Gilpin's (1981) thesis. This set of arguments has received a great deal of empirical scrutiny in the preceding two chapters. The empirical outcome has supported the emphasis on technological innovation but has failed to sustain the centrality of consumption-investment tradeoffs as root causes of rise-and-fall dynamics. These tradeoffs include the consumption associated with military spending, which is hardly an exclusively domestic undertaking. Even so, modeling potential tradeoffs between investment and public and private forms of consumption does not necessarily tap directly into the concept of imperial overextension. Since the overextension argument is potentially important to our understanding of rise-and-fall dynamics, it demands some further consideration. A brief overview of Kennedy's theoretical interpretation should help delineate precisely what is at issue here.

As a historian, Kennedy might not be comfortable with the charge that he possesses a theory. Nonetheless, the "accusation" seems appropriate. The core of his theory can be summarized in the following statements extracted from his 1987 discussion:

1. The central dynamic of change in international politics is driven primarily by developments in economic growth and technology. These developments, in turn, bring about changes in social structures, political systems, military power, and the hierarchical position of actors.

2. The pace of change is nonuniform due to irregularities in the unevenness of growth, technological innovation, entrepreneurial invention, and other intervening factors such as climate, geography, and war.

3. Different regions and states have experienced faster or slower rates of growth due to shifts in technology, production, and trade as well as to their variable receptivities to adopting new modes of increasing wealth.

4. Military power ultimately depends upon economic wealth derived

from an infrastructure integrating production, technology, and finance. Uneven economic growth, therefore, significantly impacts the relative military power and strategic position of states.

5. Great power warfare has been closely related to the rise and fall of major actors. The new territorial order established at the end of each great coalitional war, in which victory always goes to the side with the greatest material resources, confirms longer-term shifts in economic capabilities and the redistribution of international power.

6. A peculiar set of historical and technological circumstances facilitates the emergence of states that are enabled to acquire, temporarily, a disproportionate share of the world's total wealth and power. As the favorable circumstances disappear, the leading states revert to or toward their normal proportional share of wealth and power.

7. While the relative erosion of disproportional wealth and power is inevitable, the pace of erosion can be accelerated by attempts to maintain commitments that exceed the diminishing means to sustain them.

Assuming that we have correctly summarized the heart of Kennedy's argument, there is obviously a great deal of overlap connecting his approach with our own. Both of us emphasize the economic and military implications of technological innovation. We are more specific about the nature of these innovations. We also are much more impressed by their uniformities and regularities than Kennedy is. But we share with him the linkage between uneven growth and coalitional warfare, even if we might not agree perfectly with him on which coalitional wars are most significant in ratifying redistributions of power.

Whether we disagree about the significance of the commitments-means imbalance ("imperial overstretch") as a source of relative decline is a matter of interpretation. As we read Kennedy, he places the primary explanatory burden for shifts in wealth on technological change. That is essentially our argument in chapter 6.[1] Perhaps because our emphasis on technological change is more concrete, however, we do not argue that relative decline is inevitable. Instead, we see it as highly likely because, historically, no one has figured out how to monopolize innovation for more than a finite period of time.

Yet differential success in monopolizing economic innovation is also reflected in the same historical record. For example, the British managed to develop more spurts of growth and innovation than either the Portuguese or the Dutch. The migration of the site of the global economy's lead economy is not inevitable. The lead can at least be extended if the conditions favoring the next round of leading-sector growth are close at hand or susceptible to timely manipulation. Conceivably, it would even be possible to extend a lead indefinitely without suppressing technological diffusion, as long as an explicit effort was made to maintain innovational leadership and the resources were readily available to do so. Still, it must be acknowledged that no society has yet demonstrated that what we have termed conceivable is anything more than hypothetical.

More important to our consideration of the role of overconsumption in the etiology of relative decline, however, is the process of imperial overstretch. Kennedy's identification of this concept is straightforward. At some point, the system's leading state tends to be afflicted with more interests and obligations than it has the power to defend simultaneously. Indeed, according to Kennedy, the external claims on the resources of leading states are likely to expand as their relative wealth base declines: "Even as relative economic strength is ebbing, growing foreign challenges to their position have compelled them to allocate more and more of their resources into the military sector, which in turn squeezes out productive investment and, over time, leads to the downward spiral of slower growth, heavier taxes, deepening domestic splits over spiraling priorities, and a weakening capacity to bear the burdens of defense" (Kennedy 1987b: 533).

As long as Kennedy portrays this overstretch problem as a secondary cause, or consequence, of decline, it is difficult to argue with the phenomenon as a potential management problem for declining powers. Diminishing resources for external political commitments—or internal political commitments—obviously spell trouble for politicians who feel obliged to maintain or expand programs conceived in more prosperous times unless they are willing and able to discontinue other programs and obligations.

Nevertheless, Kennedy does two things that tend to muddy the conceptual waters and with which we do disagree. First, in his treatment of specific states, he refers to overstretch as one reason for their decline. For instance, the French threat to the Netherlands in the late seventeenth century is said to have had three effects. The Dutch were forced to divert limited financial resources to military defense and war debts. As a consequence, the Dutch economy was saddled with high interest payments, high taxes, and high wages—all of which undercut commercial competitiveness. Also, the relatively static Dutch population could ill afford the losses of life incurred in the warfare with the French. Finally, the nature of the Anglo-Dutch alliance in the 1688-1713 fighting meant that the Dutch had to concentrate their resources on land-based military capabilities while the British specialized in sea power. The upshot was that "as London and Bristol merchants flourished . . . Amsterdam traders suffered" (Kennedy 1987b: 88).

Another example offered by Kennedy is the case of Britain, which he describes, quite accurately, as having experienced resource-draining "overstrain" in World Wars I and II. We do not dispute the fact that late seventeenth-century warfare left the Dutch with high debts and taxes or that British assets were heavily consumed in the warfare of the twentieth century. The point we wish to make is that the relative decline of the system leader had begun well in advance of the advent of global war in the 1680s, the 1910s, and the 1930s.

The costs of these global wars only finished off the incumbent leaders, thereby facilitating the more clear-cut emergence of their successors. These examples of imperial overstretch, therefore, tell us more about the consequences of relative decline than about its roots.

The second aspect of Kennedy's treatment of imperial overstretch with which we disagree is his tendency to draw upon different types of examples to illustrate the points he wishes to make. In addition to the Netherlands and Britain, he also cites the Ottoman Empire and seventeenth-century Spain and Sweden as states that encountered serious overstretch problems. Once again, we do not dispute the fact that these states experienced difficulties in attempting to defend commitments that exceeded their means to do so. But lumping all great powers together as a single category overlooks some interesting hypotheses about overstretch behavior. As Snyder notes, there are two basic types of overstretch or overextension. One kind, which we will call type I overextension, is the true imperial variety: one state expands too far into "the hinterland beyond the point where costs begin to outstrip benefits" (Snyder 1991: 6). The other type (type II) occurs when the actions of an expansive great power provoke an overwhelming coalition of opposing states. We suggest that the leading global power is far more likely to commit a type I overextension than a type II strategic error. The leading regional power, in marked contrast, is more likely to provoke the overwhelming coalition, a type II error, than to have the opportunity to indulge in a type I error. We would also suggest that type II errors are far more fatal for leading regional powers than type I errors are for either leading regional or global powers.

To elaborate the underlying logic and to test these hypotheses would require much more space than we currently have to spare for questions somewhat tangential to the main inquiry. The incidence of type II errors is straightforward and is central to our earlier discussions of the balance of power and global wars. Type I errors, on the other hand, represent much more controversial and awkward terrain. Ascertaining when costs begin to outstrip benefits remains a highly subjective undertaking in large part because we have no widely accepted metrics for the strategic costs and benefits of imperial expansion. In any event, evaluating grand strategies in a theoretical vein over a long period of time is a subject best left to another book. There is an alternative approach to type I overextension problems, however, that can be encapsulated under the rubric of the "territorial trap hypothesis."

The Territorial Trap Hypothesis

The territorial trap hypothesis makes two assumptions: global leadership is predicated on the development of capabilities of global reach, and a global network of bases that minimizes the direct control of extensive amounts of territory provides the infrastructure for maintaining global-reach capabilities. Extensive territorial holdings and commitments drain attention and resources from the maintenance of the global network. Since global leadership in part depends on avoiding or minimizing territorial commitments, the tendency or temptation to acquire responsibilities on land creates long-term strategic traps for the global leader.

Initially, decision makers recognize the advantages of minimizing territorial obligations, but they often drift toward the stance that their systemic position can only be assured by assuming responsibility for ever larger territories and more people. What begins as a lean strategic commercial maritime network is transformed into something that increasingly resembles a land-based empire. Expanding territorial responsibilities create an increasing need for land-based armies, first to conquer the new lands, then to protect them against rivals, and finally to suppress subsequent tendencies toward revolt, unrest, and disintegration. All this armed activity also requires the financial means to meet the armies' associated expenses. The territorial expansion of empire, while seemingly a "sun never setting" hallmark of politico-economic success in the world system, can become the quagmire of world power.

The territorial trap hypothesis suggests that global leaders tend to lose track of the geopolitical roots of their own path to success. An initial low overhead strategy gives way to centralized empire (Chase-Dunn 1981: 39). Some historical examples illustrate the workings of this process.

Portuguese and Dutch strategists debated the question of network control early in the expansions of their respective colonial empires (Boxer 1965, 1969). How much or how little Asian territory needed to be controlled in order to monopolize the European trade with Asia? Portugal's first permanent commander in the Indian Ocean, Almeida, argued for scattered commercial outposts reinforced by mobile naval power: "The greater number of fortresses you hold the weaker will be your power. Let all our forces be on the sea, because if we should not be powerful at sea (which the Lord forbid), everything will at once be against us. . . . Let it be known for certain that as long as you may be powerful at sea you will hold India as yours, and if you do not possess this power, little will avail you a fortress on shore" (Danvers 1966, 1: xxix-xxx).

Almeida's successor, Albuquerque, argued that it was imperative to build imposing coastal fortresses, to intervene in hinterland politics, and, ultimately, to acquire de facto control over gradually increasing segments of Asian and African territory: "Your Highness cannot be lord over so extensive a territory as India by placing all your power and strength in the navy only (a policy at once doubtful and full of serious inconveniences); for this and not to build fortresses, the very thing which the Moors of these lands wish you to do, for they know well that a dominion founded on a navy alone cannot last" (Danvers 1966, 1: xxxi).

A century later, two successive Dutch East India governors-general, Peter Both and Jan Pieterszoon Coen, disagreed on Dutch strategy in Asia along remarkably parallel lines. Both was reluctant to build forts, but Coen was much less averse to doing so (Diffie and Winius 1977: 241-42). In the short run, the proliferation of commitments seems the more pragmatic solution to pressing problems of network control. Only later do the full costs of territorial empire become evident.

Britain's story was a longer-playing version of its predecessors'. Despite official reluctance to encourage territorial expansion, the British Empire eventually become one of the more extensive collections of real estate ever assembled. In degree and timing, the process of British expansion was not identical to the Portuguese and Dutch experiences in Asia. Still, the initial incentives—trade and plunder (Andrews 1984)—were certainly similar. Early advice on British Asian policy also sounds familiar. Sir Thomas Roe, one of the earliest emissaries (1615-19) of the English East India Company sent to the Mughal court, said that "it hath also been the errour of the Dutch who seek plantation by the sword. . . . Lett this be received as a rule that if you will profitt seek it at sea and in quiet trade for . . . it is an errour to affect garrisons and land warrs in India" (quoted in de Schweinitz 1983: 78).

Subsequent British expansion departed from this advice. One of the important constraints on earlier territorial expansion—the strength of Asian military and political capabilities—gradually eroded. The eventual disintegration of the Mughal Empire in particular no doubt increased the likelihood of British expansion ashore. Later, technological developments in firepower, transportation, and preventive medicine also increased the European ability to rule on land.

The scale of British settlement in North America, Australia and New Zealand, and southern Africa constituted another deviation from the global leader pattern. The consequent vulnerability to "sub-imperialism" or the "metropolitan dog being wagged by its colonial tail" increased (Fieldhouse 1973: 80-81). The ambitions and impulses of distant imperial agents were always difficult to restrain. The problem was compounded by the desires of relatively large settler populations on the coasts to move inland.

Britain's first empire encountered the territorial trap problem in the effort to hold on to large amounts of North American territory. The greatest threat to the pre-1792 British global position occurred during the internationalized American War of Independence. The subsequent, second British empire experienced quantitative and qualitative transformations in the nineteenth century. As late as 1815, the British

still saw their empire as a collection of ports, islands, and coastal regions, held together by the navy and dependent on it for prosperity and even survival. The navy dominated the seas of the whole world and to an extent that had no parallel . . . it

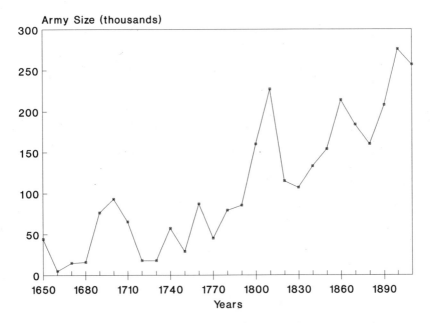

Figure 8.1 Change in the Size of the British Army

could be sent all over the world, and could be used to make Britain's power supreme at any point which lay within a cannon shot of the sea.

The British government rarely wanted to push its power any further than this and made no particular effort to advance inland (Lloyd 1984: 138).

Even so, the land size and population size of the empire increased by factors of seven and twenty respectively between 1800 and 1900 (Headrick 1981: 3). The reason for this expansion continues to be debated. World economy analysts attribute periodicities in territorial control increases almost exclusively to increased intracore economic competition (Chase-Dunn and Rubinson 1977; Bergesen and Schoenberg 1980). Others argue for the gradual expansion of the British Empire via "creeping colonialism" (Porter 1975), the "imperialism of free trade" (Gallagher and Robinson 1953), or the pull of the "turbulent frontier" (Galbraith 1960). Other emphases involve the undeniable technological changes that made hinterland expansion feasible (Headrick 1981) or preemptive strategies to deal with real or potential threats from great power rivals (Fieldhouse 1966, 1973; Baumgart 1982). These arguments are not all that incompatible. Yet whatever the reasons, Britain's maritime network became increasingly territorially based. Nonessential commitments increased. The question remains: What, if any, impact did these commitments have on British strategic capabilities and priorities?

One answer to this question involves one of the consequences of territorial commitments—the expansion of ground forces. Even though European army sizes are thought to have increased more or less steadily since 1500 (Howard 1976; Parker 1979b), the intermittent expansion of the British army often proved temporary (see table A.1). After expansion during wartime, the return to peace was accompanied by rapid demobilizations. In figure 8.1 we demonstrate the transient nature of these spurts in growth that are not particularly difficult to explain. The constraints on British army size included a seventeenth-century political phobia about standing armies, the strong reliance on the Royal Navy (and the English Channel) for national security, governmental preferences for limited spending, and the low domestic demand for the services of an army.

The British army began to expand permanently after 1763. The usual army growth spurt took place in the Seven Years' War; this war, too, was followed by immediate postwar downsizing. But the size of the army did not return to its prewar size or even to the size that prevailed before the 1739-48 warfare. A major reason for permanent growth is linked to the Canadian conquests of the 1750s-60s. Before the 1750s the North American colonies had been required to defend themselves. At the end of the Seven Years' War, London decided to maintain ten thousand regular troops in North America. As Fieldhouse put it, the era of British colonization on the cheap had come to an end (1966: 94-95).

Even after the loss of the American colonies, two-thirds of the peacetime British army remained scattered throughout the empire (Barnett 1970: 226). After 1815 the number of troops assigned to colonial duties was proportionally larger despite a doubling in army size since 1783. Barnett captures one "turbulent frontier" aspect of this dynamic:

Although the empire seemed an encumbrance, it nevertheless kept on expanding by a piecemeal but irresistible process. This process is illustrated by the case of India, the greatest single "colony." Corrupt or warlike Indian potentates on the fringes of British territory would threaten trade or order; the British would therefore take military action against the potentates. This would lead to a further extension of British rule, and by thus bringing the British up against another set of native potentates, the forward process would begin all over again. Long before the renewal of deliberate imperial expansion in the 1880s and 1890s, the British Empire therefore expanded in Africa, India, Burma, Malaysia, and China, despite hapless attempts to arrest the process. [1970: 273]

Along with this imperial growth, the nineteenth-century British army grew to levels that continued to be low by European standards but that had been matched at home only by British wartime standards. Such growth cannot be attributed to the Napoleonic revolution in military mobilization. Al-

Table 8.1 Mean British Military Budgetary Proportions, 1671–1913

Period	Navy	Army	Navy/Army Ratio
1671–1713	27.5	32.4	0.96
1714–1815	21.4	27.8	0.83
1816–1913	11.5	23.2	0.53

	Wartime				Peacetime		
Period	Navy	Army	Navy/Army Ratio		Navy	Army	Navy/Army Ratio
1671–1713	27.8	33.1	0.94		24.4	23.3	1.23
1714–1815	23.2	32.2	0.77		18.1	20.1	0.92
1816–1913	11.3	24.0	0.51		12.1	21.4	0.58

Source: Thompson and Zuk 1986: 262.

Note: Each number represents a mean of the annual data for the selected periods. British Indian military expenditures are incorporated from 1858 to 1913.

most all of it was caused by an increase in the scope and scale of the problems associated with the control of far-flung territories, reluctant subjects, and hostile neighbors. We know that Britain's naval lead declined in the nineteenth century. To what extent did the territorial trap contribute to the erosion of Britain's position?

Success as a global leader is predicated in part on the creation and maintenance of global maritime networks. Demands that drain attention and resources from the global network can contribute to the decay of a leadership position. The perceived need to sustain large land-based military forces is one type of resource-draining demand that accompanies growing territorial commitments. Normally, the global leader would be expected to allocate more resources to its naval operations than to its land-based forces. Territorial trap considerations, however, suggest that the navy-army spending ratio should decline as the need for larger armies increases.

These expectations represent testable propositions, which, in the British case, have already been tested empirically by Thompson and Zuk (1986). They first constructed a ratio of navy-to-army spending in the period 1671-1913. Since the British relied heavily on Indian troops for colonial campaigns in Asia, the Middle East, and Africa, the total army accounts of the British India (after 1857) and British governments were combined to create one total army expenditure.[2] After an initial interval of naval favoritism, the eighteenth century was one of fluctuation above and below the spending equality line. Between 1792 and 1914 the army was clearly favored. Before 1713 the navy-army spending ratio averaged 0.96. It fell to 0.83 in the 1714-1815 period and

Table 8.2 Periods of British Imperial Warfare, 1661–1913

Period	Imperial Warfare
1715–16	Scottish Rebellion
1766–69	First Mysore
1775–77	American Independence
1789–92	Third Mysore
1816–18	Gurkha, Third Maratha
1823–31	First Burmese, First Ashanti, Bhurtapore Intervention
1838–49	First Afghan, First Opium, Second Turco-Egyptian, Sind, First Maori, First Sikh, Second Sikh
1852–53	Second Burmese
1857–70	Second Opium, Anglo-Persian, Indian Mutiny, Second Maori, Bhutan, Abyssianian Expedition
1873–74	Second Ashanti
1878–85	Second Afghan, Zulu, First Boer, Basuto Revolt, Egyptian Intervention, Mahdist Revolt, Third Burmese
1887	Zulu Rebellion
1893–1904	Mashona Intervention, Third Ashanti, Fourth Ashanti, Matabele Revolt, Sudan, Afridi Revolt, Northern Nigerian Conquest, Uganda Mutiny, Second Boer, Boxer Rebellion, Ashanti Revolt, Tibetan Expedition, Nigerian Revolt

Source: Thompson and Zuk 1986: 259.

Note: The data on periods of ongoing imperial warfare are based on information reported in Wright 1965, Singer and Small 1972, and Dupuy and Dupuy 1977. Some years of imperial warfare that overlapped with years of global warfare (1689–97, 1701–13, 1793–1815) or interstate warfare (1663–67, 1672–74, 1718–20, 1727–28, 1739–48, 1756–63, 1778–83, 1854–56) have been excluded. The exclusions help to explain why no imperial warfare is reported between 1661 and 1714.

to 0.53 in the 1816-1913 era. During peacetime, the initial bias toward the navy was more pronounced, but much the same negative trend in the spending ratio was registered (see table 8.1).

To assess the pace of territorial expansion, it was assumed that periods of imperial warfare (nonglobal and noninterstate wars), delineated in table 8.2, would lead to ratchetlike, permanent increases in army personnel. Assuming further that more soldiers meant more army spending, imperial warfare should have a permanent and negative impact on the navy-army spending ratio.

Unfortunately, it was not always possible to distinguish years of imperial warfare from years of global and interstate fighting. Imperial wars, attempts to expand or defend British interests in the face of local opposition in the system's hinterland, were often fought in conjunction with, or as a subordinate theater of conflict within, wars fought between the major powers. The solution was to code any year of warfare according to the most politically significant type of war—global, interstate, and imperial, in descending order—that was ongoing in that year.[3] Major power warfare, it was argued, should boost the sizes of both armies and navies, leading to some oscillation in the navy-army spending ratio during wartime, but the impact of global and interstate wars, to the extent that they can be distinguished from imperial warfare, should be temporary (Rasler and Thompson 1985, 1989). Two other possible influences were also examined. A dummy variable was introduced to control for the Anglo-German naval arms race toward the end of the period examined. The two periods of British leadership, 1714-1815 and 1816-1913, were examined separately to gauge what appeared to be a very slow territorial trap process. The expectation was that the impact of imperial warfare should have been stronger in the nineteenth century than in the eighteenth century.

A Box-Tiao impact assessment analysis produced evidence supporting the territorial trap hypothesis. The omega coefficient for the impact of imperial warfare, after controlling for other types of warfare and the late nineteenth-century naval arms race, was negative and statistically significant over the entire 1714-1913 period. When the two centuries were analyzed separately, only the 1816-1913 findings were significant. Thus, the evidence indicates that the British experienced some form of tradeoff between territorial commitments and the maintenance of naval preponderance in the nineteenth century.

Such a finding requires careful interpretation. Does this mean that Britain lost its global lead primarily because of its expanding territorial commitments? That is certainly not our argument. Other factors were at play that are more difficult to model. In the era of wooden ships of the line, British decision makers were reluctant to build new ships except in periods of military crisis (Thompson 1988). The reluctance was probably not all that illogical, since wooden ships were fairly durable, their design changed only slowly, and there was little competition for naval supremacy in the first half of the nineteenth century. All three of these factors contributed to the reductions in British naval spending.

In the second half of the nineteenth century, naval technological innovation, thanks to steam engines, explosive shells, armor plating, and iron and steel hulls, was rapid. New naval competitors emerged as well. Still Britain managed to hold on to its naval lead. But holding on to a lead and exercising overwhelming preponderance are not the same things. In the latter context, potential rivals are reluctant to issue challenges. In the former case, they are more likely to be tempted.

The late nineteenth-century buildup of the German navy helps to illustrate this point. How large a navy the Germans intended to build is arguable (Kennedy 1983), but one of the factors facilitating the challenging of the British navy was the impression that the British navy was spread too thin around the globe and could not be quickly reconcentrated in Northern European waters (Lambi 1984). The German battle fleet, lacking responsibilities for extended territorial defense, could be concentrated easily. As it turned out, the German decision makers were wrong. The British fleet was reconcentrated in home waters well in advance of 1914 but at the expense of maintaining the global naval network—much of which had to be reduced, stripped, or abandoned to the Americans, Japanese, and French (Kennedy 1976).

Does this suggest that the real trap is not territorial commitments but a global network that makes a home defense more difficult? Again, it is a matter for interpretation. Our reading is that the root of the problem is the emergence of a threatening regional leader that resurrects the intermittent problem of home defense. While the gradual accumulation of British territorial commitments is relatively unique in the history of global leaders, the emergence of a proximate threat is not unique to the British case. The Portuguese and the Dutch experienced it as well. Before this threat emerges, the global network serves the purposes of world power quite well. It is hard to imagine the successes of the global leaders in its absence. But the network must be maintained by new resources, which in turn depend heavily on renewed spurts of technological innovation. In the absence of new innovation, decline sets in and eats away at the global leader's commanding position. It is the posited erosion that encourages competition and challenges.

Territorial commitments are a problem for global leaders. They do represent a drain of material resources and a distraction for decision makers. Moreover, the possession of empire may also inhibit tendencies to pioneer new forms of economic innovation by cushioning the effects of an increasingly noncompetitive economic position (Hobsbawm 1969; Walker 1980). Merchants and industrialists can always fall back on the imperial markets they control exclusively. While some factors discourage innovation, they are not necessarily a major source of decline. Rather, they resemble quite closely the tradeoffs examined in chapter 7. The resemblance is most striking in the sense that territorial commitment problems and consumption-investment tradeoffs seem to become problems only after the onset of decline. In this respect, they are secondary sources of decline. They make policy problems worse, but they are not at the heart of the matter. Therefore, reducing territorial commitments or consumption is not likely to be sufficient to rejuvenate a declining position.

The ongoing U.S. case of relative decline offers a test of this proposition.

One explanation for U.S. decline has been the country's extensive military commitments and expenditures. Commitments and spending, fueled by cold war containment strategies, began to escalate shortly after the end of the last global war. The Truman and Eisenhower doctrines, for instance, added or attempted to add commitments to defend parts of the Northern Mediterranean littoral, Southwest Asia, and the Middle East to earlier commitments to the defense of Western Europe and Japan. The incorporation of South Korea, once regarded as outside the perimeter, was brought about during the Korean War, just as much of the former French presence in Indochina was gradually assumed by Americans in the decade leading up to the Vietnam War. Similarly, the former British role in the Indian Ocean and Persian/Arabian Gulf was also taken over by the United States in the 1970s, eventually leading to the Gulf War in the early 1990s.

A relatively large number of U.S. troops have been maintained in Europe, Southeast Asia, and East Asia. The collapse of the Soviet Union and the demise of the cold war appear to be leading to a substantial reduction in the number of troops stationed in Germany and South Korea. At the time of this writing, of course, it is much too soon to assess its impact on U.S. economic competitiveness. We expect, however, that the impact of military downsizing on the relative economic position of the United States is likely to be minimal. At best, the retrenchment suggests that global leaders are not so entrapped by territorial commitments that they cannot withdraw when confronted with an opportunity to reduce costs in the presence of a declining resource base. The British did much the same before World War I. But retrenchment alone neither expands nor rebuilds the resource base.

The Soviet disintegration may offer another sort of test. There can be little doubt that expensive and resource-draining territorial commitments to Eastern Europe and other places such as Cuba and Afghanistan played some role in bringing about the breakup of the empire (Wolf 1985). Here again, more work needs to be done in sorting out the various hypotheses available to explain the Soviet collapse. In the interim, though, we suggest that the subsidies paid to allies and even the enormous number of ground forces will not prove to be key factors. Instead, the Soviet disintegration more closely resembles the sort of resource exhaustion experienced by regional leaders defeated in global war. The Soviet case, thus, seems more like a type II overextension than the type I variant more common to global leaders. Attempting to catch up with Western economies and military strength, the Soviet Union was unable to generate sufficient economic growth to pay for its incipient challenge. Its ability to stay in contention as long as it did was probably facilitated by access to marketable natural resources such as petroleum. Ultimately, Soviet leaders realized that they could no longer pursue their increasingly ambitious foreign policies. Nor could they expect their economic planning to generate the type of domestic growth so critical to catching up with the West. More moderate retrenchment policies sometimes get out of hand and lead to more radical approaches. The Gorbachev-Yeltsin transition seems to represent just such a case.[4]

Global leaders drift into territorial traps in a process not unlike the process by which consumption-investment tradeoffs emerge. An initial sensitivity for developing and maintaining a global network gives way to short-term considerations of the perceived need to expand territorial commitments. Whatever the short-term gains in maintaining order and security along the network's fringe, they become longer-term positional hindrances as the initially limited network is transformed into entities resembling traditional empires. The burdens of this transformation are real. The question is whether they are primary or secondary contributions to the relative decline of the global leader. Our conclusion is that, for the most part, they constitute secondary factors.

Overconsumption and overextension by no means exhaust the inventory of possible explanations for relative decline. The roles of foreign investment, education systems, cultural attitudes, and distributional coalitions—to name but four—have received little attention in this examination. A number of other topics might be discussed and explored under the rubric of relative decline. But considerations of time and space preclude an exhaustive analysis of the relative decline syndrome at present. In any event, a much different kind of book, one with detailed and illustrative case histories of the global leaders in decline, would be necessary to pursue the processes of decline in more depth. Suffice it to say that we suspect that many of the other topics in the decline inventory will also prove not to be primary when examined more closely.

We leave that investigation to another study. Our more pressing concern now is to pull together the multiple assumptions, hypotheses, and findings of previous chapters into a coherent whole. Once that whole is reassembled, we will also explore the question of just where our approach fits in with other attempts to explain structural change and war.

9.
The Model Recapitulated

Global wars are periods of intensive combat that may last twenty-five to thirty years. Since 1494 five cases have been observed: 1494-1516, 1580-1608, 1688-1713, 1792-1815, and 1914-45. While global wars are relatively rare events, occurring roughly once a century, they have profound impacts on the ways in which the world works because they essentially resolve succession struggles in the global system. Global wars thus help to determine whose rules and visions of world order will prevail in world politics and the world economy. But calling these events succession struggles only categorizes them; it does not explain why they take place. To account for these watershed events, it is necessary to tap into the heart of the world system's politico-economic processes. Figure 1.3 summarizes our explanation of why global wars occur.

Beginning at the lower right corner of the figure, a critical factor, global-regional power transition, establishes the basic context for global wars. At the global or intercontinental level, power concentration and the resource base on which the lead power relies has declined. At the central regional level, historically Western Europe, power concentration and the resource base on which the regional lead power relies has increased. Conceivably, there can be all sorts of power transitions in which one state catches up and passes another, but the type that is most important for global wars involves an ascending regional leader catching up to a declining global leader. The latter perceives the former as threatening or potentially threatening its global interests. The ascending regional power perceives the declining global leader as a barrier to further ascent. The repeated outcome has been acute conflict, consistently won by the coalition organized by the declining global leader to contain the threat of regional expansion.

Global wars, therefore, are partially caused by dissynchronized tendencies toward power concentration and deconcentration at the global and regional levels. But what causes power concentration and deconcentration? The explanatory framework sketched in figure 1.3 primarily attempts to account for concentration dynamics at the global level. This bias is due to the assumption that regional concentration dynamics are comparatively simpler. The regional concentration processes experienced in Western Europe have been a function of size and strategic ambition. Each European leader has controlled the region's largest population, the region's biggest economy, and the region's most numerous army. These size attributes have not come together entirely coincidentally; they represent years of state building and expansion.

Yet regional concentration dynamics still boil down to processes of aggregation and local territorial expansion, with a healthy element of chance thrown in for good measure. All that is missing are rulers who are interested and willing to exploit their size advantages for expansion on a more ambitious scale than is normal. For this reason, global wars are often personified by the regional leader's ruler: Philip II, Louis XIV, Napoleon, and Hitler. An ambitious ruler is almost always necessary, but never as sufficient a cause as many people seem to think.

Implicit to the global-regional distinction are dualities of strategic orientations and related capability preferences. Regional leaders tend to be continental powers that stress territorial expansion and armies. Global leaders are maritime powers, heavily engaged in long-distance commerce and industrial production, that stress the development and maintenance of global-reach capabilities and networks. Why these basic dualities in strategic and economic orientations have emerged can be traced back to several factors listed above "Prerequisites for Ascent" in figure 1.3. Small size, a fortunate location for maritime activities and commercial centrality in Europe, and a high degree of economic cohesion, especially in comparison with continental leaders, initially encouraged the development of specialization in long-distance trade and sea power. The commercial powers developed sufficient sophistication at raising revenues through taxation and loans in order to defeat their powerful, but often underfinanced, continental rivals. Representative governments, a political attribute highly associated with economic leadership, have been less likely to persist in international political activities that prove to be too costly or self-defeating.

For a number of reasons related to winning global wars and supporting long-distance economic activities in war and peace, global leaders must develop sea power to be successful. Historically, naval leadership has been vital to both attaining and maintaining the ability to project force over long distances. That is why the global leader's naval capability share, one method of indexing the level of military power concentration and deconcentration at the global level, is highlighted in figure 1.3. That is also the main reason why so much stress is placed on long-term fluctuations in naval capability shares within the leadership long cycle framework.

Naval leadership in turn is predicated on a lead in technological innovation. Innovation in leading sectors of the world economy bestows a temporary quasi-monopoly status in economic activities critical to high growth, profits, and development. This is not an abstract component of our model. It is not technological innovation per se that we choose to emphasize. Rather, we focus on specific, radical transformations of commercial and industrial activities that have periodically revolutionized the emerging world economy over the past few centuries: for Portugal, West African gold and Asian spices; for the Netherlands, Baltic and Asian commerce; for Britain, American plantation production, Asian commerce, textiles, iron production, steam engines, and railroads; for the United States, steel, chemicals, electricity, automobiles, electronics, and aerospace industries.

Bursts of radical innovation come in waves. What drives these waves remains largely obscure in the current structural transition model. Various analysts have claimed causal primacy for investment, profits, innovation, food and raw material shifts, prices, demographic shifts, and war, among other phenomena, as the main drivers. However interesting this highly contested terrain is, its complexities force us to postpone closer examination until a future date.

What we do know is that global leaders are the primary beneficiaries of at least two innovational spurts. The first one immediately precedes the onset of global war. By accelerating the processes working toward uneven growth and destabilized power hierarchies, this first spurt increases the probability of global war. The old global leader's relative decline is hastened. Rivals may be strengthened, and rivalries are apt to become more heated. The first spurt also enables the next global leader to continue its ascent and finance the combat of its coalition in the ensuing global war.

Pioneering the first spurt of innovation and winning the subsequent global war make it more likely that the global leader will benefit from a second spurt of innovation. A third spurt is not impossible, but it becomes less likely because the second wave is particularly associated with the diffusion of principal innovations. Other major economies catch up. Economic competition becomes more equal and, at the same time, more subject to nationalistic barriers. Foreign markets become less open; the leader's share of those markets is reduced (Thompson and Vescera 1992).

But an internal dimension to relative decline dynamics is equally significant. Innovations have a finite potential for contributing to spectacular economic growth. As the innovations become more routine, so too does the corresponding input to the aggregate growth trajectory. The problem of complacency also arises when few genuine competitors exist. Various types of institutional rigidities are also likely to emerge and interfere with attempts at adjustment. Finally, two spurts of innovation will raise the stan-

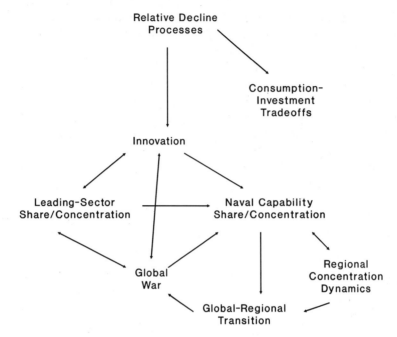

Figure 9.1 The Empirically Substantiated Portion of the
Structural Transition Model

dard and cost of living. Affluent economic leaders may find themselves increasingly priced out of markets as their production costs increase.

The internal and external processes of relative decline increase the probability of consumption-investment tradeoffs, which we regard as secondary manifestations of decline. While it is impossible to dismiss the possibility that these tradeoffs make decline worse, they do not appear to be primary sources of decline. We treat overcommitment in much the same fashion. For the most part, we think, global leaders do not begin to decline because they have overextended themselves; overextension is perceived because the processes of relative decline are in progress.

Developing an elaborate model is one thing. Demonstrating its validity is quite another. Still, we have made considerable headway. Figure 9.1 illustrates the connections among variables that have been empirically tested. Table 9.1 lists eighteen propositions associated with the structural transition model that have been found to be empirically supported.

No doubt, some readers will perceive that our model and the propositions suggest a strongly deterministic outlook. We talk about paired innovational spurts in leading sectors, cycles of capability concentrations at the regional and global levels, and leadership transitions without much reference to human agency. Do we mean to imply that these processes work as if

Table 9.1 Key Tested Propositions of the Structural Transition-Global War Model

- The modern global distribution of power has been characterized by a five-peaked pattern of concentration and deconcentration.
- The modern global distribution of power has been characterized by a five-peaked pattern of concentration and deconcentration.
- Each of the five global waves rises and declines gradually, with peaks in the 1510s, 1610s, 1720s, 1820s, and 1950s.
- The central regional distribution of power historically has been characterized by a four-peaked, negatively shaped pattern of concentration and deconcentration.
- The first two waves of regional concentration, peaking in the 1580s and 1690s, were gradual; the last two waves, peaking in the 1800s and around world wars I and II, were abrupt.
- The concentration of global sea power alternates with the concentration of regional land power.
- Global wars are followed by a statistically significant period of reconcentration in sea power capabilities.
- Nonglobal wars are not followed by a statistically significant period of reconcentration in sea power capabilities.
- Wars, especially global wars, are more likely when a regional leader catches up to and passes the relative capability position of a declining global leader.
- Other things being equal, wars are more likely when a new regional leader catches up to and passes the relative capability position of a declining regional leader.
- Other things being equal, wars are more likely when a new global leader catches up to and passes the relative capability position of a declining global leader.
- The probability of global war increases as the global system deconcentrates and as the central regional system reconcentrates.
- The preeminence of each global system leader is predicated on two sequential spurts of commercial-industrial innovation.
- The first spurt of each innovation set accelerates the relative decline of the previous global leader.
- The first spurt of each innovation set accelerates the ascent of the next global leader.
- The first spurt of each innovation set encourages the emergence of a perceived threat to the global status quo in the form of an expanding regional leader.
- The consequent global war outcome facilitates the reconcentration of economic and military capability concentration at the global level.
- Consumption-investment tradeoffs are more likely to be the consequences than the antecedents of the relative decline of global system leaders.
- Overcommitment problems are more critical to the defeat of regional leaders in global war than they are to the relative decline of global leaders.

there were a politico-economic clock timing the ostensible choices of national decision makers? And do global wars begin at midnight regardless of what decision makers do? We do think that something like a structural clock is at work. But the winners of the last global war, coupled with their economic innovations and military prowess, wind the clock and allow the mechanism (i.e., the capability concentration) to run down. The winding down is facilitated by challengers who aspire to substitute their own clocks and competitors who desire to expand or protect their shares of the prevailing division of rewards.

Nowhere is it preordained that system leaders will enjoy two and only two spurts of radical technological innovation. It is not axiomatic that the system's leading sea power must lose its edge in global reach. Nor is it written in the stars that some nation will seek to dominate the system's leading region and, in the process, come to be perceived as a threat to the global hierarchy. Yet as we have seen, these developments do tend to occur with some regularity. To the extent that the probabilities of the past have predictive powers for the future, we can say that they will probably continue to occur along roughly the same patterns until something fundamental changes in the basic environmental and behavioral parameters that shape the way things happen.

There remains considerable room for deviation from the pattern. Britain had two turns at the helm of the system and four innovational spurts. U.S. decision makers chose to bypass the global window of opportunity to re-structure world order that was first opened by World War I. For that matter, in our Dehio-inspired interpretation, World War I was unlike all of the other global wars: the German threat to dominate Europe became more likely after the war began than before its outbreak.

Moreover, a host of what-ifs remind us that the transitional patterns we are attempting to model are based on events that might well have worked out differently if different strategies had been employed, if decision makers had been cleverer, or, in some cases, if the weather had turned out differently. What if Castile had conquered the entire Iberian peninsula in 1492? What if the 1588 Spanish Armada had conquered England? What if the Dutch stadtholder William had been unsuccessful in his seizure of the English Crown in 1688? What if, after centuries of trying to get it right, a French or German challenger had decided to invest in a concerted strategy of commercial raiding at the outset of global war, rather than drifting into it after other strategies failed? What if Hitler had not launched an invasion of the Soviet Union?

The list of what-ifs could be expanded many times. If some things had worked out differently, the transition pattern might also look markedly different. Modeling macroprocesses need not imply that human beings are merely spear carriers playing out a predestined script over which they have no control. At the same time, human actors rarely have as much control as they think—certainly less than complete control—over the regional and global environments in which they maneuver. Leading-sector innovations, naval capability leads, and global orientations are not equally available options to all parties. Some actors in world politics are privileged before and after their ascent to global leadership because they reside in areas where it is more likely that ways of doing things will be innovated, ships will be built, and transcontinental orientations will develop.

Our speculations in chapter 4 about the possible applicability of these arguments to a non-European-centered world are a case in point. If in the twenty-first century we begin to see developments that appear similar to those of the past five centuries, it will not be because all political economies must operate in the fashion that we schematized in figure 1.3. Our argument is that a constellation of factors made repetitive confrontations between global and regional leaders in Europe probable between the late fifteenth and mid-twentieth centuries. Many of those same factors—such as innovational spurts and tendencies toward capability concentration or deconcentration, to name two of the most important—may continue to operate in the twenty-first century despite the decreased probability of Europe's remaining the system's central region. As far as one can tell, the world system's political theaters can still be differentiated along global (transoceanic) and regional lines. Rival leadership confrontations, therefore, remain conceivable as long as the region in question is sufficiently significant that its capture would pose a major threat to the functioning of the global system and as long as the aspiring regional leader controls or could control sufficient resources to threaten directly the incumbent global leader's position.

Between the 1490s and the 1940s only one region was paramount in the dynamics of these processes. In the future, more than one region may satisfy the "sufficiently significant" threshold. Other things being equal, that should mean a greater possibility and perhaps probability of transitional conflict. At this writing, in 1993, the number of candidates for the role of regional challenger are not infinite. But it is still possible to tick off the most obvious suspects on the fingers of one hand. Moving from west to east, Germany, Russia, China, and Japan presumably represent the most liberal slate of candidates imaginable. The question that must remain open is whether twenty or thirty years down the road, when the probability of global transition is more likely to be conspicuous, the identities of the most probable candidates will be more or less obvious. Should the dynamics of the past five hundred years persist into the near future, the slate of candidates for regional challenger should be reducible to one or two, and the prospects for another global-regional leadership confrontation should be much less ambiguous than they are at present.

Other Interpretations

What does the strong affirmation for our model say about the arguments of other analysts? Naturally, our assumptions and findings put us at odds with a number of authors. In general, we disagree with analysts that

1. see no purpose in empirically testing hypotheses about relatively complicated processes;

2. treat all wars as if they represented a single generic phenomenon;

3. regard "big" wars as the same or only slightly different from small wars, except that, for one reason or another, additional actors have chosen to enter the fray, thereby transforming a small war into a big one (see Blainey 1973; Bueno de Mesquita 1981; and the debate on this question found in Midlarsky 1990);

4. focus primarily on the number of actors involved or the number of people killed as the defining criteria for categorizing types of warfare (e.g., Goldstein 1988; Conybeare 1990, 1992);

5. contend that wars or their macroenvironments are not really comparable across the past five centuries (Luard 1986; Holsti 1991);

6. argue that personalities, decision making, and domestic politics are the only factors relevant to explaining war (see Bueno de Mesquita and Lalman 1988; Kaiser 1990);

7. insist that the rise and fall of various global powers are not sufficiently comparable (see Mjoset 1990); and

8. maintain that the relative decline of the current global leader is principally a figment of analytical imagination (e.g. Nye 1990a, 1990b).

In addition to the rejection of these specific arguments, we also must examine the larger question of paradigmatic allegiance. A number of authors have suggested that analyses of international relations can usually be placed within one of three paradigms: realism, Marxism, and an in-between category that holds a heterogenous collection of approaches that take issue with some aspect of the assumptions of realpolitik (see, among others, Thompson 1988). The identifying criteria most often attributed to approaches belonging to the realism column are emphases on nation-states as the primary actors of importance, an emphasis on the international environment of anarchy, and an overriding concern with the problematic of war.

Our analysis does not fit comfortably within the realist paradigm. The focus on war is strong, and we devote little attention to nonstate actors. But we seek to explain not all wars but only one type—the rare global war. Nor do we seek to explain war for its own sake. We focus on global war because of its critical role in the long-term structural change process of world politics: this does constitute our primary focus. Similarly, we ignore most nation-states and focus only on regional and global elite states. Again, our concern is not so much with the explanation of state behavior per se but rather with how the roles of system and subsystem leaders and challengers interact to produce conflict.

As for anarchy, we see much more structure, hierarchy, and authority in world politics than most realists are likely to accept. At best, we might be able to compromise in the sense that we could agree with the observation that the degree of global anarchy increases as the global leader's position erodes. Yet a dynamic approach to anarchy is rare in the annals of realism. Anarchy is a constant, and so too are the relative capabilities of the most significant actors. This is much too static a view for our taste. Changes in the pecking orders of world politics are persistent and far too critical to ignore. Moreover, these changes have a strongly patterned history that realists prefer to overlook, minimize, or, most often, simply reject.

Whereas realists stress anarchy, Marxists and neo-Marxists emphasize divisions of labor within a capitalist system. Instead of war, inequality is the principal problematic (Holsti 1985). We share some of these assumptions, but our analysis is not a neo-Marxist one. We have shown little interest in either the concepts of class or capitalism. Attention to divisions of labor is important because it highlights the hierarchy created by technological innovation. A few economies specialize in innovation, while the rest of the world consumes innovations originated elsewhere. In that respect, most of the world has become increasingly dependent on the economies that pioneer leading-sector innovations. Yet the technological hierarchy is no more static than the hierarchy for relative capability. Phases of catch-up and diffusion occur with some regularity even though the number of economies that are able to match or surpass the leaders remains limited. Inequality is important too, but for our immediate purposes, the changes in inequalities among the most powerful states most concern us. Thus we are interested in specific divisions of labor and inequalities because they have important analytical roles to play in our interpretation of world politics.

Since we are neither fish (realists) nor fowl (neo-Marxists), we must fall into that nebulous category in between the two major paradigms. If anyone should accuse us of being in the process of incrementally crafting a new paradigm that facilitates the development of theories with the potential for synthesizing and co-opting good ideas regardless of their paradigmatic origin, then so be it.

Besides these general points of contention, our argument is fairly distinctive even though it has points of overlap with a number of other theories. Only rarely do the arguments converge as much as many of us might prefer. For example, Gilpin (1981) emphasizes the general importance of technological innovation, but he places an even greater stress on consumption-investment tradeoffs as a primary cause of hegemonic decline. We find em-

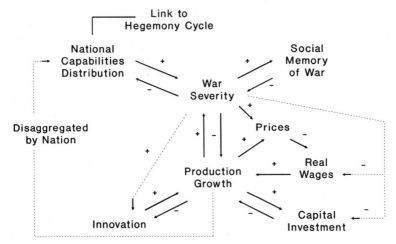

Source: based on Goldstein 1991b: 311.

Figure 9.2 Goldstein's War Economy Theory

pirical support for the former but not the latter. Choucri and North (1975, 1989) also emphasize technological change as a basic driver of their model, but in their interpretation generic technological developments, in combination with population pressures, encourage expansionary probes in search of raw materials and other resources needed for domestic consumption (lateral pressure). The probability of conflict increases as these probes multiply and intersect. Our approach does not examine lateral pressure intersections, but we can at least suggest whose conflict intersections should be of utmost concern: those of the declining global leader and the ascending central regional leader. We also suggest a more concrete interpretation linking specific technological changes to the outbreak of war.

Similarly, we have already incorporated the core of the Organski and Kugler power transition model (Organski and Kugler 1980; Kugler and Organski 1989) but have given it a geopolitical twist by demonstrating that the key transition to watch for is the one between global and regional leaders. We also think that the transition concern has a longer history than most transition analyses concede and that it is not aggregate economic wealth that is at stake in transitions. Depending on the setting, relative military standings (regional) and relative leading-sector production (global) provide useful indicators of positional flux.

Doran's (1991) cycle of relative power model is another structural one that seems reasonably compatible with ours in a general sense. His emphasis is on the uncertainties of decision makers associated with certain transition points in the rise and fall of great powers. Interestingly, the most dangerous points tend to be located roughly midway on the trajectories of ascent and decline. While it is not clear whether all great powers react, or why they should react, similarly to parallel circumstances, the conceptual gap between Doran's critical points and our stress on ascending regional leaders and descending global leaders is certainly bridgeable.

Nevertheless, the research that is closest in spirit to our analysis is Goldstein's (1988, 1991b) war economy theory, outlined in figure 9.2. At its core, the theory explains how growth and war alternate through time. Production increases supply great powers with more resources for waging war.[1] The more severe the war, the greater the negative impact on economic growth. Wars also increase prices and depress real wages.

Other components in the model include innovation and capital investment. Innovation stimulates production, but subsequent growth in production discourages further innovation. Growth in production encourages investment, but a tendency toward overinvestment slows growth. In the figure, war severity is connected to innovation and capital investment by dotted lines, which indicate some uncertainty about the general relationships. In most cases, though, war is expected to have a negative effect on investment and a positive effect on innovation.

Three other components in figure 9.2 are labeled more inherently "political" in nature. In the upper right corner of the figure is the Toynbeean idea that severe wars have a psychological impact on the participant societies that for a while, at least, inhibits the recurrence of war. On the left side of the figure, production and innovation are related to the distribution of capabilities. Here the idea is that severe wars have an asymmetrical impact on the capabilities of the participants. Winners tend to do better than losers. Another severe war is unlikely until the former losers, aided by innovation and economic growth processes, regain or surpass their former positions of rough equality. As the capability distribution equalizes, the probability of another severe war increases.

The last component is the linkage between capability distribution and the hegemony cycle. Goldstein considers this relationship to be one of the weaker ones in his model. Among the most severe wars, hegemonic wars—such as the Thirty Years' War, the Napoleonic Wars, and World Wars I and II—produce new hegemons. Goldstein defines the hegemon as "the leading country on the winning side that survives with its economy intact and reorganizes the world around itself" (1991b: 305). Yet Goldstein regards the hegemonic cycle as only weakly connected to the system's long waves of economic growth because there seems to be no definite pattern relating hegemonic cycles and long waves. While hegemonic peaks coincide with some of the peaks in war, war peaks that occur in the absence of hegemonic shifts still influence economic growth.

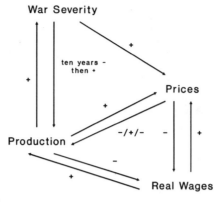

Source: Goldstein 1991b: 315.

Figure 9.3 The Outcome of Goldstein's 1991 Modeling

Much of Goldstein's empirical work has addressed the question of whether long waves exist (Beck 1991; Goldstein 1991a). Since that is not our present concern, Goldstein's most pertinent analysis for us is a test of part of the model outlined in figure 9.2 (Goldstein 1991b).[2] Using statistical techniques (VAR modeling) somewhat related to those we have employed, Goldstein examined the relationships between five variables: war severity (logged battle deaths), production (world industrial production), prices (British wholesale price indices), innovation (frequency of major innovation), and real wages (real wage index of south England). Because of several methodological considerations, the analysis was restricted to the 1779-1935 period.

Goldstein's results are summarized in figure 9.3. On the whole, the anticipated relationships were found. War increases prices and depresses production and real wages. Prosperity, as measured by production, makes severe war more likely. A few more relationships between prices, production, and real wages than were expected, however, did emerge. Moreover, no significant connection to innovation was uncovered.

It is an intriguing coincidence that while our explanation overlaps with Goldstein's, we have chosen to place our modeling emphases on entirely different aspects of the variable ensemble depicted in figure 9.2. Goldstein adopts as his primary focus the long-wave dynamics involving war, prices, investment, profits, and so on. What Goldstein has yet to examine, the links shared by innovation, capabilities, war, and systemic leadership, have been our primary concern.

There are, to be sure, other differences in our respective approaches. We have different preferences for how best to tap war severity (battle deaths versus resources expended). Our leading-sector interpretation of innovation does not incorporate the same sort of variable envisioned in Goldstein's more subjective list of innovations. We make geopolitical distinctions (global/maritime versus regional/continental leaders) that do not appear in Goldstein's model. We also have a different approach to conceiving what is being modeled. Goldstein's model is explicitly systemic, even though some of his indicators are not (e.g., British prices and real wages). We view our own model as equally systemic but choose to focus on processes involving the global leaders. Thus our indicators are seemingly national in scope, but the nations on which we focus are believed to be fundamental to systemic processes. For example, we contend that the global system leader's innovation drives the system's economic growth. Similarly, the global system leader's share of leading-sector production and naval capabilities can be read alternatively as indices of systemic capability concentration. One advantage of such an approach is that it helps to make systemic analyses less abstract. Our interpretation of systemic processes is clearly actor-rooted.

No doubt caused at least in part by all these assumptive differences, our findings are different from those of Goldstein. They must be to some extent simply because we have chosen to stress the relationships among a different set of variables. But they also substantively diverge in the areas in which they overlap. Goldstein argues for a weak connection between the hegemony cycle and economic long waves. We argue for, and demonstrate empirically, a very tight connection between system leadership and long waves of innovation-sparked growth. Goldstein argues for, and demonstrates empirically, an alternating pattern between war severity and economic growth. We find instead that a burst of radical innovation leads to a global war, which in turn leads to another innovative spurt. World industrial production and a global leader's innovational spurt are clearly not the same thing. If we are right, the former lags behind the latter. Even so, a way to reconcile the two divergent findings is not obvious, unless the problem is traceable to emphases on war severity versus global warfare. Some stimulation (more precisely, every other stimulus) of the rate of growth in world industrial production should be linked less directly to global war.

The two findings would not necessarily be in disagreement, however, if relatively severe, nonglobal wars occurred systematically at the appropriate times. The question would then be why this was the case, because there are fairly strong differences in our explanations of the linkage from innovation and growth to war. For Goldstein, prosperity builds war chests. States are more likely to go to war because they possess the sinews of war. In our interpretation, everyone's war chests are not affected equally. Nor are we convinced that decision makers are more likely to opt for war when they can afford it. Too often, decision makers foresee extremely short, inexpensive

Table 9.2 Hegemonic Phases and Economic Long Waves in the
World Economy Perspective

Hegemon	Economic Expansion	Economic Contraction	Hegemonic Phase
Netherlands	1575–90		Ascent
		1590–1620	Victory
	1620–50		Maturity
		1650–1700	Decline
Britain	1798–1815		Ascent
		1815–50	Victory
	1850–73		Maturity
		1873–97	Decline
United States	1897–1913/20		Ascent
		1913/20–45	Victory
	1945–67		Maturity
		1967–	Decline

Source: Based on information in Research Working Group 1979.

wars as opposed to the long, costly wars that populate the history books. For us, an initial innovational wave (of a two-wave set) accelerates rise-and-fall processes, thereby increasing the tensions and perceptions of threat associated with structural change and transition.

Hence, despite some important areas of convergence, our assumptions and findings are markedly different from those of Goldstein's 1988 and 1991 investigations. We agree that war and economic long waves are systematically related. We disagree in explaining precisely how they are related.

A second analytical cluster that overlaps with our work are the studies of Wallerstein and other world economy analysts who have developed a framework that relates the hegemonic cycle to long economic waves and major power conflict. In the world economy canon, three, not necessarily overlapping, hegemonic iterations have been experienced (see table 9.2). Hegemons ascend largely on the basis of their superiority in productive efficiency. Their decline is brought about by technological diffusion, overproduction, and rising production costs.

Each hegemonic cycle is divided into four phases. Either economic expansion or economic contraction characterizes every hegemonic phase. A new hegemon begins to emerge in the hegemonic ascent phase. Intense competition among the leading rivals for succession marks this period. A new hegemon is established in the hegemonic victory phase, although the third phase, hegemonic maturity, represents the phase of full hegemony. The fourth phase, hegemonic decline, is one in which the main conflict axis is centered on the struggle between a declining leader and its principal rivals.

All world economy analysts do not subscribe to all of these generalizations (compare Chase-Dunn and Rubinson 1977; Bousquet 1979, 1980; Vayrynen 1983; Bergesen 1985; Chase-Dunn 1989). Whether the schedule described in table 9.2 is internally consistent is dubious. For instance, the Dutch hegemonic maturity phase coincides with the Thirty Years' War, which, according to Wallerstein (1984), was the world war that "encrusted" the Dutch edge. One would think that a war that is supposed to have facilitated the Dutch ascension would have had to precede the hegemonic maturity phase. Nor is this problem restricted to the Dutch era. Each of Wallerstein's three world wars (1618-48, 1792-1815, and 1914-45) occurred in a different phase of the hegemonic cycle. This timing clouds the relationship of the big wars not only to the hegemonic cycle but also to the periodicity of the economic long waves. Not surprisingly, the theoretical relationship between the hegemonic cycle and the economic long waves is murky as well.

The underspecification of the world economy model has had predictable consequences for assessing the validity of its arguments. Empirical outcomes associated with testing this set of ideas have been at best mixed. Although Vayrynen (1983) changes the dating somewhat, he found no major power warfare associated with the phase of hegemonic decline after 1825. Thompson (1988) found that the four phases did not differentiate among 1575-1986 major power conflict very well. Boswell, Sweat, and Brueggemann (1989) and Boswell and Sweat (1991) found more statistical support for Goldstein's price-based periodization of long waves and war than they did for the hegemonic cycle.

We wish to suggest that while some striking parallels between the world economy approach and our transition model approach certainly exist— namely, the common assertion that major power conflict, systemic leadership, and paired economic long waves generated by productive superiorities are all systematically related—the world economy argument proceeds from considerably different assumptions and is considerably less well developed on the matters that most concern us. The empirical support aligned with our arguments is also considerably stronger, we think.

The regional and global systems that we are studying represent historically contingent phenomena. So too are the explanations that have been advanced to explain behavior taking place within these systems. Exactly when the global system began to take shape is disputed (Abu-Lughod 1989; Modelski and Thompson forthcoming), but we can at least agree that the 1490s was a decade of significant transformation, both globally and regionally. Four hundred fifty years later it was evident that Western Europe had lost its claim to being the central region. By 1945 it was no longer clear whether that region would ever regain a semblance of its former autonomy.

One of the implications of emerging and submerging systems is the possibility that the world has changed so dramatically that the 1494-1945 story no longer applies.[3] If that is the case, then our elaborate framework may be useful in explaining a historical puzzle but offers little explanatory power for the twenty-first century. The obsolescence of our explanation would not be a bad thing if it meant that we humans had figured out how to extricate ourselves from a recurring and ever-escalating, but still primitive, system of governmental change.

While there can be no question that structures change and people learn, the question that must remain open is whether change and learning have proceeded to the point that we can relax and worry more about other, more proximate sources of threat. In chapter 10, we review six sets of arguments that favor a radically altered future environment for major power warfare. Many of these arguments are seductive, but as we outline their points, the reader should look for the places where uneven growth and global-regional transitions fit into the pictures of the future they sketch. If they do not seem to fit in at all, does that not suggest that something fundamental is being overlooked?

10.
The Future of Transitional Warfare

Several authors have contended that the world is changing and that it has already changed sufficiently to restrict severely the future likelihood of major power warfare. If they are right, and we would be among the first to hope that their forecast is correct, then our work in the preceding chapters is not invalidated. But it would suggest that our argument is dated, that its future applicability will be close to nil. Yet is it safe to assume that the world has changed so much that tendencies manifested over several hundred years of the evolution of the major power war system have been radically transformed? We take this to be a theoretical question, and we will turn to theory in an attempt to answer it. In particular, we propose to examine six "endism" theories. These are theories about the end of something—ranging from war itself to predictability—that lead to the expectation that the chances of a future major power war are slim to nonexistent.[1]

To make a forecast about the probabilities of transitional war, one needs an understanding of why these affairs come about in the first place. In the preceding nine chapters we have sought to advance just such an understanding. Prominent features of our explanation include concentration and deconcentration processes at the global and regional levels, waves of innovation, lead economies, and global wars. After reviewing the endism arguments, we will explore in this concluding chapter the basic question of whether a case can be made for substantially modified expectations about future probabilities of transitional warfare because of changes in the way the world works. More concretely, do we have reason to believe that changes have occurred in the way processes of innovation and concentration operate?

The End of History

Francis Fukuyama garnered a great deal of attention in 1989 with a provocative article in *National Interest* entitled "The End of History?" What he had in mind was the Hegelian notion that history ends when there are no more fundamental contradictions that cannot be resolved within the context of Western liberalism. This does not mean some form of convergence between rival ideologies nor does it mean an end to ideology per se. Rather, it means the universal triumph of liberalism, the final and highest form of ideology, and the exhaustion and rejection of any systematic alternatives. Interestingly, Hegel thought this point had been reached after Napoleon's victory at Jena in 1806. Fukuyama thinks the point has been reached or nearly reached in the more developed world only during the past few years.

Fukuyama acknowledges that the universalization of liberalism has some way to go. Most of the Third World remains "very much mired in history," as he puts it (Fukuyama 1989: 15). Neither Russia nor China are liberal societies, he argues, but there is at least some possibility that their foreign policies will no longer be driven by Marxist-Leninist doctrine. Hence the triumph of liberalism is at best an ideational victory, with its full implications yet to be worked out in the real world.

For Fukuyama, the implications for the future of world politics are optimistic, if a bit monotonous. He assumes that great power national interests are predicated on ideological foundations. World War I was a battle between liberalism and the remnants of absolutism. World War II was fought between liberals and fascists. The cold war was a struggle to defeat bolshevism and Marxism. If you remove ideological tensions from world politics, there should be much less chance of large-scale conflict. Large-scale conflict requires large states that are still mired in history. If such dinosaurs should no longer exist—and on this point Fukuyama is prepared to waffle a bit—conflict will persist, but only at a small scale. In the part of the world no longer caught up in history, politics and strategy will cease to hold much interest. Economic strategy, consumerism, and the "Common Marketization" of international relations will prevail as the principal mode of interaction across borders.

The End of Autocracy

The argument of Immanuel Kant (1970), produced in an earlier end-of-the-century era, has a number of components. Several of these intriguingly foreshadow more modern turns in international relations theory.[2] In essence, the argument can be reduced to substituting republican hesitation for monarchical caprice, giving fellow liberals the benefit of the doubt, and avoiding costly interference with commerce. To the extent that conditions develop along these lines, perpetual peace is conceivable.

Kant began his elaboration of this position with a strong evolutionary assertion. Republics emerge and survive because they are best equipped to deal with two fundamental political problems: external threats and overly ambitious rulers. These republics are identified by a complex of major institutional characteristics. They must have sovereignty, market economies with private property rights, individual rights, and representative governments with effective legislatures. The development of these institutions produces three by-products. Representation and rights have evolved from a sequence of exchanges between rulers and citizens. Citizens receive some participation in government in exchange for ruler legitimacy, authority, and tax revenues. Tax revenues, of course, are particularly critical in market economies. Moreover, the legitimacy and authority of governments facilitate unity among the population—something that is essential to coping with foreign threats. The legal infrastructure associated with the complex of rights and duties of representative government also serves as a restraint on aggressive rulers.

Once republics are firmly established, wars in general are more easily avoided. To the extent that popular consent is necessary for a declaration of war, the population is likely to balk. War is both dangerous and costly. Lives and wealth must be placed at risk during the fighting. Even worse, the costs of war continue after the fighting has ended. Wartime destruction must be repaired. Debts contracted during the war must be paid, even though it is unlikely they can ever be paid in full as long as the probability of more warfare remains high. Thus it is only natural that republican populations, as well as their rulers, would hesitate to sanction a war effort.

In contrast, nonrepublican rulers interested in engaging in warfare do not need to seek the permission of their populations. In Kant's view, they also will sacrifice much less: "War will not force [a nonrepublican ruler] to make the slightest sacrifice so far as his banquet, hunts, pleasure palaces and court festivals are concerned. He can decide on war, without any significant reason, as a kind of amusement, and unconcernedly leave it to the diplomatic corps (who are always ready for such purposes) to justify the war for the sake of propriety" (cited in Doyle 1986: 1161).

Yet republican caution and the whims of monarchies are only part of the war avoidance equation. A second factor of some importance is the axiom that, given a world of separate nations and states, the more in agreement people are about their philosophical principles, the more likely they are to assume that accommodation and cooperation are the appropriate strategies to pursue. Apparently Kant saw this generalization influencing interactions among republican regimes. His explanation centered on the assertion that regimes based on consent are likely to be viewed by other representative regimes as similarly organized and just. Therefore they will be given the benefit of the doubt when disputes arise. In a concept reminiscent of more modern neofunctionalist themes, Kant asserted that initial experiences with successful cooperation make subsequent cooperation more likely.

Again, in contrast, republican regimes are likely to suspect nonrepublican regimes, which are by definition differently and unjustly organized. Doyle nicely summarizes this part of the Kantian argument: "Fellow liberals benefit from a presumption of amity; nonliberals suffer from a presumption of enmity" (1986: 1161). Conflicts and wars, as a consequence, are less likely between republican states and more likely between republican and nonrepublican states.

This relationship between regime type and the propensity to conflict is buttressed further by the observation that as republican regimes multiply, the "spirit of commerce" should expand accordingly. As it does, the costs of war and therefore inhibitions against assuming such costs should also increase. In sum, the elimination of war and the achievement of perpetual peace depend on doing away with nonrepublican regimes. As they disappear from the scene, the reasons for going to war and the likelihood of war will decline commensurately.

The End of War

For John Mueller, war has become similar to dueling, foot binding, bear baiting, slavery, lynching, and the Spanish Inquisition. All of these practices became obsolete because they were viewed as absurd ways of doing things. They are no longer viewed as acceptable and therefore have become "subrationally unthinkable."

An idea becomes impossible not when it becomes reprehensible or has been renounced, but when it fails to percolate into one's consciousness as a conceivable option. Thus two somewhat paradoxical conclusions about the avoidance of war can be drawn. On the one hand, peace is likely to be firm when war's repulsiveness and futility are fully evident—as when its horrors are dramatically and inevitably catastrophic. On the other hand, peace is most secure when it gravitates away from conscious rationality to become a subrational, unexamined mental habit. At first, war becomes rationally unthinkable—rejected because it is calculated to be ineffective and/or undesirable. Then it becomes subrationally unthinkable—rejected not because it's a bad idea but because it remains subconscious and never comes off as a coherent possibility. Peace in other words can prove to be addictive. [Mueller 1989: 240]

Mueller's analogy is to a person who wishes to descend from the fifth floor of a building. The two main choices are walking down the stairs or jumping out the window. No rational person, he says, would ever consider the second choice to be a real choice. As a consequence, it is unlikely that jumping out of a fifth-floor window would ever emerge as a conscious alternative.

Why is war like jumping from a fifth-floor window? Basically, it has become viewed as increasingly ineffective and counterproductive. It accomplishes little but destruction. Therefore, it serves no point. While advocates of the view of war as futile have been around for some time, they had always been in the minority. Now, says Mueller, they are in the majority in the developed world.

Traditionally, a more romantic view of war as a test of heroic valor prevailed in great power circles. At worst, war was regarded as something distasteful but occasionally necessary. A few states, such as the Netherlands, had chosen to drop out of the great power club because they no longer wished to engage in war. These states, though, were the exceptions to the rule that war was a way of life for great powers.

World War I altered this perception. A repetition of this degree of bloodletting and material destruction had to be avoided at all costs. After 1918 advocates of war as an institution were relegated to a minority position. World War II came about only because of Hitler, Mussolini, and the persistence of Bushido values in Japan. Hitler, correctly at first, thought he could attain German goals through risky, incremental manipulation and still avoid a world war. Mussolini thought a new Roman empire could be resurrected in the Mediterranean area at little cost. Japanese values concerning the utility of war remained unfashionably old-fashioned. In the absence of these factors, especially in the absence of Adolf Hitler, a second world war might not have occurred. But by the time it was over, the entire developed world had become "Hollandized." That is to say, war in the developed world had become subrationally unthinkable.

Of course, war was somewhat less unthinkable in the East-West cold war. Fortunately, though, Communists tended to eschew war as a vehicle for spreading their ideological faith. Western containment policies threatened escalation to World War III as the probable price of territorial expansion. In view of the likely destructiveness of such a war, Mueller suggests that the presence of nuclear weapons may have been a redundant element of cold war deterrence. The idea that war, or at least war between major powers, was entirely counterproductive to national goals was the primary inhibiting factor. But the additional threat of nuclear devastation didn't hurt.

The End of War's Profitability

Carl Kaysen (1990) agrees with Mueller's main conclusion that war is obsolete. He parts company with Mueller on the steps taken to reach the conclusion. From Kaysen's perspective, Mueller has emphasized sociocultural change at the expense of changes in technology, economies, and politics.

Kaysen thinks that, in doing so, Mueller has misinterpreted how the obsolescence of war came about.

Kaysen's starting point is the proposition that wars will not occur if all parties involved see the prospective costs as outweighing the probable benefits. People must perceive some potential gains before they will be prepared to go to war. Historically, wars have proved profitable for their winners. Fundamental politico-economic change since the late eighteenth century, however, has altered the cost-benefit calculus. "Winners," especially in the twentieth century, are no longer likely to profit.

In feudal Europe, the basis of politico-economic power in an agrarian economy was the ability to control land and its labor force, as well as the capacity to convert agricultural surplus into military capability. Victory in war meant greater resources in land and people at relatively little cost. The limited scale of the combat meant minimal economic destruction and relatively few people killed. Even if this were not the case, war remained a predominately elite sport, hardly subject to popular constraints or resistance.

Between the fifteenth and eighteenth centuries, things began to change. The scale of war expanded. Armies became larger. Gunpowder increased the level of firepower attainable. State institutions became more complex. The relative significance of agrarian output compared with urban output and trade began to decline. Yet since the general level of wartime destructiveness continued to be limited, it was still possible to view war gains as outweighing war costs. Although elites of a state were increasingly unlikely to participate on the battlefield, they still retained most of the power to decide whether wars would occur.

The Industrial Revolution and its consequences brought about a fundamental transformation of the war cost-benefit calculus. The ways of making things became increasingly mechanized and electrified. Synthetic materials and factories replaced natural materials and handicraft production techniques. Urban populations expanded. Rural populations contracted. Industrialization increased the level of conceivable firepower. Armies grew. Logistical improvements and advances in communications also contributed to the ability to fight on a larger scale than ever before. At the same time, nation-states became more integrated, with expanded numbers of literate and middle-class people who possessed greater political significance thanks to taxes and ballots.

These changes in political economy increased tremendously the costs of war and decreased accordingly the possible benefits. Territorial control declined as a significant way to enhance wealth or power. Populations also became more attached to their national allegiances, which made transfers of political control less legitimate, more costly, and more difficult. The scale and cost of war expanded immensely, increasing the difficulty of recovering the wartime sacrifices of life and economic growth. From a rational perspective, it made more sense to invest national treasure for future productive purposes or to spend it in international exchange than to try to gain wealth through force. It also became more difficult to mobilize consent and support for wars from populations concerned with matters other than issues of national prestige.

In a sense, Kaysen's argument is about innovations. Innovations in ways of making war and innovations in the ways elite-mass relationships were structured led to innovations in the ways people thought about war. World Wars I and II, rather than serving as Mueller's anachronistic displays, catalyzed the solidification of the innovations as ways of life. The new ways of warfare were brought home, literally and figuratively. The old regimes were swept away, and new ones dedicated to popular welfare replaced them. The nuclear weapons introduced at the end of the World War II, far from being redundant, managed to escalate the cost of war even further. Decision makers became even more cautious. More people became convinced that war could serve no rational purpose.

Still, Kaysen does not think that war has yet become subrationally unthinkable. The attitudinal change is real, but it has outpaced equivalent reorientations in the technology of war and the institutions of the state. The cold war also prolonged thinking about the possibility of war. It continues to be possible to reap political gains from short and inexpensive military victories. Nonetheless, the processes leading to the total obsolescence of war continue and have been facilitated further by the failure of Communist ideology in the former Soviet Union and Eastern Europe. As more nations experience the modernizing consequences of the eighteenth-century Industrial Revolution, the processes should approach completion. Therein lies the contemporary rub, however, for Kaysen acknowledges that his "fully modern" societies remain a minority in the world system. War is in the process of becoming obsolete, but it is not there yet.

The End of Westphalian Simplicity

James Rosenau (1992) suggests that scholars of international relations who study the causes of war tend to share two biases. First, they are likely to treat the tendency for states to go to war as a constant rather than a variable that is subject to the possibility of institutional and attitudinal transformations. Second, an examination of the causes of war tends to exaggerate the weight of war-promoting factors vis-à-vis war-thwarting factors. If one focuses on the obstacles to war, according to Rosenau, it is difficult to escape the conclusion that the probability of interstate war is already low and continues to decline.

Interstate wars are singled out for special attention because, unlike most forms of internal warfare, conflicts between states are highly visible, unambiguous affairs that demand extensive societal mobilization. In interaction with four sets of processes involving complexity, war weariness, governmental paralysis, and attitudinal revulsion, the attributes of war make it more likely that interstate wars are doomed to extinction.

The concept of complexity refers to the increasing density of societal networks that organize groups of people within and across states. These networks can be used to resist efforts to mobilize a society for war; they can also be used to resist efforts to conquer territory and to control postwar territorial gains. In general, the "thickening" of societies makes it less likely that outcomes can be controlled by decision makers. Therefore, the probability that leaders will attempt solutions relying on military force should diminish.

Rosenau believes most people are simply tired of interstate violence (war weariness) that costs too much, achieves too little, and diverts attention from more pressing local problems. While there is a well-known hypothesis that war weariness is a cyclical phenomenon, Rosenau argues that the current sentiment is not likely to be temporary. In particular, the aversion to war, if it leads to political and constitutional prohibitions against military involvement, can become habit forming.

In addition to growing complexity and widespread war weariness, governments are said to be paralyzed by their inability to overcome differences of opinion and to resolve policy problems. The resulting crisis of national authority structures reduces state legitimacy, encourages popular resistance to national leadership, and makes it more difficult to mobilize for war.

Finally, Rosenau asserts that the increased homage paid to the status of human rights around the world carries with it corollary implications for forms of collective violence. To the extent that state-sanctioned violence is seen as an abuse of human dignity, popular revulsion to the institution of war will be all the greater.

The four processes or dynamics are interactive and mutually reinforcing. None are seen as likely to fade away in the near future. All work to reduce the probability of interstate war. Societies are no longer ready to do battle for remote national goals as the world transits away from a state-centered system toward a multicentric system (see Rosenau 1990). As a consequence, national decision makers are left with little room to maneuver their societies into bellicose situations.

The End of Predictability

Robert Jervis's (1991-92) argument evidently is a more general response to the Mearsheimer (1990) argument on the future of Europe. Some background on the nature of Mearsheimer's contentions will help us understand why Jervis chooses to emphasize certain points over others.

Mearsheimer's essay was a theoretically guided speculation on what might happen if the military forces of the United States and what was then the Soviet Union were to be withdrawn from their respective Western and Central European bases. Essentially, he predicts multipolarity and increased instability. This conclusion rests on a number of assumptions. Mearsheimer assumed that the distribution and character of military power are the root causes of war and peace. Consequently, the long post-1945 European peace could be attributed to the symmetrical bipolarity of the United States and the Soviet Union and their large nuclear arsenals.

Symmetrical bipolarity is a desirable power distribution for four reasons. There is only one conflict dyad that really counts; therefore, the possibilities of war breaking out are fewer. Power imbalances are less likely. So are miscalculations of relative power and resolve. These factors contribute to the likelihood that policies of deterrence will be successful. Finally, the system is likely to be polarized, which means that minor powers will have less room to maneuver and manipulate the polar powers into situations that will escalate political conflict.

The presence of nuclear weapons is also viewed from a deterrence perspective. The basic assumption is that deterrence is most likely to be successful when the costs and risks of going to war are great. Nuclear weapons promise horrible destruction if employed. They also suggest the futility of territorial conquest, which should discourage temptations toward aggressive expansion.

All of these alleged advantages of nuclear bipolarity would be lost if Soviet and American troops were withdrawn from Europe. Interestingly, the crux of this argument hinges on still another set of assumptions, which are very curious. Mearsheimer argues that from 1945 on, the Soviet Union and the United States constituted not only the global poles but also the European poles. If they withdrew from Europe, then Germany, France, Britain, and possibly Italy would then rise to major power status—presumably on the regional level. Given its proximity, the Soviet Union would also be counted as a major European power. Thus the European region would have four or five major powers, with or without relatively equal nuclear arsenals, competing in an unstable multipolar setting. Increased conflict and war were therefore more probable in the future than they had been in the recent past.

The easiest criticism to raise would focus on Mearsheimer's curious polar assignments. Did it make sense to treat the United States and the Soviet Union as European actors? Could not one argue just as easily that Europe's long peace was predicated on the disappearance or at least the eclipse of the indigenous European poles because of defeat and exhaustion in World War

II and the ascendance of the two global superpowers? If so, then the withdrawal of superpower forces from the European theater might have little impact on the distribution of the military power that counts most. The eclipse of the European major powers meant that the regional distribution of power had become secondary to the global distribution. For the regional distribution of power to become more significant, one of two things would have to occur. Either the significance of the global distribution would have to be reduced substantially, or one or more European powers would have to be elevated to a position roughly on par with the two global powers. Otherwise, one is forced to dismiss the influence of the global power distribution as entirely irrelevant to behavior within the region.

Jervis chose a different approach. His argument amounts to a series of assertions explaining why the future of world politics is unlikely to resemble its past. He advances eight different reasons, based on a mixture of analytical prudence, common sense, and assumptions about the history of international relations.

First, students of international relations do not know all that much about how things work in world politics. Few generalizations about how relationships operate have gone uncontested. Forecasting is therefore quite difficult in the absence of a solid theoretical base.

Second, it is unlikely that a single variable will determine the course of events in world politics. Even if it has done so in the past, it may not continue in the future. Jervis cites the example of polarity. While he is dubious that evidence exists to support the contention that bipolarity is always a more stable arrangement than multipolarity, he thinks it may not matter. Whatever its effect was in the past, interaction with other variables in the future may nullify or alter the historical impact.

Third, familiarity with social science findings can influence the way actors behave. Decision makers may even learn not to behave as they have in the past, thereby diluting the predictability of generalizations based on earlier behavior.

Fourth, unless outcomes in world politics are completely determined by external environments, there will always be ample room for the values, preferences, beliefs, and choices of decision makers to play some role. To the extent that foreign policy is strongly influenced by these individual-level factors, predicting their future values is a highly dubious undertaking.

Fifth, even if one concedes the dominant influence of the external environment, the current state of affairs is unprecedented. Opportunities for reordering world politics have depended on major wars in the past. And even though the disintegration of the Soviet Union resembles what might have happened if the Soviet Union had lost a war, no clear-cut winner is in a position to lead the restructuring process. Moreover, despite the weakness of the cold war's major loser, it remains the only country that could destroy the surviving superpower, the United States. At the same time, the principal allies of the United States are also its principal economic rivals. Thus, the uniqueness of the present and the near future make it difficult to categorize the prevailing distribution of power, let alone use it as a basis for prediction.

In some respects, Jervis's sixth point is a more general elaboration of his second argument. If there is a system of external factors that are tightly interconnected, even small changes anywhere in the system can significantly influence relationships elsewhere. Such a system is much too complex for its possible future to be reduced to the nature of the interaction of two actors, such as the former Soviet Union and the United States. Knowledge of a radical change in the superpower dyad is not sufficient information to allow one to map the ramifications for the rest of the system.

Continuing the point of view expressed in the previous observation, Jervis also points out that international relations are sensitive to the influence of chance and accidents. The history of world politics is a sequence of specific events that caused future developments to take a different path than they might otherwise have done. Imagine, for example, the history of the 1919-45 period in the absence of the First World War in 1914-18 or the course of the cold war without the Korean War. Similarly, it is not yet clear whether the Soviet Union's disintegration will be peaceful or bloody, permanent or temporary. The way it works out is likely to make some difference to the future of world politics. Hence, contingencies matter; since we do not know what they will be, prediction is exceedingly difficult.

Jervis's last argument against predictability is the most complex and most interesting of the eight. Employing the familiar metaphors of time's arrow and time's cycle, Jervis suggests that analysts tend to interpret macrohistory from one perspective or the other. Arrow interpretations are based on the assumption that change is gradual, constant, and unidirectional. Cyclical interpretations assume that change moves systems to and from one phase to another without altering the essential patterns. Assuming further that both points of view have something to offer, the main questions are Which one has more to offer or provides a better fit? and What are its implications for predicting the future?

If arrow interpretations are more appropriate than cyclical interpretations for world politics, for example, then predictability will be diminished by new elements introduced by change. In contrast, cyclical interpretations should lead to enhanced predictability, because the basic features oscillate rather than mutate. But what if both interpretations have utility? Or what if their relative advantage varies from time to time and place to place?

Jervis contends that the time's arrow metaphor fits the developed world best because it is hard to imagine a war breaking out among developed states. This development is a radical departure from the past and is predicated on three processes: increases in the costs of war, decreases in the benefits of war, and changes in domestic values and regimes.

The costs and benefits of war are viewed largely through the lenses of nuclear capabilities and interdependence. The development of nuclear weapons has magnified the potential negative impact of war many times over. Interdependence is so great that no developed state could forgo access to the flows of capital, investment, and trade from the world economy. Moreover, the high level of interdependence is made possible in the first place by expectations of a low probability of war. The idea that a state might become wealthier through territorial conquest than through trade has disappeared.

Changes in attitude are at the heart of the emphasis on regime change as well. What Jervis has in mind is his view that, in the developed world, war is no longer seen as an appropriate technique unless all other options have failed or are blocked. It helps also that there is much less to fight over. In addition to the economic costs, territorial disputes are not particularly salient. Nor is nationalism: presumably Jervis has Western Europe primarily in mind here, as a factor that is as potent as it was before World War II. Noting that democratic states rarely, if ever, have fought one another, Jervis points out that developed states are liberal democracies and need not fight each other because they are comfortable with the prevailing status quo.

One might think these changes are sufficiently compelling in themselves to make Jervis's case. His argument, however, goes much further. He asserts that the changes in the costs and benefits of war and domestic regimes are powerful influences on political behavior—more powerful than structural considerations such as polarity. So even if polarity retained some explanatory value in the future, its effects would be overwhelmed by the other types of change. In addition, the cost calculations, benefit calculations, and domestic regime factors are not three autonomous variables. They reinforce one another. The high cost of war facilitates higher levels of economic interdependence. Interdependence raises the costs of conflict. Value shifts reduce the perceived benefits of war. Finally, these developments, even though they may have been assisted mightily by perceptions of the Soviet threat and the need to preserve a united front, are irreversible as long as the most developed states retain their democratic values.

These revolutionary changes mean that predictability in the developed world is unlikely:

These changes represent time's arrow; international politics among the developed nations will be qualitatively different from what history has made familiar. War and the fear of war have been the dominant motor of politics among nations. The end of war does not mean the end of conflict, of course. Developed states will continue to be rivals in some respects, to jockey for position, and to bargain with each other. Disputes and frictions are likely to be considerable; indeed the shared expectation that they will not lead to fighting will remove some restraints on vituperation. But with no disputes meriting the use of force and with such instruments being inappropriate to the issues at hand, we are in unmapped territory; statesmen and publics will require new perspectives if not new concepts; scholars will have to develop new variables and new theories. [Jervis 1991-92: 55]

Outside the developed world, Jervis is less optimistic. Time's cycle seems a more appropriate metaphor in Eastern Europe and the Third World. Nationalism, ethnic disputes, and regional rivalries are likely, but they are probably containable as security threats to the developed world. The one possible exception is that widespread unrest and conflict in Eastern Europe and Russia might draw German intervention, thereby raising renewed fears concerning German continental dominance. Nevertheless, the possibility of the development of this scenario seems quite slight to Jervis.

Endisms and the Future of Transitional Warfare

The six endism theories reviewed above do not exhaust the array of possible arguments. Nevertheless, they are representative and certainly encompass most of the themes: interdependence, economic costs, nuclear destruction, liberalism, democratization, attitudinal and institutional change, and complexity.[3] Taken individually, each theory has variable appeal; taken as a group, the force of the aggregated argument is quite powerful.

Given all these changes, how is it even possible to contemplate the future prospects for major power war? Even while acknowledging the power of the forces presumably working against the likelihood of major power war, we argue that structural change is also a powerful force. It persists and will continue to persist into the future. Historically, it has been an important promoter of systemic warfare. The question, then, should not be Is the world changing? Of course it is. Rather, the question should be Are the changes sufficiently powerful to overwhelm the destabilizing consequences of structural change in the political, military, and economic positions of major powers? Ultimately, that is difficult to tell. We lack the theoretical sophistication at present to know how much, say, increasing interdependence is "worth" in equations concerning persisting uneven growth and positional change. In the interim, though, we can at least reexamine skeptically the asserted obstacles to war. Are the obstacles and arguments that accompany them really as powerful as they seem?

One way to evaluate the six sets of arguments about the future of world politics would be to take each one and discuss its individual merits and liabilities. Such an approach, however, would be both time-consuming and redundant. Fortunately, the six arguments share a number of common features that make our task easier. Of course, some idiosyncrasies of the various arguments deserve selective attention as well.

Perhaps the most pervasive commonality of these stories is the myth of developmental modernization. In the subfield of comparative politics, scholars once argued that political development was the process by which states came to be more like the states that were most advanced, modernized, and, not coincidentally, democratic. In other words, as other states in the world system came to resemble the home states of the development analysts, they could then be said to have become more developed. Naturally, some analysts still hold this view of political development. But for many others, the perspective has become an uncomfortable one. How can it be anything but arrogant to say that other societies and polities should become more like one's own, as if one's own structures and processes are the only ideal way to organize civic affairs?

The application is not quite the same in the endism literature, but it is similar. Essentially, most of these arguments assert in different ways that more of the world is becoming Western in values, institutions, and preferences. Fukuyama stresses liberal ideology. Kant, Doyle, and Jervis emphasize liberal, representative regimes. Mueller stresses subrationally unthinkable ideas no longer entertained in the West. And Kaysen notes the significance and importance of the ascendance of Western versions of the welfare state. As more of the world becomes westernized, major powers become less likely to fight one another. Again, the precise reasons for this reluctance to war against states that are similar vary by argument. Nevertheless, the conclusion is always the same. As the rest of the world becomes more like us, the world will become more harmonious. This generalization may prove to be correct. We merely wish to suggest that in our scholarly hubris we should be careful, if not downright hesitant, about painting too rosy a picture of what the West represents and what a more Western future is likely to resemble. In this case, we are unlikely to be the most objective observers available. Nor should we forget that the modern great power war system was also a Western invention imposed on the rest of the world.

All of the various endism arguments, whatever their validity, may be somewhat irrelevant to the future of transitional warfare. The observers, with perhaps Rosenau as the major exception, recognize explicit spatial limitations on the applicability of their interpretations. They tend to delimit the structural and psychocultural changes in which they are most interested to a subsystem of developed, democratic states in North America, Western Europe, Japan, and Australia and New Zealand. The arguments are always expressed in such a fashion that they relate most directly to interactions and probabilities for conflict within that subsystem. Conflict probabilities between states within the subsystem and states outside the subsystem usually are seen as not having changed all that much. Thus one can read most endism arguments as implying that transitional warfare is unlikely within the developed, democratic subsystem but is no less likely between states inside and outside the subsystem.

The question then becomes whether there are states outside the subsystem that are powerful enough or have sufficient growth potential to cause the type of trouble involved in transitional warfare. Is it possible, in other words, for a nondeveloped, nondemocratic state to emerge that could pose at least a major regional challenge? Africa and Latin America seem unlikely sites. But Russia and China, in various possible configurations, remain prominent possibilities in Eurasia. As some of the endism arguments state explicitly, the outcome depends in part on what happens in these states. Regardless of whether that is the only requirement, both candidates have a long way to go before they will resemble states in North America and Western Europe.

Allusion to a temporal dimension invokes another common denominator. Endism arguments tend to emphasize the near future. For example, it is most difficult to imagine another war between Germany and France for control of Western Europe occurring in the next one or two decades. But is it equally difficult to imagine another war between Russia and Germany or China and Japan forty years down the road? The problem is that one must adopt a long-term perspective to study the prospects of transitional warfare. The near future is too short-term.

At the same time, endism arguments also tend to talk about transitional stages. The world is becoming more liberal, more democratic, more interdependent, more multicentric, and so on. How long will these transitions need to persist before the probability of war, according to the various arguments, is truly zero? What if the transitional phase takes another hundred years to complete its transformation? Another hundred years of a warfare probability greater than zero may represent enough time and threat to caution against our assuming that the transformation is "almost" complete.

A fifth commonality is that change is seen as irreversible. Democratic states will remain democratic and presumably become even more democratic. The ideological hegemony of liberalism will not be assaulted by the resurgence of old ideas or the invention of new systems of thought. Revulsion to war and its horrific costs will not fade with time or new military technology. Levels of economic interdependence will not decline. Yet none of these trends are guaranteed to endure forever.

Most of them are not even likely to be perfectly linear in the first place.

The number of democratic states is a good example of this problem. While the trend over time is certainly positive, the trend line has been punctuated by major wars, indeed transitional wars, that have done two things. First, they have facilitated the survival of the older democracies in the face of attacks from more authoritarian enemies. Second, they have created circumstances in which either new states emerge with democratic political systems or older states have democratic political systems imposed upon them (Modelski and Perry 1991). If the other sides had won in the fighting of 1580-1608, 1688-1713, 1792-1815, and 1914-45, there would be far fewer democracies around today. However one chooses to define the meaning of *democracy*, most states in the system continue to be less than ideal candidates. Presumably, there may still be room for more war-induced democratization just as external pressures continue to contribute to movements in the opposite direction.

The irreversibility problem is even more obvious when we examine Mueller's argument. If World War II can be blamed primarily on Adolf Hitler and Benito Mussolini, as Mueller contends, can we ignore the possibility that environmental deterioration will restore the same type of electoral circumstances somewhere that permitted Hitler and Mussolini to be elected to office? At the very least, it is impossible to argue that right- and left-wing extremists have had increasing difficulty in garnering votes in Western democracies. Nor can we say that with time all democracies have only become more democratic. We might wish otherwise, but neither democratization nor economic development, for that matter, is an irreversible process.[4] Yet endism arguments insist on the opposite.

A sixth feature common to these arguments is what we would characterize as weak interpretations of previous transitional warfare. By *weak*, we mean that the portrayals of these wars, principally World Wars I and II, are unconvincing. Most of the arguments do not differentiate types of warfare other than by referring to their escalating costs. Nor do most of these arguments address the role of structural change as it relates to positional rise and decline.[5] Fukuyama views the big twentieth-century wars as primarily ideological in inspiration, despite the fact that the winning coalitions in both cases represented a mixture of ideological types. Mueller is even less convincing in his suggestion that World War II might never have happened if Hitler had never been born.

Thus, by omission or commission, most endism arguments tend to overlook the possibility that different types of war need different types of explanations and lead to different types of expectations. Different types of war need explanations of varying complexity, too. None of the six arguments, for example, operate on the assumption that, historically, one must make a distinction between global and regional theaters of operation. None suggest that "Hollandization" happens to states that are squeezed out of the major power ranks because larger, more powerful newcomers have upped the competitive ante—as opposed to decision makers' electing to opt out of competition because they no longer wish to participate. Nor do any of the six arguments rest on the assumption that, for a generation or two at least, geopolitical developments outside Europe, in conjunction with wars in Europe and elsewhere, worked to eliminate the transition potential of Western European actors.

Who is right? It would only display another type of arrogance to argue that the geohistorical story is superior to stories emphasizing democracy, liberalism, war costs, or war abhorrence. The point is that none of these endism proponents appear to have considered the possibility that what they are describing may have been caused by factors other than those they chose to stress. Some of the arguments will likely prove to be spurious. At this point, it is difficult to say, with any definitive evidence as corroboration, which stories are most accurate.

A seventh characteristic that is particularly appropriate to the arguments that incorporate a war cost feature—Jervis's end of predictability, Kaysen's end of war profitability, Mueller's end of war—is that they bestow an enormous amount of rationality and even omniscience on decision makers who must decide whether or not to wage war. There can be no disagreement about the impressive escalation in the costs of war over the past several centuries. And given those rising costs, it makes a great deal of sense that decision makers would think twice—and maybe a few more times—before choosing to go to war. There are some well-known problems with this perspective, however. Most notably, decision makers do not always demonstrate a great deal of sense. Given their track record of misperceptions in war decisions, one hesitates to give them the benefit of the doubt.

Another problem is that for most of the participants the costs of transitional warfare in particular have often been greater than the benefits for some time. The major winners are the leaders of the victorious coalition. They get to try to shape the world in their own image. Some of their allies are counted in the winner column despite losing a great deal. The Netherlands and Britain avoided losing their political autonomy to the French and Germans, respectively, only to lose much of their economic autonomy to one of their coalition partners. Transitional wars also sealed their fates as declining leaders of the global system. In contrast, the regional challengers invariably lose. With all this repetitive loss, one might think some learning would take place. Between the sixteenth and twentieth centuries, though, this seems not to have been the case.[6]

Yet perhaps this observation hints at another side of the coin of cost-benefit calculations in transitional wars. War costs are frequently indexed by lives lost, property destroyed, and resources consumed. War benefits are more traditionally restricted to territorial gains. Territorial gains and losses are part of transitional warfare too, but they are only a part and are primarily of interest to expanding regional challengers. The cost-benefit calculation becomes even more problematic if we add the opportunity to structure the global political economy. How much is it worth to "rule the world"? How much is it worth to make sure the other side does not rule? At root, that is what transitional wars are about, or they become such if they do not start that way. If the past is any judge, this benefit for one side and cost for the other are worth quite a bit.

Even so, the huge stakes that emerge in these contests must be weighed against the misperceptions of decision makers about the probable durations of wars and the identities of adversaries. Decision makers often expect short wars, just as they tend to overestimate their own capabilities and underestimate those of their opponents. If we take into account the pathologies of decision makers, which may or may not have been influenced by the presence of nuclear weapons, along with the great stakes involved in transitional warfare, then we should be extremely cautious about the straightforwardness of the cost-benefit calculations likely to be associated with these infrequent bouts of global bloodletting.

Does that leave Jervis's more general unpredictability argument as the safest approach to adopt? That course will no doubt appeal to some, but several points need to be made about the Jervis position. First, we will all agree that the predictability of the future is limited. Just because certain types of wars have come about in a consistent fashion for several centuries does not mean that they must continue to do so. Transformational change is conceivable. Practices, institutions, and attitudes are susceptible to change. The ambiguities surrounding the probability of the persistence of cyclical processes create their own sense of unpredictability.

The argument that the future is entirely unpredictable will be most appealing to analysts who have consistently maintained that prediction in world politics is difficult and unlikely. That is to say, one needs to be careful in differentiating between perennial factors working against predictability and newly erected barriers. Jervis's position on this question has been fairly consistent, before and after recent developments. Much of Jervis's argument in the early 1990s resembles points that he advanced in the 1960s and 1970s. Presumably this is more a function of his general skepticism about explanation and prediction and not necessarily a function of new developments in world politics. Thus, much of Jervis's argument betrays an ingrained skepticism, as opposed to a newfound one. If many of his reservations about predictability preceded more recent developments, they probably could have been made in earlier centuries just as easily. Yet despite these reservations, strong structural patterns have emerged from the battle-scarred history of the last half millennium.

But what should we make of his belief that the significance of structural variables such as polarity have been eclipsed by war cost-benefit calculations and domestic value changes? Unfortunately, that is all that it is at this juncture—a belief. Jervis presents neither evidence nor much argument that this is the case. He simply asserts it.[7] Something more concrete would be preferable before we heed his radical advice to develop new variables and new theories, especially in a period of flux and especially if some of the old variables and theories possibly retain utility.

These endism arguments give too much credit to time's arrow and not enough to time's cycle. Indeed, these exclusively arrow arguments give no credit to time's cycles. The closest we come to a cyclical argument is Jervis's attribution of cyclicity to Mearsheimer's bipolarity-nuclear weapon argument. But this is not really much of a cyclical argument. Most realism arguments are really flat arrows: change is minimal, but behavior does not oscillate back and forth between phases.

Clearly, we should strive to avoid the analytical trap of being forced to choose between these arrow and cycle alternatives. Both types of interpretation can improve our understanding. Neither is likely to be sufficient to the exclusion of elements from the other end of the continuum. We need integrated interpretations that combine arrow and cycle. The long cycle argument contains elements of both types of change (see, for example, Modelski 1990). But when you combine the transitional arrows of endism and the historical-structural cycles of world politics and economics, you cannot yet reach the sanguine conclusion that only the arrows count and the cycles have lost their significance. The cyclical element appears to remain too strong, and the arrows of endism are not yet strong enough. We may wish it were otherwise, but it will probably take more time to eliminate the legacies of the past. Until that happens, we do not yet have enough theoretical reason to anticipate that the future of transitional warfare will stray too far from the trodden path of its own destructive history.

This conclusion does not mean that future transitional warfare among the major powers is inevitable, only that its demise within the next generation or two is less than a sure thing. Indeed, if we assume that it cannot happen again, we are more likely to facilitate its reoccurrence than if we assume that it remains an unfortunate possibility.[8]

Appendix A.

The Army Data and Sources

In principle, any definition of *power* is likely to be best addressed by multiple indicators that tap the degree to which influence is successfully realized. A multiple indicator system for the 500-odd years between 1490 and 1990, however, is not very realistic. While analysts focusing on post-1815 world politics may be in a position to use five or six indicators of relative power potential (Singer, Bremer, and Stuckey 1972; Doran and Parsons 1980), the state of pre-1815 data discourages complicated indexes. These multiple indicator systems are also intended to combine economic, demographic, and military dimensions of capability in an across-the-board fashion. Fortunately, the concept of regional power does not require information on all conceivable dimensions of capability. Similarly, the regional power concept does not require that attempts to influence be successful or even executed. We are attempting to capture a type of state, not the relative success of its strategies.

A regional power is a state that organizes its resources, especially bureaucratic and military ones, to advance its territorial, economic, and security interests in its roughly immediate neighborhood. It is a continental power that gives primary emphasis to its landward strategic orientations. Land powers with limited resource bases, as exemplified classically by Prussia, can be overachievers, just as land powers with unlimited resource bases, as exemplified by pre-1917 Russia, can be perennially sleeping giants.

The antithesis of the regional power is the global power. Regional powers are allowed some interest in sea power, but their principal orientation remains fixed on adjacent territorial concerns. Since we typically and not coincidentally associate states with interests that are primarily maritime with large navies and small armies, regional powers should be states with large armies and small navies. A primary emphasis on developing military strength on land via armies should suffice as an indicator for determining which states possess what proportion of continental resources.

Historically, regional leaders have had the largest armies. A focus on the concentration of power among regional powers may therefore result in asking the question Who has the largest proportion of army personnel at any given time? Some things may be lost in the translation, but such a circumstance is inevitable in moving from concept to variable to indicator. It is also easy to argue that despite a number of technological changes, large numbers of troops have retained some semblance of their historical military significance into the late twentieth century.

To operationalize the indicator of army size, we surveyed historical references. The sources examined—approximately 160—cannot claim to exhaust all possible sources of information. The more sources that are examined, however, the more conflicts emerge between the pieces of information that are collected. At some point, unless one has access to a large number of governmental archives, it is actually counterproductive to continue expanding the field of search. Just where that threshold between productive and counterproductive data collection lies remains a fairly subjective matter.

Not surprisingly, the problems encountered in extracting data on army size are similar to those experienced in collecting information on the historical distribution of warships (see Modelski and Thompson 1988). One must be careful to discriminate between total armed forces and field armies. Governmental claims of specific army sizes cannot be taken at face value. Some independent verification is always desirable. Similarly, there are always problems with military units that are chronically understrength and, in some cases, underarmed. It is also clear that some state decision makers from time to time simply had no idea what the actual size of their army was.

Moreover, historians are often more interested in army size at specific battles, usually representing only a fraction of total army size. Or depending on the subject at hand, a historian will often find it adequate to give an army size that is taken as representative for as long as an entire century. For these purposes, numbers tend to be borrowed from earlier published authorities, even though they are not always accurate. The number of times a particular army size is repeated, regrettably, is not necessarily a good indicator of its accuracy.

Despite the problems likely to be encountered, the task is not as impossible as it may seem. The general growth of armies since the sixteenth century has fascinated many analysts. Accordingly, a number of discussions are rich sources of specific numbers. The evolutionary development of national armies is another fertile area for extracting indicators of size. The data collection problem ultimately reduces to one of finding and inspecting a wide enough number of sources to be able to piece together a composite array of army sizes for those countries considered to be most important for constructing proportional indices.

A secondary problem remains: How does one discriminate among the conflicting reports for a given army in a given year? The task is made easier by constructing long series. Spectacular increments and decrements in army size are not inconceivable, but they need to be explicable in concrete terms. In the absence of collateral information on intensive mobilizations and demobilizations, gradual change in a uniform direction can be expected. Aside from major discrepancies, the dilemmas of choice often revolve around choosing between reports that give an analyst a general impression of the best figure to use. For example, if several sources give a range of estimates that vary between, say, a low of 175,000 and a high of 205,000, then a working compromise of 190,000 should not be too far off the mark. Splitting the difference may not be the most desirable approach to the creation of data, but it will often serve the purpose of developing relative indices without creating too much distortion.

As noted in the text, Levy's (1983: 47) guidelines on identifying great powers have been followed for the most part: England/Britain (1490s-1945), France (1490s-1945), Austria (1490s-1918, with a break at 1520-55), Spain (1490s-1800, with Spain assuming the united Hapsburg identity between 1520 and 1555), the Netherlands (1590s-1800), Sweden (1590s-1809), Prussia/Germany (1640s-1945), Russia/USSR (1700 on), and Italy (1860s-1943). Data on non-European great powers—the United States (1816 on) and Japan (1870s-1945)—are included as well because of Dehio's (1962) emphasis on the increasing significance of extra-European resources. The dates of inclusion and exclusion are broader than Levy's in some cases in order to smooth the impact of states breaking in and falling out of the elite circle.

Inevitably, information is more readily available on some countries' armies than on others. The worst case is the Ottoman Empire, for which we have located little specific information on army size. One could argue against including the Ottoman army as an early extra-European resource. The absence of data makes the issue moot at this time. In general, data availability improves after the sixteenth century and is best for the most prominent land powers (France and Prussia/Germany). Data on states such as the Netherlands, Sweden, Austria, and Russia are variably available. That is to say, little information appears to be accessible concerning particular periods of time. In these cases, it is assumed that, barring periods of warfare, army size is fairly stable between the better-discussed periods. Extrapolation between known points is utilized when necessary.

Finally, the available information base simply precludes annual series from the 1490s on. Observations encompassing five-year intervals (e.g., 1490-94, 1495-99) are as specific as can be expected. This choice of temporal unit, however, creates another type of problem. If a war breaks out toward the middle or the end of the interval, it is likely that the half decade will encompass information on very different army sizes (pre- and post-mobilization). Should one record the highest army size or attempt to average across the full information available for the interval? Wherever possible, we chose to average. Averaging, we think, is apt to be less misleading than reporting only the highest figure, which may represent accurately only one year in the interval. The cost of this approach is that the peak size of each national army will be artificially depressed unless the army maintains that peak through the entire five-year span. But this type of downward bias holds equally for all states and thus should not create any major problems for comparison purposes within the data set. It may prove to be a problem, though, when one attempts to compare army size figures from this data set with size estimates cited in other sources. Frequently, our size estimates will seem to be smaller than those given by other sources. The reader should keep in mind that other sources often give numbers referring to the size of a total military apparatus and sometimes even reserves. They also are not constrained by the need to average across the five-year intervals.

Sources of Data on Army Size

Austria: Adams 1990; Addington 1984; Anderson 1984; Baldwin 1962; Barker 1982; Betts 1961; Black 1991; Chandler 1971; Childs 1982; Clark 1971a; Connelly et al, 1985; Corvisier 1979; Dorn 1940; Duffy 1974, 1977, 1981; Fuller 1984; Hale 1985; Herwig 1984; Hufton 1980; Kann 1974; Keim 1906; Koch 1981; Lynn 1990; McKay and Scott 1983; Mallett and Hale 1984; Mulhall 1903; Parker 1987, 1988; Roberts 1967; Rothenberg 1976, 1978, 1982; Sked 1979; Strachan 1984; von Pflugk-Harttung 1906; Webb 1911; Weigley 1991; Western 1968.

England/Britain: Addington 1984; Anderson 1984; Baldwin 1962; Barnett 1970; Best 1982; Black 1991; Bond 1980; Chandler 1971; Childs 1982; Clark 1971a, 1971b; Connelly et al, 1985; Corvisier 1979; Dorn 1940; Doyle 1978; Ehrman 1956; Fortescue 1911; French 1990; Godechot, Hyslop, and Dowd 1971; Hale 1985; Hayter 1978; Howard 1972; Institute for Strategic Studies (1959-1988-89); Mallett and Hale 1984; Mulhall 1903; Oman 1937; G. Parker 1979a, 1979b, 1988; H.M.D. Parker 1957; Roberts 1967; Rothenberg 1978; Scouller 1966; Sheppard 1974; Spiers 1980; Strachan 1983, 1984; Tilly 1990; Warner 1973; Webb 1911; Weigley 1991; Weygand 1953; Wilson 1986; Young and Lawford 1975.

France: Adams 1990; Addington 1984; Ambler 1968; Anderson 1988; Baldwin 1962; Barker 1906; Barnett 1970; Best 1982; Black 1991; Chandler 1971; Childs 1982; Clark 1971a; Connelly et al. 1985; Corvisier 1979; Delbruck 1985; Dorn 1940; Doyle 1978; Duffy 1981; Ellis 1973; Elting 1988;

continued on page 198

Table A.1 Army Sizes (thousands)

Years	Spain	France	Britain	Austria	Nether-lands	Sweden	Germany	Russia	United States	Italy	Japan
1490–94	60	29	20	10							
1495–99	39	27	20	10							
1500–1504	18	18	25	10							
1505–9	20	30	25	10							
1510–14	22	30	24	10							
1515–19	24	30	27	10							
1520–24	26	30	31	—							
1525–29	63	32	34	—							
1530–34	100	35	37	—							
1535–39	113	53	41	—							
1540–44	126	35	44	—							
1545–49	138	40	42	—							
1550–54	150	44	40	—							
1555–59	125	39	37	—							
1560–64	100	10	35	9							
1565–69	75	18	33	9							
1570–74	50	26	31	20							
1575–79	67	34	28	20							
1580–84	83	42	26	20							
1585–89	100	50	26	20							
1590–94	108	50	25	20	33	15					
1595–99	117	29	25	20	33	15					
1600–1604	125	10	24	20	25	15					
1605–9	125	40	29	20	62	15					
1610–14	30	45	34	20	30	15					
1615–19	30	20	40	20	30	15					
1620–24	150	20	45	62	48	15					
1625–29	200	30	50	107	70	27					
1630–34	200	140	57	98	70	120					
1635–39	180	150	64	89	70	150					
1640–44	160	150	70	79	70	110	4				
1645–49	140	150	70	70	44	70	8				
1650–54	120	150	44	25	40	70	12				
1655–59	100	111	25	45	36	75	26				
1660–64	64	61	5	65	32	60	13				
1665–69	27	101	16	50	28	60	18				
1670–74	49	139	15	50	24	63	20				
1675–79	70	228	15	45	40	63	23				
1680–84	62	179	16	40	57	63	28				
1685–89	55	214	48	35	73	63	24				
1690–94	48	334	76	30	83	90	29				
1695–99	41	268	50	50	95	90	34				

continued

Table A.1 Continued

Years	Spain	France	Britain	Austria	Nether-lands	Sweden	Germany	Russia	United States	Italy	Japan
1700–1704	34	195	93	70	87	100	39	52			
1705–9	50	321	93	100	79	105	43	150			
1710–14	30	263	65	133	71	110	42	220			
1715–19	38	122	35	165	62	110	61	200			
1720–24	46	133	18	161	54	45	80	215			
1725–29	55	133	35	157	46	45	70	210			
1730–34	63	169	18	153	38	45	60	132			
1735–39	71	174	49	131	30	45	71	130			
1740–44	80	241	57	108	55	45	112	141			
1745–49	73	356	80	104	55	45	138	152			
1750–54	65	249	29	137	48	45	136	163			
1755–59	58	305	129	171	44	45	150	291			
1760–64	98	285	87	200	40	45	150	313			
1765–69	88	159	45	200	37	45	160	357			
1770–74	79	168	45	200	33	45	168	400			
1775–79	69	178	78	171	29	45	175	400			
1780–84	60	187	79	307	25	45	185	413			
1785–89	50	140	50	300	25	45	195	426			
1790–94	51	440	85	300	24	45	200	450			
1795–99	52	442	140	340	23	45	200	450			
1800–1804		750	160	267		45	220	415			
1805–9		575	200	284		45	110	503			
1810–14		811	227	359			153	645			
1815–19		75	125	360			136	800	22		
1820–24		400	115	333			145	749	9		
1825–29		331	107	307			153	860	6		
1830–34		262	107	280			162	553	7		
1835–39		352	117	305			200	677	10		
1840–44		259	133	330			200	800	11		
1845–49		366	139	417			200	790	10		
1850–54		478	154	445			273	996	14		
1855–59		565	197	376			300	869	16		
1860–64		434	214	306			300	852	509	220	
1865–69		409	203	588			320	834	37	224	
1870–74		444	184	429			792	794	32	207	45
1875–79		500	178	270			410	748	27	220	36
1880–84		488	160	297			419	767	27	220	73
1885–89		515	192	323			492	785	27	255	67
1890–94		564	208	340			507	896	27	268	150
1895–99		623	253	358			495	948	132	282	240
1900–1904		673	276	375			495	1,000	85	295	577
1905–9		678	257	410			601	1,225	75	323	625

continued

Table A.1 Continued

Years	Spain	France	Britain	Austria	Nether-lands	Sweden	Germany	Russia	United States	Italy	Japan
1910–14	1,075	1,447	850				2,296	1,282	94	597	498
1915–19	2,128	2,072	1,975				2,075	5,050	1,252	1,135	371
1920–24	675	251					125	3,014	171	250	244
1925–29	588	230					100	617	138	250	250
1930–34	626	208					300	1,093	139	400	325
1935–39	1,650	652					2,075	2,150	204	800	544
1940–44	155	2,013					4,066	4,840	4,269	2,125	3,118
1945	500	2,920					—	6,289	8,268	—	5,500
1950	525	527					—	3,200	593	170	—
1955	565	523					—	2,425	1,109	170	—
1960	812	317					230	2,100	873	250	—
1965	350	208					246	2,000	969	292	172
1970	328	198					281	2,000	1,323	313	169
1975	332	178					294	1,800	767	307	154
1980	321	176					308	1,825	772	255	155
1985	300	163					314	1,995	648	270	155
1989	281	158					320	1,900	776	265	156

Note: All data reported after 1940–44 are single-year estimates.

Fisher 1906; Fuller 1985; Godechot, Hyslop, and Dowd 1971; Hale 1985; Herwig 1984; Hood 1988; Hufton 1980; Institute for Strategic Studies (1959-1988-89); Jones 1981; Keim 1906; Kennett 1967; Koch 1981; Lee 1967; Lundkvist 1973; Lynn 1980, 1984; Maland 1983; McKay and Scott 1983; Mallett and Hale 1984; Michel 1975; Mitchell 1984; Mulhall 1903; Parker 1987, 1988; Porch 1976; Riley 1986; Roberts 1967; Rothenberg 1978; Rude 1964; Snyder 1984; Sonnino 1987, 1988; Strachan 1983; Tilly 1990; Trevelyan 1934; Vagts 1959; Warner 1973; Webb 1911; Weigley 1991; Western 1968; Weygand 1953; Wolf 1951.

Italy: Addington 1984; Baldwin 1962; Gooch 1984; Herwig 1988; Institute for Strategic Studies (1959-1988-89); Knox 1988; Mulhall 1903; Roberts 1967; Sullivan 1988; Whittam 1977.

Japan: Addington 1984; Barker 1980; Beasley 1963, 1987; Boyd 1988; Butow 1961; Coox 1988; Institute for Strategic Studies 1959-1988-89; Kennedy 1924; McGovern 1920; Mulhall 1903.

Netherlands: Adams 1990; Anderson 1984; Barker 1906; Black 1991; Carter 1971; Chandler 1971; Childs 1982; Clark 1971a, 1971b; Doyle 1978; Hale 1985; Hufton 1980; Israel 1982; Jones 1981; Kossmann 1970; McKay and Scott 1983; Mulhall 1903; Parker 1988; Tilly 1990; Treasure 1985; Trevelyan 1934; Veenendaal 1971; Weygand 1953; Wijn 1970.

Ottoman Empire: Lybyer 1913; Oman 1937.

Prussia/Germany: Addington 1984; Anderson 1984; Baldwin 1962; Barnett 1970; Best 1982; Black 1991; Carsten 1961; Childs 1982; Clark 1961; Connelly et al. 1985; Cooper 1978; Corvisier 1979; Craig 1956; Delbruck 1985; Dorn 1940; Doyle 1978; Duffy 1974, 1981; Ellis 1973; Elting 1988; Forster 1988; Fuller 1984, 1985; Gibbs 1965; Godechot et al. 1971; Goerlitz 1975; Herwig 1984, 1988; Hufton 1980; Institute for Strategic Studies 1959-1988-89; Irving 1977; Koch 1978, 1981; Liddell Hart 1960; Lundkvist 1973; Lutz 1969; Lynn 1990; McKay and Scott 1983; Maland 1983; Mulhall 1903; Muller-Hillebrand 1969; Parker 1988; Pennington 1989; J.M. Roberts 1967; P. Roberts 1947; Rothenberg 1978; Rude 1964; Scott and Scott 1979; Seaton 1971, 1981, 1982; Shanahan 1945; Snyder 1984; Strachan 1983, 1984; Treasure 1985; van Creveld 1982; von Pflugk-Harttung 1906; Ward 1908; Warner 1973; Webb 1911; Weigley 1991; Western 1968; Westphal 1951; Weygand 1953; Willems 1986; Wolf 1951.

Russia/Soviet Union: Addington 1984; Adelman 1985; Alexander 1989; Alexinsky 1915; Anderson 1971, 1988; Askenazy 1907; Best 1982; Black 1991; Bloomfield, Clemens, and Griffiths 1974; Childs 1982; Collins 1980, 1985; Connelly et al. 1985; Corvisier 1979; Dmytryshyn 1977; Duffy 1981; Dukes 1990; Erickson 1962; Erickson, Hansen, and Schneider 1986; Garder 1966; Golovine 1931; Haumant n.d.; Herwig 1984; Institute for Strategic Studies 1959-1988-89; Jessup 1988; Jones 1988; Keep 1985; Koch 1981; Lynn 1990; McKay and Scott 1983; Parker 1978; Pennington 1989; Roberts 1967; Rothenberg 1978; Rude 1964; Scott and Scott 1979; Strachan 1983, 1984; Stschepkin 1906; Tilly 1990; Treasure 1985; Werth 1964; Western 1968; Wilson 1986; Wolfe 1970; Ziemke 1988.

Spain: Adams 1990; Anderson 1984; Barker 1906; Black 1991; Childs 1982; Corvisier 1979; Dorn 1940; Jones 1981; Kamen 1969, 1980; Mallett and Hale 1984; Mulhall 1903; Oman 1937; Parker 1972, 1988; Stradling 1981; Thompson 1976; Tilly 1990.

Sweden: Adams 1990; Anderson 1984; Black 1991; Chandler 1971; Childs 1982; Clark 1961; Corvisier 1979; Hatton 1971; Jones 1981; Koch 1981; Lundkvist 1973; McKay and Scott 1983; Mulhall 1903; Parker 1979a, 1979b, 1988; Reddaway 1908; Rosen 1961; Tilly 1990; Treasure 1985.

United States: Institute for Strategic Studies 1959-1988-89; U.S. Department of Commerce 1975.

Appendix B.
Identifying Systemic Wars

One of the more encouraging developments in the study of international politics is the increased appreciation for the special significance of certain wars. Scholars have assigned these wars a variety of labels: global wars, world wars, hegemonic wars, systemic wars, and general wars. Despite the irony that the subject of war has long preoccupied students of international relations, the idea that a series of infrequent outbursts of intensive combat and their consequences has a special role to play in explaining several hundred years of the evolution of the world system has been slow in emerging. We have always known that some wars seem unique because they kill more people, consume more material resources, involve more participants, and tend to spread throughout the system. Yet scholars have conventionally placed the emphasis on individual representatives of this distinctive class of warfare. What we sorely lack are lengthy studies on the system's benchmark wars viewed as a categorical phenomenon.

Our specific dilemma in this book is that we need to know which wars should receive the most attention in our search for an understanding of how structural change brings about systemic warfare. We know, for instance, that we need not spend much time on ostensibly nonsystemic clashes such as the Spanish-American War or the iterative Arab-Israeli warfare. But do we need to spend as much time with, say, the Thirty Years' War or the Crimean War as we presumably do with World Wars I and II? Which wars best qualify as examples of systemic warfare, and which ones do not?

In this appendix, we first briefly review five different definitions pertaining to the identification of the system's most important wars. With this foundation in hand, we will be in a better position to evaluate a recent critique of the adequacy of existing definitions. These preliminary considerations will serve as a platform for our main objective: empirically assessing and validating the set of global wars provided by leadership cycle theory as appropriate targets of explanation. Our entire explanatory apparatus is geared to interpreting the relationships linking structural change and systemic warfare. If we are focusing on the wrong wars, it is not likely that our explanation will be very fruitful.

Defining Systemic Wars

The process of extracting definitions is not always as simple as it seems. For many of us, the boundaries between our definitions of various phenomena and less definitive observations about the same phenomena are not always precisely drawn. Similarly, separating a brief definition from its supporting elaboration and qualification does not always do justice to an author's original intention. Yet if we wish to compare several definitions that seem to overlap in interesting ways, we have little choice but to assume the risk of potential misinterpretation. What follows, therefore, is our interpretation of five different definitions of the wars that constitute important transitional points in the evolution of systemic structure.

Robert Gilpin's (1981: 199-200) *hegemonic war* is essentially a mechanism for realigning the way in which an international system is governed with a newly emerged distribution of power. The war is a direct contest between the dominant power(s) and the rising challenger(s), in which all major powers and most minor powers become participants. Because the basic legitimacy of the system is at stake and because so many actors are drawn into the fray, the conflict rapidly becomes unlimited in the means employed and the extent of the territory encompassed by the combat. The most important consequence of a hegemonic war is that it "determines who will govern the international system and whose interests will be primarily served by the new international order" (Gilpin 1981: 198).

George Modelski's (1984: 4-5) *global war* is a product of the periodic structural crises of the global political system. A long period of capability deconcentration leads to a lack of leadership and greatly increased competition among rising powers. The outcome is a sequence of interrelated wars of generational length in which all global powers become involved. The fighting is widespread, encompasses several continents, and features a strong oceanic dimension. The outcome of each global war, in turn, is a new leadership structure, based on the reconcentration of global-reach capabilities, for the management of the global political system.

Immanuel Wallerstein's (1984: 41-42) *world war* is an extremely destructive, thirty-year, land-based struggle that tends to involve most of the major military powers at some point in the fighting. Each world war produces a new period of hegemony and a restructuring of the interstate system. Indeed, world war is thought to be a necessary factor in the creation of hegemony and the new hegemonic power. "The winner's economic edge is expanded by the very process of the war itself, and the postwar interstate settlement is designed to encrust that greater edge and protect it against erosion" (Wallerstein 1984: 44).

Manus Midlarsky's (1984) *systemic war* is a war fought over such serious and fundamental issues that the stakes involved draw in all of the major actors as combatants. The duration of the war is long, the casualty count is high, and the intensity of the conflict is such that a substantial proportion of the civilian population becomes involved in the combat. The number of structural and processual similarities exhibited in systemic war suggest that it belongs to a separate category of systemic conflict that also incorporates mass revolutions and civil wars at the domestic level.

Finally, Jack Levy defines *general war* "as one in which a decisive victory by at least one side is both a reasonable possibility and likely to result in the leadership or dominance by a single state over the system, or at least in the overthrow of an existing leadership or hegemony" (1985: 371). More specifically, a war must satisfy three criteria to qualify as a general war: the participation of the system's leading power, the participation of at least half of the other major powers, and the attainment of a conflict-intensity level exceeding one thousand battle deaths per one million European population.

These five definitions are hardly identical. Each reflects somewhat different interests and purposes on the part of its author. Yet in important ways the five converge. The commonalities become even more clear when we categorize the definitions by the elements their authors choose to stress (see table B.1). All five authors stress the participation of most or all of the system's major actors. The fact that some analysts elect to stress the participation of leaders and challengers and others do not does not seem particularly significant, at least in the context of those definitions. For instance, the leader-challenger terminology, even though it is not made definitionally explicit, is certainly compatible with the long cycle and world economy perspectives. Moreover, if all major actors are participating, then so must any leaders and challengers.

Three of the authors emphasize long durations, and all five focus attention, albeit in ways that reflect their different theoretical perspectives, on the broad scope of these wars. Again, these differences are not always meaningful. For example, Modelski (1984: 6-7) does not emphasize severity as one of his definitional criteria, but he does point out that the five global wars that meet his definition accounted for 79 percent of the battle deaths between 1494 and 1945. Alternatively, Midlarsky's emphasis on the generic term *fundamental issues* is hardly incompatible with the other four authors' stress on succession struggles. The difference in this case is partially attrib-

Table B.1 Conceptual Elements in Five Definitions of Systemic War

Conceptual Elements Stressed	Authors				
	Gilpin	Modelski	Wallerstein	Midlarsky	Levy
Participation					
Most or all major actors	X	X	X	X	X
System leader					X
System leader and challenger(s)	X				
Most minor actors	X				
Long Duration		X	X	X	
Scope					
Broad geographic scope	X	X			
Land-based			X		
Great severity/intensity	X		X		X
Fundamental issues				X	
Substantial civilian involvement				X	
Necessary Structural Causes	X	X	X	X	
Consequences					
Concrete structural change	X	X	X		
Potential structural change	?				X

utable to Midlarsky's interest in a definition that could apply to both regional and global systems.

More important, four of the five authors integrate, or can be interpreted as integrating, necessary but not sufficient structural causes as part of their definitions. A different set of four draws attention to the significant structural consequences of the wars they describe. In respect to both causes and consequences, however, Levy explicitly stakes out a different position, eschewing any discussion of causes and preferring an emphasis on potential rather than concrete consequences. Indeed, the argument over whether to include or exclude structural consequences may be the most interesting definitional disagreement discernible among these five scholars.

The Levy Critique

Levy's definitional position was developed in explicit reaction to what he perceived to be the main flaws of earlier attempts. As a consequence, it is appropriate to consider the nature of his critique in more detail. According to Levy, defining general war by the systemic consequences of the war is difficult to justify because:

1. The consequences of war are open to a wide variety of interpretations . . . and are difficult to define operationally.

2. . . . One of the key propositions . . . —that the constitution or authority structure of the system is determined by general war—is established by definition and becomes impossible to investigate empirically. . . . Unless the general war (the predictor variable) is defined independently of its systemic consequences (the dependent variable) the empirical utility of the concept of general war is greatly restricted.

3. . . . [It] generates a danger that the causes of war may also become more difficult to test empirically.

4. . . . the dispute between Modelski and others over the question whether global wars follow a regular cyclical pattern . . . cannot be resolved until operational indicators for the identification of global war are defined independently of the hypothesized cycles. Otherwise, it is impossible to determine whether particular wars . . . do not fit the long cycle because they do not fit the cycle or whether they are empirical anomalies in a cyclical theory of global wars. [Levy 1985: 359-60]

These four criticisms are not equal in magnitude. Of the four, the first and third ones appear to be the least compelling. Consequences of war are indeed subject to multiple interpretations. But so too are causes and definitions of war. The proclivity for multiple interpretations has hardly precluded analysis. Whether war consequences are any more difficult to define operationally than, say, the causes of war remains to be seen. After all, we do have much more experience with causes than with consequences (Stein and Russett 1980; Rasler and Thompson 1992). The real question in this instance is how well the war consequences are specified, not whether they are prone to specification.

Levy's concern that an emphasis on the functional consequences of some wars will spill over into the analysis of war causes presumably stems from an understandable distaste for tautology. If certain wars alter the system's structure, then their occurrence can be explained by systemic imperatives. They occur because the system's continued functioning requires them to occur. Functional explanations such as these, once very much in vogue in the social sciences, can be found in historical-structural writings on world politics.[1] But they are not foreordained by an initial definitional focus on functional consequences.

Rather than interfering with empirical tests of war causes, we would argue that identifying some wars as special cases—because of their systemic consequences—actually facilitates the empirical study of war. All wars cannot and should not be treated as if they represented exactly the same phenomenon. Nor is it likely that any explanation will fit all wars equally well. If theory suggests, for example, that World War II was something more than a more deadly version of the Korean War or the Iran-Iraq conflict, we should be wary of attempting to account simultaneously for the variance in all types of warfare.

Levy's most important criticism, that it is conceptually restrictive to define key wars by their actual structural consequences, is an interesting point of view—especially when it is advanced by someone who would prefer that we focus on wars with less concrete *potential* for structural change. As a general principle of concept formation, we would agree that definitions should be parsimonious, in the sense that they should not be burdened with less relevant features. But which facets of systemic warfare are most and least dispensable? If the focus is placed on determining who will govern the system and whose interest will be served by the new order (Gilpin 1981), the creation of a new leadership structure based on the reconcentration of global-reach capabilities (Modelski 1984), or the introduction of a new period of hegemonic dominance and a restructuring of the interstate system (Wallerstein 1984), then a number of the definitional attributes pale in significance. The number of participating states, the number of people killed, the number of years of fighting, or even the geographic scope of the fighting—all of which are likely to be considerable in systemic wars—retain some relevance, to be sure. Yet they must take second place to the fundamental reordering consequence of the war. Such an approach is restrictive, but the restriction is made intentionally.

In addition to conceptual restrictiveness, Levy is also concerned with empirical restrictiveness. According to him, if one defines certain wars as the struggles that alter the system's authority structure, it is then "impossible to investigate empirically" (1985: 359) the hypothesis that those same wars are associated with alterations of the authority structure. While this criticism may appear quite appealing, the position has at least two problems. On the one hand, Levy recognizes that the war-authority structure relationship is a basic premise of some theories. The theory construction literature fairly well recognizes that all of the components of a theory need not be tested or even be testable. What one tests are deductions from a theory and not its central assumptions or axioms. The war-authority structure relationship, therefore, cannot be both a basic premise and a hypothesized deduction.

Thus, one defense is to fall back on the accepted canons of theory building and argue that theoretical utility is more important than "empirical utility." But it is not necessary to rest solely on one's theoretical laurels. That some wars have altered the system's authority structure is not a particularly bizarre assertion, especially since we are only four decades away from the last structure-altering war. What is far more contentious and certainly empirically testable is how many or which wars are associated with the consequence of structural alteration. Do the specific periods identified in historical-structural theories of world politics qualify as genuine periods of systemic war? Do other periods of warfare qualify as well? Three questions, then, are testable: whether there is such a thing as a war that ushers in a new phase of reconcentrated capabilities, whether there have been X number of wars that qualify, and whether war X qualifies while war Y does not.

Finally, Levy's most specific criticism—To investigate whether global wars follow a regular cyclical pattern, as suggested by Modelski's leadership long cycle argument, requires an identification of global war independent of the hypothesized cycles—is highly misleading. The argument is not so much that global wars follow a regular cyclical pattern. Rather, global wars are part of a cyclical pattern of concentration-deconcentration of capabilities that creates conditions for varying amounts of systemic order. The occasional struggles for systemic leadership, the global wars, in effect switch the system from a long period of deconcentration to a short-lived period of reconcentration and greater order. The leadership long cycle question is therefore not simply whether "major wars" occur cyclically or randomly (Thompson 1985). The question is whether specific wars halt the system's deconcentration drift and facilitate structural change and reconcentration. To throw out the notion of structural change is thus tantamount to abandoning the basic processes that are, it is asserted, cyclical in nature.

Fortunately, there is an alternative approach to throwing the proverbial baby out with the bathwater. Moreover, it is an approach that offers an empirical demonstration of the appropriateness of some of these counter-assertions to Levy's critique. Focusing on the leadership long cycle version of systemic transformation, we need, for an empirical test, a series measuring the fluctuations in global capability concentration and a list of global war candidates. The problem then becomes one of ascertaining which wars, if any, have been associated with significant levels of systemic reconcentration. While this may seem to be a relatively uncomplicated task, a variety of research design problems are encountered in juxtaposing a long capability series and a list of war candidates. To make analysis as convincing as possible, considerable preliminary attention must be devoted to several potential threats to the validity of such an exercise.

Identifying Systemic Wars

Information on the wars that might qualify as systemic transformation breakpoints is not difficult to find. Each of the five authors reviewed earlier explicitly designates the wars that qualify according to his own definition. The set of wars, variously described as hegemonic, global, world, systemic, or general, encompasses nine to thirteen conflicts between 1494 and 1945. The total count varies depending on whether the following four groups of conflict are merged or treated as separate events: League of Augsburg and Spanish Succession, Jenkins's Ear and Austrian Succession, French revolutionary and Napoleonic wars, and world wars I and II. In table B.2 we follow

Table B.2 The Set of Hegemonic, Global, World, Systemic, and General Wars

War Candidate	Gilpin	Modelski	Authors Wallerstein	Midlarsky	Levy
Italian/Indian Ocean (1494–1516)		X			
Dutch Independence (1580–1608)		X			X
Thirty Years' (1618–48)	X		X	X	X
Dutch War (1672–78)	X				X
League of Augsburg (1688–97)	X	X			X
Spanish Succession (1701–13)	X	X			X
Jenkins's Ear/Austrian Succession (1739–48)					X
Seven Years' (1755–63)					X
French Revolutionary/ Napoleonic (1792–1815)	X	X	X	X	X
World War I (1914–18)	X	X	X	X	X
World War II (1939–45)	X	X	X	X	X

what seems to be the most common practice, by merging two pairs and listing two separately.

No disagreement is registered on the status of the three candidates after 1792. All five authors accord special status to the French revolutionary and Napoleonic wars and world wars I and II. Four of the five bestow the same distinction on the Thirty Years' War, and a majority (three of five) treat the League of Augsburg/Spanish Succession wars as having comparable systemic significance. Beyond this apparent core of candidate wars, disagreement proliferates. Thus, regardless of how one counts the events, something approaching consensus applies to half the candidates, while the other half (Italian/Indian Ocean, Dutch Independence, Dutch War, Jenkins's Ear/ Austrian Succession, and Seven Years') remain objects of dispute.

Measuring Capability Concentration

Stressing the significance of sea power (and later aerospace power) is hardly novel in the study of international relations. Nor is the significance of sea power entirely alien to some of the other historical-structural perspectives.[2] But leadership long cycle theory is fairly unique in arguing that sea power is a necessary, although not a sufficient, prerequisite to global power and systemic leadership.

The nature of sea power has evolved considerably over the past five hundred years. Its modern manifestation began with the development, roughly in the late fifteenth and early sixteenth centuries, of armed sailing vessels capable of oceanic voyages. As Cipolla (1965) and others have noted, guns and sails were critical in the expansion of European power throughout the world. They were also crucial in many of the intra-European competitions of the emerging nation-states. In time, specialized vessels for war were developed and became indicators of national military strength, used by state decision makers in calculating comparative capabilities. Throughout the technological transitions, decision makers have emphasized those ships capable of serving in the first line of battle; leadership long cycle theory's approach to measuring sea power capabilities also focuses on these warships.

To create a long sea power capability series that captures a variety of changes in naval technology requires some amount of flexibility in measurement principles. Armed with a more theoretically neutral capability series, we might be able to proceed immediately to a discussion of techniques and analytical outcomes. The sea power capability series, however, is unorthodox, not only because it is linked closely to a theoretical point of view but also because it encompasses a number of analytical interventions. Furthermore, these interventions were designed by analysts who also assumed that they knew which wars deserved to be labeled global, owing to the wars' impact on systemic reconcentration. Readers may have some reason to suspect the validity and reliability of an analysis designed to test war impacts on a concentration series whose construction already presumes the outcome of the undertaking. We will therefore devote some attention to inspecting the capability distribution series for possible biases in construction that could influence the outcome of a war-reconcentration examination.

Several aspects of the capability index require further consideration. First and arguably foremost, table 2.4 only summarizes the shifts in the ways in which the series was developed. Each century requires additional intervention (see table B.3). In the sixteenth century, the major states—Spain and France—still had not established regular state navies. Yet these same states were able to obtain the ships they needed for exploration, colonization, or military crisis. In this era, merchantmen often were interchangeable with warships and could be purchased, leased, or seized when necessary. To avoid misleadingly low capability scores, we increased the capability shares of Spain and France by fixed percentages (25 and 10 percent, respectively) of the other states' total number of warships. We ended the augmentation procedure in 1579 for two reasons. By that time, the Spanish had begun to build a state navy, and they would soon acquire control of the Portuguese fleet. Also, the internal warfare of late sixteenth-century France makes a very low capability score much less misleading. Only one of the wars listed in table B.2 occurred before 1579. Even so, increasing the relative shares of Spain and France is hardly likely to benefit the Portuguese relative share

Table B.3 Analytical Interventions in Naval Capability
Concentration Measurement Procedures

Year	Index Shifts
1494	Beginning of augmentation of Spanish/French scores
1579	End of the augmentation of Spanish/French scores; beginning of Dutch discount procedure
1608	End of Dutch discount procedure
1655	30+ gun minimum threshold
1671	40+ gun minimum threshold
1691	50+ gun minimum threshold
1757	60+ gun minimum threshold
1816	Ship focus supplemented by additional focus on naval expenditures
1861	Ship focus shifts from wooden ships of the line to battleships
1880	Ship focus shifts from battleships to pre-Dreadnoughts
1910	Ship focus shifts from pre-Dreadnoughts to Dreadnoughts
1914	Naval expenditures excluded during wartime
1919	Naval expenditures reintroduced
1939	Naval expenditures excluded during wartime
1946	Ship focus shifts from Dreadnoughts to aircraft carriers; naval expenditures are not reintroduced
1960	Aircraft carrier focus supplemented by additional focus on nuclear submarines and attributes of submarine-launched ballistic missiles (counter military potential and equivalent megatonnage)

position early in the sixteenth century. The first intervention is therefore an indirect discounting of the Portuguese naval capability lead and works against finding postwar reconcentration.

The second analytical intervention is a direct discounting of the Dutch capability share by 50 percent between 1579 and 1608. This intervention can be traced to the many but relatively small and lightly gunned vessels the Dutch initially used as part of their fight for independence from Spain.[3] On a one-to-one basis, the Dutch ships were outclassed by the more formidable Spanish and Portuguese galleons. To compete, the Dutch were forced to operate in groups, so that two or more of their ships would be in a position to engage an adversary. The number of cannon carried and the size of the Dutch ships used for war gradually increased, even though the Dutch continued to lag behind their rivals in this area.

The ending of the discount in 1608 is partially arbitrary, but it also reflects the decline in the size disadvantage during the war. Ending the discount at the end of the war, however, does increase the probability that the Dutch relative capability share will expand and exceed the 0.5 threshold for world power status. Actually, though, the effect of the intervention is simply to delay the numerical leadership of the Dutch by seven years. Without the discount, the Dutch share exceeds 0.5 for only one year, 1589, after the first Spanish Armada disaster, and then declines as the Spanish rebuilt. The Dutch surpassed the 0.5 threshold again in 1601, this time on a more permanent basis. With the 50 percent discount, the Dutch share reached the 0.5 mark in the last year of the war. This suggests a bias with rather minimal consequences for our current purposes.

The subsequent interventions tend to be more technologically oriented and can be treated as a cluster sharing a number of features. The minimal number of guns needed to qualify as a ship of the line gradually became more concrete and then escalated. In many respects, the ships remained much the same from the mid-seventeenth through the mid-nineteenth centuries. It was their firepower that increased. In the mid-nineteenth century, the Industrial Revolution finally caught up with naval power, rendering the wooden ship of the line obsolete almost overnight. Through experimentation in the second half of the century, new battleship standards evolved from the first crude ironclads, to the relatively standardized pre-Dreadnoughts of the late 1880s-90s, to the Dreadnoughts built after 1906, which again revolutionized the minimal competitive standards for a first-class battleship.

We introduced naval expenditures for the 1816-1945 period to help smooth the discontinuities introduced by technological innovation primarily from the 1860s on. The expenditures might have been introduced much earlier if it were not so difficult to generate reliable and comparable series for most of the states before 1815. Reliability and comparability are also a problem for naval expenditures during World Wars I and II, owing to a combination of secrecy, inflationary pressures, debt practices, and the fiscal advantages of conquest. Expenditures, therefore, are not used during 1914-18 and 1939-45.

Soviet naval expenditures are simply unobtainable for more than a very few years after 1945. The focus of the index shifts accordingly to the aircraft carrier, which supplanted the battleship as the principal or capital warship during World War II. This singular focus is expanded by the introduction of nuclear propulsion in submarines, which gave these craft their first genuine undersea capability. Stationing nuclear weapons at sea in the form of submarine-launched ballistic missiles also transformed the nature and meaning of naval firepower.

Obviously, greater detail and justification could be supplied on these multiple index changes. For present purposes, though, the primary question is whether they introduce important biases to the series that might under-

Table B.4 Analytical Interventions and Index Distortion

t_0	t_{-5}	t_{-4}	t_{-3}	t_{-2}	t_{-1}	t_0	t_{+1}	t_{+2}	t_{+3}	t_{+4}	t_{+5}	Mean Percentage Change
1655	0.321	0.321	0.408	0.358	0.352	0.331	0.329	0.335	0.356	0.342	0.335	-3.6
1671	0.357	0.370	0.355	0.344	0.320	0.342	0.333	0.303	0.278	0.270	0.235	-18.7
1691	0.224	0.229	0.260	0.273	0.242	0.228	0.228	0.223	0.240	0.231	0.230	-6.2
1757	0.428	0.432	0.426	0.433	0.419	0.364	0.401	0.431	0.423	0.427	0.433	-1.1
1816	0.505	0.503	0.483	0.516	0.523	0.660	0.609	0.615	0.589	0.588	0.586	18.1
1861	0.505	0.504	0.489	0.467	0.493	0.574	0.574	0.401	0.449	0.490	0.401	-5.8
1880	0.443	0.434	0.432	0.431	0.429	0.522	0.508	0.498	0.489	0.481	0.477	13.1
1910	0.411	0.392	0.363	0.368	0.373	0.442	0.404	0.389	0.391	0.436	0.422	7.1
1914	0.373	0.442	0.404	0.389	0.391	0.436	0.422	0.424	0.415	0.411	0.374	2.4
1919	0.436	0.422	0.424	0.415	0.411	0.374	0.371	0.356	0.320	0.346	0.335	-18.0
1939	0.288	0.279	0.273	0.278	0.285	0.259	0.273	0.283	0.300	0.294	0.286	2.3
1946	0.283	0.300	0.294	0.286	0.350	1.000	1.000	1.000	1.000	1.000	1.000	230.5
1960	1.000	1.000	1.000	1.000	1.000	0.724	0.724	0.740	0.736	0.762	0.770	-25.4

mine its utility. In table B.4 we explore this possibility empirically by listing eleven-year slices of the series that encompass the year in which the index procedures changed, as well as the five years before and after the change. Operationally, the question can be reduced to whether the index change alters the level of the series in some significant way. One way to assess significance in this case is to compare the pre-five-year means with the post-five-year means. A change greater than, say, an arbitrary 10 percent might bear closer inspection.

About half—seven of thirteen—of the index changes can be associated with marginal changes (less than 10 percent) in the series: 1655, 1691, 1757, 1861, 1910, 1914, and 1939. Three of the remaining six cases are not very troublesome. The 1880 and 1960 cases do not occur particularly near critical wars. The 1919 case takes place during what will be considered here as one long period of systemic war (1914-45). As we will see, the years during which the candidate wars were fought will be excluded from our analysis.

The 1671 case is quite proximate to one of the wars of interest (the Dutch War, 1672-78). The problem is that it is difficult to disentangle the deterioration of Dutch competitiveness from the naval expansionary efforts of the English and the French. It is clear that the Dutch were increasingly outgunned in this period—a handicap traceable in part to the shallowness of Dutch harbor entries and the consequent need for ships with shallow drafts. In this respect, the 1671 index change, raising the minimal gun threshold, influences the series, but probably not in an artificial way.

The remaining two cases (1816 and 1946) are the most important ones. Both involve periods in which wars gave way to systemic reconcentration, according to the long cycle premise. Even though neither the Napoleonic Wars nor World War II is a particularly controversial candidate for a structural watershed war, some additional attention is still warranted. Only 5 percent of the change attributable at least in part to the 1816 index shift was actually caused by the introduction of naval expenditures as half of the indicator system. This means that a significant increase would still have been encountered if the expenditures had been introduced at a later point and only ships of the line had been counted. Far more critical to the reconcentration process was the fact that the Allied victory in 1814-15 enabled the victors to substantially reduce the size of the French fleet.

The most glaring change linked to the index interventions is the complicated 1946 case. The case involves a shift from battleships to carriers, a shift from one world power (Britain) to another (the United States), and loss of four other global players (France, Japan, Germany, and Britain). Limiting the discussion for the moment to the types of ships counted, substituting carriers for battleships at an earlier point—either before 1941, when the relative value of the two ship types was still being argued in naval circles, or

Table B.5 Three Capability Indices in the Post-World War II Era

Year	Naval Capability Index	Ha Strategic Nuclear Weapons Index	Ward Military Stockpile Data Index
1946	1.000	1.000	—
1951	1.000	1.000	0.959
1955	1.000	0.903	0.877
1960	0.724	0.717	0.860
1965	0.770	0.728	0.863
1970	0.714	0.620	0.713
1975	0.707	0.726	0.674
1979	0.639	0.611	0.531

Note: Ha's (1983: 35) index represents the U.S. proportion of strategic nuclear warheads deliverable by bombers, land-based missiles, and sea-based missiles. The U.S. share is based on an $\underline{N}$ encompassing the Soviet Union, Britain, France, China, and the United States. Ward's (1984: 312) military stockpile data combine two indices. One measures the conventional forces (manpower x firepower x mobility) of the Soviet Union, East Germany, West Germany, and the United States. The second series focuses on U.S. and Soviet strategic forces (total number of weapons weighted by lethality). The two indices are added and then divided by 1000. The series in this table is the U.S. (and the West German contribution to the conventional index) share of the total stockpile data.

after 1941, when the superiority of the carrier was established in the Pacific fighting—would not reduce the dramatic amount of postwar reconcentration. By 1945 the United States possessed 71.9 percent of the carriers of the six global powers. In any event, the abrupt change in 1945-46 is traceable far more readily to the changes in world and global power status than to precisely what is counted.

It might be argued, of course, that a focus on carriers is unfortunate in a two-actor situation in which only one actor has carriers. But the high global-reach capability scores bestowed on the United States after World War II are not all that unrealistic. And even if the focus on sea power was abandoned after 1945 for a more conventional emphasis on general weapon systems, it is not clear that the change would affect at least the initial 1945-46 shift all that much. This point can be illustrated (see table B.5) by comparing sea power distribution scores with some alternative calculations comparing nuclear weapons in general (Ha 1983) or both strategic and conventional weapons (Ward 1984). The point is not that each index behaves identically. Instead, it is that the levels of the American scores are fairly similar despite the varying emphases.

The discussion of the 1946 index change does raise a different source of possible indicator bias—the question of changes in actor status (see table B.6). As noted previously, actors are introduced as global powers as early as possible in order to minimize distortion. The introduction of Russia in 1714

Table B.6 Changes in Actor Status

Year	Actor Introduced	Actor Exits	Change in Systemic Leadership	
			From	To
1494	England, Spain, Portugal, France			
1579	Netherlands			
1580		Portugal		
1581			Portugal	
1609				Netherlands*
1714	Russia		Netherlands	Britain
1808		Spain		
1810		Netherlands		
1816	United States			
1871	Germany			
1875	Japan			
1946		Britain, France, Germany, Japan	Britain	United States

*The measurement of the leadership gap between 1581 and 1609 can be filled in more than one way. Spain gained control over the Portuguese navy and led briefly. One could also rely on the Dutch share at an earlier date. These problems are avoided when using the Ray-Singer concentration algorithm.

and the United States in 1816 actually works against British numerical leadership. Technically, the Netherlands (1579 entry) and Germany (1871 entry) did not exist before their global power status began. Japan had no real navy before the early 1870s.

The exit side of the coin offers even fewer degrees of freedom. Portugal, Spain, and the Netherlands lost their independence in war. When they regained their autonomy, they no longer met the minimal qualifications for global power status. Any dispute about the post-1945 status of Britain, France, Germany, and Japan pertains more to what is counted than to whether the four states failed to be fully competitive according to the criteria partially described in table 2.4.[4]

The interaction between the capability indicator system and the changes in systemic leadership, no doubt, raises the most disturbing potential for bias. The identity of the global leader—and the state that supplies the share score that describes systemic concentration—changes at precisely the time that is most subject to scrutiny vis-à-vis the possibility of capability reconcentration. There is simply no circumventing the vulnerability of this procedure to charges of bias and indicator contamination. Fortunately, there is a way to see whether the procedure makes that much difference.

The world power's share is used as a measure of global concentration in part because it is quite easy to interpret. There are other ways of measuring concentration that do not require the analyst to assign special status to any of the actors. One such alternative calculation formula for concentration has been proposed by Ray and Singer (1973):

$$\text{Concentration} = [(\Sigma \underline{s}^2 - 1/\underline{N})/(1 - 1/\underline{N})]^{1/2}$$

where $\underline{s}$ is each actor's percentage share and $\underline{N}$ is the number of actors in the system. As a partial control for the bias in the world power share indicator, an alternative index of the sea power distribution data, using this formulation, is also available in Modelski and Thompson (1988). We will employ it in our investigation in order to compare the results obtained with the two different approaches to measuring systemic concentration.

Linking War and Structural Change

Some wars, it is argued, bring about structural change, while others do not. To assess which wars are linked with change and which ones are not, we propose applying Box and Tiao's (1975) policy impact assessment models to measure the influence of the candidate wars on the structural concentration series. The basic Box-Tiao model is

$$\underline{Y} = f(\underline{I}_t) + \underline{N}_t$$

in which $f(\underline{I}_t)$ represents a functional relationship between the intervention ($\underline{I}$) and the affected $\underline{Y}$ series. $\underline{N}$ is an ARIMA model noise component that describes the stochastic behavior of the time series around the $\underline{Y} - f(\underline{I}_t)$ relationship. In utilizing these models, one first identifies the parameters of the noise component (ARIMA structure). Appropriate intervention components are next selected, based on a priori expectations concerning the nature of the impact (whether it is abrupt or gradual and permanent or temporary), and added to the noise component.

Leadership long cycle theory suggests that the structural impacts are apt to be fairly abrupt—in the immediate postwar sense—and relatively permanent. The new leadership structure is expected to endure for at least a generation or a quarter of a century. This expectation permits us to employ the simplest intervention component ($\omega_0 \underline{I}_t$), in which $\underline{I}$ normally would be coded as 1 during the years of candidate warfare and 0 otherwise. Some of the candidate wars, however, were waged for quite lengthy periods of time. During these long wars, the respective fortunes of the opposing sides sometimes oscillated, with challengers leading in the beginning only to lose in the end, while in other wars the challengers suffered early setbacks. Some of the longer wars also had pauses, when combat ceased for short intervals. Taking these factors into consideration suggests that we should avoid trying to model structural change while war is ongoing. All we are really interested in is whether the immediate postwar era is significantly more concentrated than the period before the war began. To address this question we will first purge the war years from the capability series and then code a set of postwar years as the intervention. Five years may seem unusually short as an intervention period, but it is sufficient to serve the modeling purpose and it avoids the potential problem of one candidate war's postwar period overlapping with the onset of another candidate war. Since this decision may also seem suspect to some, the five-year impacts will be contrasted with ten- and fifteen-year impact assessments.[5]

Given our before-after comparative design, we are forced to eliminate the 1494-1516 Italian/Indian Ocean War from most of the analysis owing to the absence of pre-1494 capability data. With this exception, the leadership long cycle argument will be validated to the extent that the immediate postwar periods of the global wars of 1580-1608, 1688-1713, 1792-1815, and 1914-45 are associated with positive (greater concentration) and statistically significant omega values that reflect abrupt and relatively permanent changes. All of the immediate postwar periods of the other four candidate wars—the wars of 1618-48, 1672-78, 1739-48, and 1755-63—should be associated with either statistically insignificant values or negatively signed values. In other words, we expect nonglobal wars to be associated with the absence of significant structural reconcentration at the systemic level.

HYPOTHESIS B.1: Global wars are followed by a statistically significant period of reconcentration in sea power capabilities.

HYPOTHESIS B.2: Nonglobal wars are not followed by a statistically significant period of reconcentration in sea power capabilities.

Assessing the Data

Table B.7 provides a first cut at the question of the war impact on concentration. Each of the eight wars is examined five times. What varies is the length of time considered in the calculations of the proportional changes, ranging from the five prewar years compared with the five postwar years to the twenty-five prewar years compared with the twenty-five postwar years. Regardless of which formula is used to measure systemic concentration, the four global wars identified by leadership long cycle theory—1580-1608, 1688-1713, 1792-1815, and 1914-45—are associated with the strongest positive postwar increases. The other four wars—1618-48, 1672-78, 1739-48, and 1755-63—are

Table B.7 War and Proportional Changes in Capability Concentration

War Years	Number of Years Compared in Prewar and Postwar Means				
	5	10	15	20	25
Power Share					
1580–1608	67.7	49.3	43.0	38.8	30.0
1618–48	-37.5	-32.9	-20.3	-17.6	-21.7
1672–78	-31.8	-32.8	-32.3	-33.1	-30.9
1688–1713	90.4	85.5	84.0	77.0	64.5
1739–48	-7.8	-9.6	-9.6	-10.5	-9.9
1755–63	3.0	-2.9	-7.7	-11.3	-13.7
1792–1815	78.4	66.7	61.4	52.3	42.8
1914–45	150.0	153.2	148.0	126.7	109.2
Alternative Concentration Index					
1580–1608	85.7	88.7	77.6	67.2	51.5
1618–48	-39.5	-34.0	-28.3	-27.2	-29.6
1672–78	8.9	-3.3	-6.0	-11.4	-6.0
1688–1713	43.8	55.6	52.2	49.4	43.2
1739–48	-10.7	-10.7	-10.0	-11.7	-10.8
1755–63	13.6	9.2	3.9	-2.7	-8.6
1792–1815	134.4	109.2	84.1	61.5	44.8
1914–45	204.0	221.5	218.2	167.9	128.4

Note: Global war periods are italicized.

for the most part associated with negatively signed changes. A clear pattern is revealed. Global wars are associated with reconcentration. Nonglobal wars tend to be associated with further or continuing deconcentration.

However clear-cut the pattern in table B.7 may be, the outcome imparts little information that will help answer the question of which impacts are statistically significant. Table B.8 reports the outcome of the Box-Tiao analyses on five-, ten-, and fifteen-year postwar impact periods. While the findings in table B.7 overlap considerably with those displayed in table B.8, the outcomes are not identical. Three of the four global wars—1580-1608, 1792-1815, and 1914-45—are again consistently shown to have reconcentration effects, across different time intervals and concentration indices. The omega parameters are positive and statistically significant. The 1739-48 and 1755-63 nonglobal wars are also consistently insignificant in impact.

The results in table B.8 pertaining to the three conflicts beginning in the seventeenth century not only disagree with the proportional changes found in table B.7, but they are also inconsistent across time periods and indicators examined. This outcome gives several causes for concern. Not only does it muddy the waters concerning which wars have significant posi-

Table B.8 The Impact of War on Capability Concentration since 1494
(Box-Tiao omega coefficients)

| | Number of Years Compared in Prewar and Postwar Means | | | | | |
| | World Power Share Index | | | Alternative Concentration Index | | |
War Years	5	10	15	5	10	15
1580–1608	0.143*	0.274*	0.263*	0.092*	0.212*	0.209*
	(0.043)	(0.037)	0.037)	(0.040)	0.045)	(0.046)
1618–48	-0.111*	0.030	0.008	-0.139*	-0.026	-0.031
	(0.034)	(0.037)	(0.037)	(0.040)	(0.045)	(0.046)
1672–78	-0.056	-0.146*	-0.150*	0.004	-0.038	-0.044
	(0.034)	(0.037)	(0.037)	(0.040)	(0.045)	(0.046)
1688–1713	0.085*	0.045	0.037	0.032	0.065	0.052
	(0.034)	(0.037)	(0.037)	(0.040)	(0.045)	(0.042)
1739–48	-0.009	-0.025	-0.024	-0.017	-0.036	0.036
	(0.034)	(0.037)	(0.037)	(0.040)	(0.045)	(0.042)
1755–63	0.014	-0.000	0.000	0.021	0.002	0.002
	(0.034)	(0.037)	(0.037)	(0.040)	(0.045)	(0.030)
1792–1815	0.166*	0.151*	0.158*	0.171*	0.165*	0.174*
	(0.034)	(0.032)	(0.032)	(0.040)	(0.039)	(0.040)
1914–45	0.358*	0.358*	0.350*	0.373*	0.373*	0.358*
	(0.034)	(0.032)	(0.032)	(0.040)	(0.039)	(0.040)

Note: All six equations (0, 1, 0 order) have white-noise parameters. Global war periods are italicized.

*Statistically significant at the .05 level.

tive impacts, but the outcome also suggests that perhaps it does make some difference how long the postwar year period is or which concentration formulation is used. Box-Tiao analyses, however, are subject to a liability that may be influencing the outcomes reported in table B.8. Statistical significance is a relative concept, not an absolute one. There is always a possibility that very strong impacts, along the lines of the 1914-45 case, for example, can depreciate the significance of comparatively weaker impacts.

To check this possibility, we shortened the capability distribution series by eliminating the pre-1608 and post-1792 periods. This serial surgery makes possible a closer examination of the unclear status of the 1688-1713 event and also permits a reexamination of all four of the nonglobal wars. The outcome is reported in table B.9. The impacts of the two eighteenth-century wars are little changed. In contrast, the findings for the Thirty Years' War (1618-48) and the League of Augsburg/Spanish Succession con-

Table B.9 Box-Tiao Impact Parameters for the 1609–1791 Period

| | Number of Years Compared in Prewar and Postwar Means | | | | | |
| | World Power Share Index | | | Alternative Concentration Index | | |
War Years	5	10	15	5	10	15
1618–48	-0.111*	-0.107*	-0.124*	-0.139*	-0.132*	-0.136*
	(0.022)	(0.017)	(0.016)	(0.021)	(0.020)	(0.020)
1672–78	-0.056	-0.146*	-0.150*	0.004	-0.038	-0.044
	(0.022)	(0.020)	(0.018)	(0.021)	(0.023)	(0.023)
1688–1713	0.085*	0.045*	0.037*	0.032	0.065*	0.052*
	(0.022)	(0.020)	(0.018)	(0.021)	(0.023)	(0.023)
1739–48	-0.009	-0.025	-0.024	-0.017	-0.036	-0.035
	(0.022)	(0.020)	(0.018)	(0.021)	(0.023)	(0.023)
1755–63	0.014	-0.000	0.000	0.021	0.003	0.006
	(0.022)	(0.020)	(0.018)	(0.021)	(0.023)	(0.023)

Note: All six equations (0, 1, 0 order) have white-noise parameters. Global war periods are italicized.
*Statistically significant at the .05 level.

flict (1688-1713) are much more consistent. Five of the six parameters for the 1688-1713 war are positive and statistically significant. All six of the omega coefficients for the Thirty Years' War are statistically significant but negatively signed. Only the Dutch War (1672-78) remains ambiguous. More accurately, its impact outcome depends on which indicator is used; this clue helps to explain the two different types of results. The world power share index is influenced by the continuing decline of the Dutch—a process accelerated by raising the ante for the number of cannon for ships of the line in 1671. The alternatively formulated index, the one applying the Ray-Singer algorithm, indicates little real change in the overall capability distribution between about 1666 and 1702, with the index values fluctuating between 0.27 and 0.24.

Aside from this difference, the two approaches to tapping the extent of systemic concentration appear to behave along fairly parallel lines. The plot of the two concentration series in figure B.1 provides visual confirmation for this observation. The figure also presents another, more visual type of evidence for the relationship between war and systemic reconcentration. Five major though irregular humps (exceeding the 0.5 level) can be discerned in the two series.

The series almost begins with a hump associated with the early Portuguese naval lead first attained during the Italian/Indian Ocean warfare.

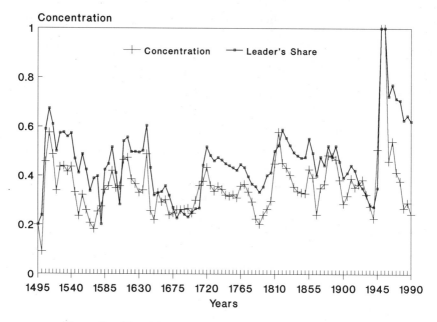

Figure B.1 Two Measurement Approaches to Concentration

Toward the end of the sixteenth century, the Spanish briefly passed the 0.5 threshold during the 1580-1608 fighting, only to lose their position to the Dutch. The Dutch ascendancy in the seventeenth century gave way to a comparatively weak British succession in the eighteenth century. The Napoleonic Wars ushered in the nineteenth century and a new era of British systemic leadership and reconcentration. The two series diverge in some respects on the depiction of the deconcentration of the late nineteenth and early twentieth centuries. The Ray-Singer algorithm highlights the brief upsurge after World War I that was caused primarily by American gains that were not translated into a leadership change. Both series converge, however, on the dramatic American rise to preeminence after 1945. In sum, the statistical and visual evidence lends strong support to the notion that five periods of global war have been uniquely instrumental in bringing about significant systemic reconcentration.

Global versus Nonglobal Wars

Why do some wars lead to systemic reconcentration and new leadership when others do not? Answering this question completely would require a fully specified theory of world system dynamics. Particular emphasis would

Table B.10 The Impact of War on the Primary Challenger's Position

War Years	Primary Challenger	Peak Position During War	Position at War's End	Challenger's Positional Change
1580–1608	Spain	0.525/0.571	0.165/0.172	-68.6/-69.9
1618–48	Spain	0.272/0.441	0.175/0.260	-35.7/-41.0
1672–78	France	0.396/0.471	0.352/0.402	-11.1/-14.6
1688–1713	France	0.433/0.484	0.236/0.213	-45.5/-56.0
1739–48	France	0.191/0.418	0.185/0.351	-3.1/-16.0
1755–63	France	0.272/0.338	0.267/0.217	-1.8/-35.8
1792–1815	France	0.353/0.537	0.175/0.108	-50.4/-79.9
1914–45	Germany	0.282/0.366	0.000/0.096	-100.0/-73.8
		0.146/0.486	0.000/0.000	-100.0/-100.0
Global War Mean		0.348/0.489	0.115/0.118	-72.9/-75.9
Nonglobal War Mean		0.283/0.417	0.245/0.308	-12.9/-26.9

Note: Positional scores are expressed first in global terms and then in regional terms. Global war periods are italicized.

need to be placed on why major states rise and fall in the system's pecking order of relative capability. We would also need a better understanding of why and how some regional wars—historically in Europe—escalated into affairs with much wider consequences.

The articulation and elaboration of such a theory receives more attention elsewhere in this book. Yet some clues to the distinctiveness of global wars are still worth pursuing. By definition, and now as established by empirical analysis, global wars bring about significant capability reconcentration. They also usher in a new era of systemic leadership and order—something we have not yet attempted to measure. Nonglobal wars accomplish none of these things. Why is that the case? One major clue concerns the process of reconcentration. Earlier, we emphasized the post-global war ascendancy of a world power controlling 50 percent or more of the system's global-reach capabilities. In this respect, global wars facilitate the rise to preeminence of the system's lead power. But where there are winners, especially when wars are involved, there are also apt to be losers. And when the winners win big, the losers' losses tend to be equally dramatic.

Table B.10 illustrates the nonrandom nature of major positional losses on the part of each war's primary challenger. Measuring from the peak position attained during the war to the relative position held immediately after the end of war, primary challengers suffer their greatest, and certainly their most abrupt, positional losses in global war combat, with declines ranging from 46 to 100 percent. While challengers can lose things other than position—for example, territorial holdings, as in the French eighteenth-century case—they are much less affected by their losses in nonglobal wars. Excepting the Thirty Years' War, the challengers' loss range for the nonglobal wars is roughly 2 to 11 percent.[6]

Reconcentration occurs, then, when the relative position of the lead state soars to a new peak and its most dangerous rival suffers a severe positional setback. The capability setback can be caused by battle losses, financial exhaustion, peace settlements, or, more likely, some combination of the three. But this very distancing of the positions of the system leader and its principal rival and what that distancing means to the ability to influence events are what is so important in creating the opportunity and positional space for imposing a new order.

The window of opportunity for generating order is neither permanent nor particularly long-lived. The sequential identity of the challengers listed in table B.10—and the fact that only three states are identified—clearly hint at this facet of the system's struggle for leadership. Spain, France, and Germany have competed with the Netherlands, Britain, and the United States for several centuries. Moreover, it is clear that while a global war can devastate a challenger's relative position in the system, one global war never quite suffices to completely eliminate a challenger. Spain was weakened severely in the 1580-1608 fighting. Yet within a decade or so, the Dutch and the Spanish had resumed their feud. The French lost two global wars and several intermediate bouts before they were ready to relinquish the role of challenger. Even so, the British continued to worry, albeit intermittently, about a renewed French threat well into the nineteenth century. The German threat eventually supplanted the French one, and dealing with it also required two world wars, separated by a twenty-year pause.

An emphasis on the sequential character of these primacy struggles does suggest that all eight of the wars listed in table B.10 have more in common than may be indicated by the labels global and nonglobal. Yet another distinction still needs our attention. If one compares the peak wartime capability position of the Spanish and French challengers in their global and nonglobal forays, the global war challenges are based on more impressive capability foundations—at least as far as sea power is concerned—than the nonglobal war quarrels. This observation suggests, in turn, that the imagery of multiple relative capability trajectories—not simply the one traversed by the system as a whole via the system leader's relative capability fortunes—needs to be considered.

Other scholars have focused on transitional capability passages and their link to war. Doran and Parsons (1980) and Organski and Kugler (1980) are two prominent examples. These approaches, however, imply a single relative capability cycle per actor (Doran and Parsons) and one major transitional war per adversarial dyad (Organski and Kugler). Table B.10 suggests otherwise. The French relative position certainly peaked more than once. Nor are challenges for leadership always once-and-for-all showdowns. Instead, they tend to involve serial confrontations. Some of these confrontations are more serious than others, owing at least in part to the challenger's initial relatively strong position. But this also implies what is expressed explicitly in the leadership long cycle argument: that what becomes the primary target of the challenge—the world power—is also in a weaker position relative to its strength at an earlier time.

A third important actor in these confrontations is the erstwhile leading coalition partner and successor to the world power (Britain in 1713 and the United States in 1945). These actors prove pivotal in those global wars in which the old system leader is too weak to withstand the challenger's threat. They are not too conspicuous in table B.10's nonglobal wars, although England did participate in phases of the 1618-48 and 1672-78 combat. Consequently, distinguishing between global and nonglobal wars with the advantage of hindsight involves tracking three types of relative capability trajectories—the system leader's, the primary challenger's, and the system leader's ultimate successor. In global wars, the system leader's position is lower than it has been in the past, while the positions of the other two types of actors tend to be improving. In table B.10's nonglobal wars, the system leader may no longer have been in the position it enjoyed immediately after the previous global war. Nonetheless, it remained sufficiently powerful to fend off the challenger's probe. As a result, there is no reason to anticipate postwar capability reconcentration in these cases.

The Question of Regional Concentration

In this appendix we have emphasized the global level because the primary question at stake has been whether global wars lead to global reconcentration and other wars do not. But what happens to regional concentration in the aftermath of global war? Figure B.2 helps answer this question. Here we plot regional army concentration between 1490 and 1945 and demarcate the global and nonglobal wars listed in table B.2.

The answer to the question of the impact of war on regional concentration is fairly uniform. In most cases, the major wars upon which we are focusing decreased regional concentration. Yet the amount of decrease was not always all that great, nor was it usually long-lasting. Particularly comparable are the postwar developments after 1580-1608, 1688-1713, 1792-1815,

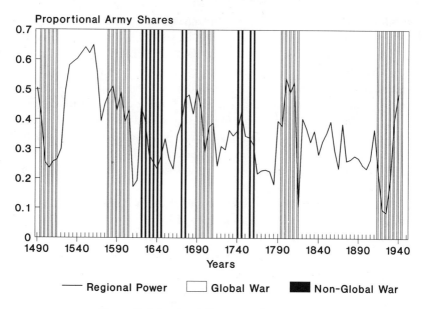

Figure B.2 Regional Concentration and War

and perhaps 1914-18 if we treat it as a separate entity. In each case, the resource-exhausted European challenger demobilized or was forced to demobilize. In each case, within roughly twenty years or so, the challenger had restored itself as the leading military power of Western Europe. Although the aftermath of the 1494-1516 global war is dissimilar, in that the continental winner went on to emerge as the main threat to European independence, it resembles the prototypical post-global war pattern. The outcome of global war did not preclude a return to high levels of regional power concentration. On the contrary, it encouraged regional reconcentration. The only exception to this rule is of course the aftermath of World War II, which, presumably, ended the European cycle of deconcentration-reconcentration.

The outcome associated with three of the four nonglobal war candidates is similar. The Thirty Years' War certainly contributed to Spain's decline, just as it facilitated France's reemergence as the leading European land power. The 1672-78 Dutch War, the one nonglobal war that is not associated with a decline in army shares, was only a preliminary bout to the main event beginning in 1688. The costs of fighting in 1739-48 and 1755-63 contributed to the coming of revolution in France, as did the French participation in the War of American Independence, but again, none of the defeats before 1815 prevented renewed Anglo-French conflict.

Thus, the historical record is quite clear that while global war reconcentrates power at the level of the global political economy and ushers in a new era of global political management, its impact on regional affairs tended to be much less significant and definitely more short-lived until quite recently. This characteristic must be considered one of the reasons for the long-term perpetuation of the intermittent fusion of global and European regional politics. The impact of global war is usually far more superficial as one moves farther away from issues concerning the regulation of transoceanic activity.

Global wars are defined by consequences because these wars have little, if any, theoretical meaning in their absence. Other wars, such as the four seventeenth- and eighteenth-century war candidates rejected in this examination, are not empirical anomalies, nor do they fail to qualify because they do not fit an arbitrarily constructed long cycle. They fail to qualify because they are not global wars. They were not succession struggles that led to a reconcentration of naval capabilities that could serve as a partial, but essential, foundation for global leadership. Evidence confirms that this pattern has been followed since 1494. The evidence also suggests that there are distinct limits on how far the impacts of global war reach.

Appendix C.

Cross-Correlations, Time Series Regressions, and Coefficients Derived from Vector Autoregression

A cross-correlation function measures the correlations between two time series at different time periods. It is sometimes referred to as a between-series correlation. The idea is to measure the degree of association between an explanatory and dependent variable at various time lags in order to discern whether past or future values of $\underline{X}$ are more strongly associated with $\underline{Y}$. Instances where past values of $\underline{X}$ yield large correlations with $\underline{Y}$ suggest that $\underline{X}$ is antecedent to $\underline{Y}$, and large correlations between future values of $\underline{X}$ with $\underline{Y}$ suggest that $\underline{Y}$ precedes $\underline{X}$. More detailed discussions can be found in the work of Box and Jenkins (1970) and McCleary and Hay (1980).

Cross-correlations are estimated as a first step in the data analysis for two purposes: to observe which of the series tends to lead or lag behind the other, and to discern at what time lags the relationships are the strongest—for example, the first five lags or later at ten to twenty lags.

The cross-correlations between war, naval capability share, leading-sector share, and leading-sector growth for the United States (1870-1980) are listed in table C.1. Theoretically, we expect to find positive rather than negative relationships among the nonwar variables. The results indicate that the correlations between leading-sector share and naval capability share are strongest at lags 1, 2, and 3. They also suggest that leading-sector share is causally prior to naval capability share, in that the correlations from naval capability share to leading-sector share are either zero or negatively related in the wrong theoretical direction.

The correlations between leading-sector growth rate and leading-sector share indicate that the strongest relationship is at lag 0, without any obvious pattern relating to causal direction. The results are also the same for the correlations between leading-sector growth rate and naval capability share. The strongest association occurs at lag 0.

The results involving the war variable show a potential one-way rela-

Table C.1 Cross-Correlations: United States, 1870–1980

i	War and Naval Capability Share Lag(-i) N W	War and Naval Capability Share Lead(+i) W N	War and Leading-Sector Share Lag(-i) S W	War and Leading-Sector Share Lead(+i) W S	War and Leading-Sector Growth Rate Lag(-i) G W	War and Leading-Sector Growth Rate Lead(+i) W G	Leading-Sector Share and Naval Capability Share Lag(-i) S N	Leading-Sector Share and Naval Capability Share Lead(+i) N S	Leading-Sector Growth and Leading-Sector Share Lag(-i) G S	Leading-Sector Growth and Leading-Sector Share Lead(+i) S G	Leading-Sector Growth and Naval Capability Share Lag(-i) G N	Leading-Sector Growth and Naval Capability Share Lead(+i) N G
0	-0.360*	-0.360*a	-0.014	-0.014	0.157	0.157	0.046	0.046	0.457*	0.457*	0.312*	0.312*
1	-0.039	-0.098	-0.067	0.015	-0.417*	-0.039	0.270*	0.017	0.170	0.022	-0.091	0.070
2	-0.032	-0.035	0.154	-0.008	-0.024	0.093	0.340*	-0.077	-0.185	-0.003	-0.018	-0.022
3	-0.049	0.093	0.081	0.108	0.074	0.274*	0.216*	-0.073	-0.129	0.004	-0.004	0.136
4	-0.040	0.369*	-0.150	0.191	0.149	-0.064	0.127	0.031	-0.017	-0.083	-0.117	0.182
5	0.080	0.266*	-0.276*	0.126	0.002	-0.089	0.174	-0.109	-0.087	0.116	-0.097	-0.003
6	0.047	0.078	-0.129	0.089	-0.097	-0.076	0.166	-0.118	0.144	0.279*	0.054	-0.005
7	-0.007	0.004	0.132	-0.090	0.027	0.077	0.033	0.073	0.207*	0.083	0.141	0.089
8	-0.057	-0.039	0.184	-0.133	-0.097	-0.118	-0.211*	0.013	0.020	-0.094	-0.112	-0.155
9	-0.010	-0.089	-0.075	-0.196	0.119	0.041	-0.043	0.111	-0.162	-0.075	-0.022	0.140
10	0.049	-0.030	-0.197	-0.043	0.124	0.064	0.066	0.013	0.020	-0.094	-0.112	-0.055
11	0.048	-0.029	-0.098	0.126	0.058	0.005	-0.021	-0.153	-0.053	0.190	0.022	-0.039
12	0.038	-0.055	0.105	0.278*	-0.141	-0.112	-0.042	0.227*	-0.093	-0.048	-0.057	-0.152
13	-0.013	-0.058	0.026	0.064	-0.056	0.056	-0.030	-0.167	-0.091	0.071	0.014	-0.089
14	-0.069	0.290*	0.095	-0.043	-0.144	0.035	-0.188	-0.088	0.053	-0.098	-0.405*	0.127
15	-0.036	0.133	-0.002	-0.098	0.062	-0.002	-0.245*	-0.049	-0.161	-0.189	-0.213*	0.089
16	0.000	0.065	0.057	-0.089	0.006	0.017	-0.158	-0.027	-0.208*	-0.106	-0.125	0.065
17	0.003	-0.053	-0.038	-0.059	0.128	0.075	0.086	-0.011	0.053	0.039	0.037	0.093
18	-0.083	-0.228*	-0.015	0.117	-0.009	-0.164	0.097	-0.040	0.005	0.007	0.123	0.030
19	0.023	-0.156	0.100	-0.042	-0.141	-0.043	-0.137	-0.128	0.047	-0.045	-0.018	-0.077
20	0.032	-0.027	-0.047	-0.207*	0.061	0.133	-0.124	0.040	0.149	0.053	-0.057	0.056
SE	0.10	0.10	0.10	0.10	0.10	0.10	0.10	0.10	0.10	0.10	0.10	0.10

Note: W = war, N = naval capability share, S = leading-sector share, G = leading-sector growth rate, SE = standard error of the cross-correlations.

*p is less than or equal to .05

[a]The -0.360 coefficient is due to a sharp decrease in the military/GNP indicator in the aftermath of World Wars I and II. A cross-correlation of these two variables from 1870–1913 shows the first cross-correlational value to be 0.445*, while the 1950–80 value is -0.021.

tionship between war and naval capability share. When naval capability is causally prior to war, the cross-correlations are weak and close to zero. When war is causally prior, however, the cross-correlations are positive and statistically significant at lags 4 and 5. The relatively large -.360 correlation at lag 0 is the consequence of extreme outliers around world wars I and II. Specifically, a sharp decrease in the war indicator occurred in the aftermath of these wars. A cross-correlation of the same variables from 1870 to 1913 shows the first correlation value to be a statistically significant 0.445, while the 1950-80 value is -0.021.

The remaining cross-correlations between war and leading-sector share and leading-sector growth rate suggest two-way relationships. When leading-sector share precedes war, there is a strong negative correlation at lag 5; conversely, when war precedes leading-sector share, there is a strong positive value at lag 12. With leading-sector growth rate causally prior to war, the cross-correlation value is strong and negative at lag 1; there is a cross-correlation value of 0.274 at lag 3 when war precedes leading-sector growth rate.

In the case of Britain in the 1780-1913 period, the results are not as clear-cut. Table C.2 shows that the correlation between leading-sector share and naval capability share is highest at lags 9 and 10. When leading-sector share is causally prior to naval capability share, the correlations are slightly higher than in the reverse situation. The cross-correlations between leading-sector growth rate and leading-sector share show that the strongest association occurs at lag 0. The correlations between leading-sector growth rate and naval capability share indicate an association at lag 0 and at lag 7 when leading-sector growth rate is positioned causally prior to naval capability share.

The war and naval capability relationship appears to be one-way, as in the U.S. pattern. When war is causally prior to naval capability, we obtain a strong, positive cross-correlation at lag 5. When the relationship is reversed, the cross-correlations are weak and near zero. Two-way relationships emerge at this stage between war and leading-sector share. The cross-correlations are positive at lags 3 and 16, respectively, when leading-sector share is causally prior to war and when the two variables are reversed. The relationship between war and leading-sector growth rate appears to be one-way, with war causally prior to leading-sector growth rate at lag 5.

Time Series Regressions

The last data analysis for chapter 5 involves obtaining a more precise estimation of the relationships between the four variables. Although up to this point we have been able to discern where the variables fit together in a

Table C.2 Cross-Correlations: Britain, 1780–1913

i	War and Naval Capability Share		War and Leading-Sector Share		War and Leading-Sector Growth Rate		Leading-Sector Share and Naval Capability Share		Leading-Sector Growth and Leading-Sector Share		Leading-Sector Growth and Naval Capability Share	
	Lag (-i) N W	Lead (+i) W N	Lag (-i) S W	Lead (+i) W S	Lag (-i) G W	Lead (+i) W G	Lag (-i) S N	Lead (+i) N S	Lag (-i) G S	Lead (+i) S G	Lag (-i) G N	Lead (+i) N G
0	-0.173	-0.173	-0.147	-0.147	-0.168	-0.168	-0.033	-0.033	0.458*	0.458*	0.132	0.132
1	-0.149	-0.057	0.005	-0.142	0.029	0.049	-0.135	0.148	0.099	-0.278*	0.015	-0.003
2	-0.019	0.038	0.041	-0.177	-0.096	-0.049	-0.112	0.111	0.025	-0.110	-0.067	-0.074
3	0.057	0.160	0.211*	-0.039	-0.021	0.012	-0.026	0.114	-0.056	-0.065	-0.045	-0.067
4	0.008	0.123	0.093	0.052	0.015	0.100	-0.064	0.165	0.023	-0.003	-0.185	0.069
5	-0.055	0.190*	0.107	0.094	0.105	0.220*	0.039	-0.116	-0.081	-0.046	-0.150	-0.145
6	-0.119	0.168	-0.025	0.061	-0.091	0.035	0.116	-0.028	-0.010	-0.028	-0.093	-0.084
7	-0.084	-0.060	-0.098	-0.006	-0.133	-0.118	0.131	0.021	0.004	-0.090	0.200*	-0.107
8	-0.047	-0.013	0.007	-0.095	-0.055	-0.095	-0.038	-0.021	-0.015	0.014	-0.036	-0.096
9	-0.038	-0.024	0.142	-0.023	0.095	-0.004	0.185	0.153	-0.004	0.024	0.157	-0.029
10	-0.017	-0.095	0.065	0.137	0.081	0.058	0.197*	0.129	0.046	0.146	-0.011	-0.044
11	0.014	-0.066	-0.001	-0.137	0.064	-0.242	0.070	0.029	0.172	0.079	0.003	-0.021
12	0.079	0.055	0.035	-0.098	0.086	0.001	-0.015	0.065	-0.022	-0.099	-0.013	0.086
13	0.040	0.078	0.019	-0.105	0.091	-0.011	-0.014	-0.009	0.027	0.115	-0.059	-0.038
14	0.025	0.044	-0.051	-0.027	0.153	-0.011	-0.061	0.007	-0.050	-0.092	-0.023	0.126
15	0.033	0.086	-0.125	0.098	0.016	-0.036	0.092	-0.030	0.136	0.027	0.121	-0.008
16	-0.055	0.042	-0.169	0.218*	-0.134	0.012	0.146	0.000	-0.078	-0.163	0.098	0.047
17	-0.046	0.001	-0.151	0.111	-0.141	-0.028	0.171	-0.045	0.079	0.087	0.162	0.043
18	-0.063	-0.078	0.062	-0.020	-0.062	-0.050	0.095	-0.019	0.183	-0.037	0.004	0.022
19	-0.043	0.055	0.029	-0.078	0.053	0.031	0.056	0.030	0.081	-0.110	-0.188	0.083
20	-0.033	0.040	-0.106	-0.110	-0.028	0.075	0.114	-0.001	-0.032	-0.091	0.107	0.062
SE	0.09	0.09	0.09	0.09	0.09	0.09	0.09	0.09	0.09	0.09	0.09	0.09

Note: W = war, N = naval capability share, S = leading-sector share, G = leading-sector growth rate, SE = standard error of the cross-correlations.
*p is less than or equal to .05

Table C.3 Parameter Estimates for Relationships between Naval-Capability Share, Leading-Sector Share, Leading-Sector Growth Rate, and War

Variable	Coefficient	t statistic	F statistic	Durbin Watson statistic
United States: 1870–1980				
Dependent variable: naval-capability share				
Constant	0.001	0.24		
Leading-sector share lagged 2 years	0.927*	3.74*	14.0*	1.82
Dependent variable: naval capability share				
Constant	0.004	0.74		
Leading-sector growth rate	14.21*	3.36*		
Moving Average	0.228	2.36*	8.9*	1.98
Dependent variable: leading-sector share				
Constant	0.003	1.54		
Leading-sector growth rate	8.10*	5.79*		
Moving Average	0.36*	3.73*	22.9*	1.99
Dependent variable: naval-capability share				
Constant	0.005	0.83		
War lagged 5 years	0.221*	2.38*		
Moving Average	—		11.36*	1.80
Britain: 1780–1913				
Dependent variable: naval-capability share				
Constant	0.001	0.55		
Leading-sector share lagged 10 years	0.163*	2.00*		
Moving Average	0.184*	1.99*	4.58*	1.99
Dependent variable: naval-capability share				
Constant	0.000	0.27		
Leading-sector growth rate lagged 7 years	0.974*	2.54*		
Moving Average	0.265*	2.92*	7.11*	1.99
Dependent variable: naval-capability share				
Constant	0.000	—		
War lagged 5 years	0.152*	2.08*		
Moving Average	0.178*	2.00*	4.49*	1.99

p is less than or equal to 0.05.

causal process, we have yet to obtain the exact nature of these relationships in parameter estimates. In all instances, we will calculate bivariate relationships, recognizing that these are preliminary findings until a full specification of our theoretical model is feasible. As a result, we do not report R-square values because the primary purpose of this exercise is to reaffirm the statistical results obtained from the cross-correlational analysis and the Granger tests of antecedence.

In the U.S. case, we have estimated four time series regression equations. The specifications of the equations are based on the earlier tests of antecedence in table 5.2. The statistically significant relationships form the basis of the parameter estimates in table C.3. The first equation in table C.3 regresses the naval capability share series on leading-sector share, and the parameter estimate is derived from ordinary least- squares calculations. As expected, the relationship yields a statistically significant coefficient. The two following equations in table C.3 are based on generalized least-squares estimation due to the presence of a significant moving average process. In the second equation, leading-sector growth rate, as the independent variable, is significantly related to the naval capability share series. And in the third equation, leading-sector growth rate is also significantly related to leading-sector share. All three of these equations yield residuals with white-noise characteristics.

Table C.3 also provides the generalized least-squares estimates for the regression coefficients for Britain. Although table 5.3 identifies several significant relationships, we have estimated only two of the relationships that do not involve the war variable because of misspecification problems. The naval capability share series is regressed on leading-sector share and leading-sector growth rate separately. As the results demonstrate, statistically significant relationships emerge. The residuals are also white noise in both of these equations.

At this point, we are only in a position to estimate a bivariate relationship between war and naval capability share for both the United States and Britain, since they have clear unidirectional associations. Estimating the remaining two-way relationships via a generalized least-squares approach would be fruitless, since we would run into both identification and misspecification problems.

Nevertheless, table C.3 provides another piece of evidence. In both national cases, the war coefficients are positive and statistically significant. In the U.S. case, the relationship appears at lags 4 and 5; for Britain, it appears at lag 5.

Table C.4 Coefficients Derived from Bivariate Vector Autoregressions:
Britain, 1831–1913 (annual data)

Independent Variable		Dependent Variable				
		EG	I	PC	GC	M
EG	(lag 1)	—	2.00*	0.06	0.88	0.88
	(lag 2)	—	0.00	0.08	0.53	0.62
	(lag 3)	—	-0.27	0.04	0.05	0.53
	(lag 4)	—	0.04	-0.03	1.50*	0.61
	(lag 5)	—	-1.80*	0.14	0.17	0.47
	(lag 6)	—	0.16	0.09	1.20	-0.18
I	(lag 1)	0.08*	—	-0.01	0.01	-0.02
	(lag 2)	0.02	—	0.00	0.02	0.01
	(lag 3)	-0.05*	—	0.01	0.03	0.06
	(lag 4)	0.01	—	0.02*	-0.03	0.09
	(lag 5)	0.01	—	0.00	0.07	-0.04
	(lag 6)	0.01	—	-0.01	0.03	-0.04
PC	(lag 1)	-0.21	-0.11	—	1.06	-1.60
	(lag 2)	0.06	-1.90	—	2.20	-0.62
	(lag 3)	0.06	1.60	—	0.39	0.25
	(lag 4)	0.15	0.58	—	0.55	-0.12
	(lag 5)	0.04	0.22	—	-1.20	0.01
	(lag 6)	-0.06	-0.71	—	-9.20	0.82
GC	(lag 1)	0.00	-0.11	-0.02	—	0.29*
	(lag 2)	0.00	-0.09	-0.02	—	0.24*
	(lag 3)	0.01	0.04	-0.01	—	0.19*
	(lag 4)	-0.01	-0.19	-0.03*	—	0.04
	(lag 5)	0.00	0.17	-0.03*	—	0.01
	(lag 6)	0.02	0.39	-0.03*	—	0.01
M	(lag 1)	0.02	-0.16	0.02	-0.61*	—
	(lag 2)	-0.02	0.14	0.01	-0.34	—
	(lag 3)	0.01	-0.08	0.00	0.16	—
	(lag 4)	0.01	-0.02	0.02	0.13	—
	(lag 5)	0.01	0.08	-0.02	-0.08	—
	(lag 6)	0.00	-0.29	0.02	-0.03	—

lag structure = 2, 6

*p is less than or equal to .05

EG = Economic Growth, I = Investment, PC = Private Consumption, GC = Nonmilitary Public Consumption, M = Military Spending.

Table C.5 Coefficients Derived from Bivariate Vector Autoregressions:
United States, 1950–1986 (annual data)

Independent Variable		Dependent Variable						
		EG	P	I	PC	GC	M	D
EG	(lag 0)	—	0.56*	6.20*	-0.43*	-0.93*	-2.60	-0.73
	(lag 1)	—	-0.33*	3.80*	-0.11	-0.91*	-0.21	-7.60*
	(lag 2)	—	0.04	2.20	-0.03	0.18	-0.31	3.70
	(lag 3)	—	-0.08	-1.50	0.07	-0.09	0.78	-4.90
	(lag 4)	—	0.19	2.30*	0.09	0.77*	-0.02	1.80
P	(lag 0)	1.10*	—	4.50*	-0.44*	1.20*	-1.50*	15.70*
	(lag 1)	-0.18	—	0.59	0.16	-0.68	-0.72	-7.30*
	(lag 2)	0.16	—	3.30	-0.13	-0.49	-0.99	-5.10
	(lag 3)	0.17	—	0.33	-0.13	0.28	0.75	5.30
	(lag 4)	0.21	—	-0.59	0.01	1.20*	1.10	4.50
I	(lag 0)	0.13	0.04*	—	-0.06*	-0.18*	-0.38*	-0.83*
	(lag 1)	-0.01	-0.06	—	0.00	-0.05	0.03	-0.90*
	(lag 2)	0.08*	0.01	—	-0.02*	-0.01	-0.08	-0.45
	(lag 3)	-0.02	-0.01	—	-0.01	0.08	0.11	-0.32
	(lag 4)	0.05	0.00	—	0.00	-0.03	-0.09	-0.21
PC	(lag 0)	-2.10*	-1.10*	-17.70*	—	-0.96	5.30*	7.60
	(lag 1)	0.02	0.63*	-4.80	—	0.96	0.35	14.10*
	(lag 2)	-0.41	-0.51	-0.94	—	-1.20	0.76	-1.00
	(lag 3)	0.12	-0.12	-5.30*	—	2.80*	-1.00	5.50
	(lag 4)	0.28	-0.02	0.04	—	-0.23	0.92	0.04
GC	(lag 0)	-0.31*	0.24*	-3.30*	-0.02	—	0.45	2.50*
	(lag 1)	0.14	0.15*	-0.56	0.01	—	-0.36	-0.43
	(lag 2)	-0.15	0.00	0.57	-0.01	—	-0.53*	2.60*
	(lag 3)	0.12	-0.04	0.34	-0.01	—	-0.88*	0.83
	(lag 4)	0.02	0.01	-0.16	-0.03	—	-0.02	0.36
M	(lag 0)	-0.21*	-0.08*	-1.70*	0.10*	0.18	—	0.62
	(lag 1)	0.04	-0.05	-0.15	0.00	0.04	—	1.20*
	(lag 2)	-0.04	-0.04	0.09	0.02	-0.20	—	-0.81
	(lag 3)	-0.02	-0.01	0.22	0.00	-0.13	—	-1.40*
	(lag 4)	-0.06	-0.03	-0.87*	0.03	0.09	—	-0.04
D	(lag 0)	-0.00	0.04	-0.29*	0.01	0.16*	0.04	—
	(lag 1)	0.02	0.04	-0.18	-0.01	-0.03	-0.02	—
	(lag 2)	0.01	0.02	0.08	0.00	-0.05	-0.09	—
	(lag 3)	-0.00	-0.00	-0.09	0.00	-0.01	-0.04	—
	(lag 4)	0.00	0.02*	-0.04	-0.00	0.05	-0.01	—

lag structure = 4, 4.
*p is less than or equal to .05
EG = Economic Growth, P = Productivity, I = Investment, PC = Private Consumption, GC = Nonmilitary Public Consumption, M = Military Spending, D = Government Deficits.

Table C.6 Partial List of Coefficients Derived from Multivariate Vector Autoregressions: United States, 1954–1986 (quarterly data)

Independent Variable		Dependent Variable			
		I	PC	GC	M
I	(lag 0)	—	0.02*	-0.04	-0.04
	(lag 1)	—	-0.01	-0.02	0.00
	(lag 2)	—	-0.02	0.02	0.00
	(lag 3)	—	0.03	0.03	-0.02
	(lag 4)	—	-0.00	0.05	0.03
PC	(lag 0)	-2.20*	—	0.73*	0.11
	(lag 1)	-1.60	—	-0.01	-0.36
	(lag 2)	-1.50	—	0.19	0.01
	(lag 3)	-2.60*	—	0.14	-0.21
	(lag 4)	-0.33	—	0.53*	0.03
GC	(lag 0)	-0.54	0.08*	—	0.00
	(lag 1)	-0.64	-0.01	—	0.02
	(lag 2)	-0.21	-0.01	—	-0.15
	(lag 3)	0.41	-0.03	—	-0.09
	(lag 4)	-0.39	0.02	—	-0.25*
M	(lag 0)	-0.29	0.01	-0.01	—
	(lag 1)	-0.43	-0.02	-0.03	—
	(lag 2)	-0.38	-0.01	0.00	—
	(lag 3)	0.06	-0.02	0.09	—
	(lag 4)	-0.26	0.03	0.08	—

*p is less than or equal to .05

I = Investment, PC = Private Consumption, GC = Nonmilitary Public Consumption, M = Military Spending.

Table C.7 Coefficients Derived from Bivariate Vector Autoregressions:
Britain, 1950–1980 (annual data)

Independent Variable		Dependent Variable				
		EG	I	PC	GC	M[a]
EG	(lag 0)[b]	—	1.39*	—	—	—
	(lag 1)	—	1.63*	0.17	0.39	0.16
	(lag 2)	—	0.88	-0.06	1.58*	-0.13
	(lag 3)	—	0.95	-0.09	-0.05	-0.15
	(lag 4)	—	0.53	0.06	0.63	-0.73
	(lag 5)	—	0.43	-0.19*	-0.49	-1.42*
	(lag 6)	—	0.26	0.09	0.21	-1.05*
I	(lag 0)[b]	0.44*	—	—	—	—
	(lag 1)	-0.36	—	0.02	0.39*	0.19
	(lag 2)	-0.06	—	-0.05	0.65*	-0.21
	(lag 3)	0.18	—	-0.09	-0.21	-0.01
	(lag 4)	0.10	—	0.03	-0.05	-0.87*
	(lag 5)	0.23	—	0.01	-0.71*	-0.81*
	(lag 6)	0.09	—	0.09	-0.15	-0.23
PC	(lag 1)	0.65	0.78	—	1.04	1.09
	(lag 2)	0.78	2.47*	—	1.94*	0.76
	(lag 3)	-0.51	-0.54	—	2.20*	1.75
	(lag 4)	0.80	0.74	—	0.89	-0.83
	(lag 5)	0.32	0.16	—	-0.44	1.72
	(lag 6)	0.76	0.66	—	-0.14	-1.68
GC	(lag 1)	0.09	0.15	-0.06	—	0.13
	(lag 2)	-0.08	-0.27	-0.04	—	0.03
	(lag 3)	0.07	-0.08	0.01	—	-0.26
	(lag 4)	0.05	-0.22	0.00	—	0.04
	(lag 5)	-0.05	0.09	0.03	—	0.37*
	(lag 6)	-0.07	-0.33	0.00	—	0.58*
M	(lag 1)	-0.01	-0.09	-0.04	0.17	—
	(lag 2)	-0.06	-0.11	-0.01	-0.42	—
	(lag 3)	-0.02	-0.12	-0.06	0.00	—
	(lag 4)	-0.08	-0.05	-0.04	-0.02	—
	(lag 5)	0.02	-0.04	-0.01	0.01	—
	(lag 6)	-0.07	-0.01	-0.01	-0.16	—

[a] Relationships involving military spending are based on 1953–80 data.

[b] Coefficients for lag 0 are used for instantaneous tests of antecedence. Only significant coefficients are displayed.

Lag structure = 2, 6.

*p is less than or equal to .05

EG = Economic Growth, I = Investment, PC = Private Consumption, GC = Nonmilitary Public Consumption, M = Military Spending.

Notes

1. An Overview of the Theoretical Argument

    1. Thompson (1988) reviews the overlap in the attributes that they discuss.

    2. Olson (1982) has developed a theory of decline focused almost exclusively on these types of institutional rigidities.

2. Tracing the Rise and Fall of Regional and Global Powers

    1. Dehio (1888-1963) was a German historian and archivist whose professional career spanned the period from the early 1920s to the mid-1950s. He developed his historical interpretation in response to mainstream German historians who he felt had seriously misread Germany's situation, especially before World War I, and thereby had contributed to the German defeat in both wars. Briefly, Dehio felt that the basic error was the assumption that Germany could attempt to improve its relative standing as a world power without being seen as an acute threat by British decision makers. This assumption, Dehio argued, stemmed from a tendency to view world politics as if it functioned along the same lines as continental or regional balancing politics, when, indeed, the two spheres operated on different principles. In his 1962 book, *The Precarious Balance*, Dehio attempted to spell out just what the rules of the world game had been in the 1494-1945 era. A second book (Dehio 1967) requires some familiarity with the 1962 book and can be misleading because it focuses almost exclusively on German foreign policy of the late nineteenth and early twentieth centuries. Dehio did not view these policies as fully isomorphic with the activities of earlier aspirants to regional hegemony. Dehio's concerns in the 1967 book also lead to his emphasizing the significance of the opposing maritime coalition at the expense of discussing the historical role of the eastern flank.

    2. It is clear that the eastern and western flanks did not always operate simultaneously. The most obvious cases include the Franco-Ottoman coalition against the Hapsburgs in the mid-sixteenth century, the French Revolution and the Napoleonic Wars, and World Wars I and II. The western flank operated in all cases of global war after the mid-sixteenth century, and the eastern flank never operated alone. Both Philip II and Louis XIV, however, found themselves fighting on two fronts. Thus, the two-front strategic error has been more common than the simultaneous operation of both flanks.

3. The question of what motivated German decision makers in 1914 is a controversial one. One clever resolution of the debate and a useful introduction to the debates within German historiography (Levy 1990-91) summarizes the preference structures of the main adversaries in terms of their policy proclivities toward a negotiated settlement, a local Balkan war, a regional war pitting Germany and Austria-Hungary versus France and Russia, and a world war involving the participation of Britain. Levy sees the German preference order as first local war, then regional war, then negotiated settlement, and finally world war. Thus, Levy and Dehio end up agreeing that war in 1914 was not initiated on the part of the Germans to seize regional hegemony but for much different reasons.

4. Note that two western sea powers (the Netherlands and Britain) are found in the regional list. They also had some leeway in deciding whether to intervene in Western European affairs. Their locations, though, despite their watery insularity, marked them as members of the region. This was particularly the case for the Netherlands and certainly applies to England/Britain most strongly before 1714. Portugal, on the other hand, was never a great land power in the European region. More generally, Tilly (1990: 171) notes that this type of Eurocentric bias in assembling a list of major powers overlooks large and powerful armies in China, West Africa, Persia, India, Mexico, and South America, especially in the fifteenth and sixteenth centuries. He is certainly right, but the current emphasis on Europe as a regional system neutralizes the power of the criticism for this examination.

5. See Zolberg 1981 for a forceful and non-Dehioan reminder of the importance of the sixteenth-century Ottoman role.

6. The maximum size of the Ottoman army in the late fifteenth and the sixteenth centuries was probably on the order of 200,000 men. In comparison, the size of the united Hapsburg army peaked at around 150,000 men in the middle of the sixteenth century.

7. See Wohlforth 1987 for an interesting discussion of the problems associated with estimating Russian capabilities immediately before World War I.

8. The dates used for splicing purposes are not quite the same as the long cycle leadership periods. The modifications are made to pick up the transitions more smoothly than would be the case if one waited for the end of the global war before switching the leadership focus.

9. An anonymous reviewer of an earlier version of this chapter once suggested that it is odd that alternating cycles should have been more conducive to European balancing than synchronous cycles, in which one type of power would have been readily available to match or balance the other type. Although synchronization seems more logical, one's view of the European alternations depends on how one interprets the pattern. The pattern might better be labeled "synchronized alternation" if one emphasizes the tendency for a declining global power to encourage an ascending regional power, which in turn leads to a reconcentration of global power in order to suppress the regional threat.

3. Global and Regional Transitions

1. See, among others, Siverson 1980; Thompson 1988; Houweling and Siccama 1988; Kugler and Organski 1989; Kim 1989, 1991, 1992; Kim and Morrow 1992; and Geller 1992a, 1992b. Geller's work is particularly innovative in its combination of transition analysis with information on systemic attributes, thereby tapping

into more than one level of analysis. The work to be published in Kugler and Lemke (forthcoming) represents the outcome of an intensive conference on the subject of analyzing transitions that was held at the Claremont Graduate School in October 1992.

2. A rather liberal twenty-year interval is the norm in power transition analyses.

3. The approach of the Portuguese can be described as crude because they were usually more interested in controlling trade than in participating in it as traders.

4. We are indebted to James Morrow for suggesting this approach at the presentation of an earlier version of this chapter.

5. In his emphasis on the German concern for Russian positional gains, Levy (1987, 1990-91) suggests an entirely different transitional focus for the 1914 case. Rather than focusing on Britain, the Germans are said to have desired a preventive war to keep from falling behind the Russians. The difference of opinion registered here seems to be reducible to whether German decision makers were more concerned, in our terms, with a global or interregional transition. The answer does not have to be one or the other; it is more likely one detailing which decision makers were more concerned about which threats at particular times and their relative influence on strategic decision making in 1914. Unfortunately, we must leave the detailed analysis of specific cases to another time and place.

4. Concentration and Transitional Warfare

1. Some of the better-known statements on the subject are found in Deutsch and Singer 1964; Singer, Bremer, and Stuckey 1972; Waltz 1979; and Gilpin 1981.

2. See, for example, Bueno de Mesquita and Lalman 1988; Doran 1989b; and Jervis 1991-92.

3. Two earlier efforts are Modelski 1974 and Rapkin and Thompson with Christopherson 1979.

4. Our interpretation can be readily translated into polarity terms, but there are additional complications pertaining to the crude measures associated with polarity categorizations that can be best dealt with in a separate analysis.

5. Empirical justification for isolating these wars as a distinctive category is presented in appendix B. While it is true that these wars are very much coalitional efforts, we do not view our task as one of predicting the identities of alliance members or of calculating relative alliance capabilities to measure concentration. The ultimate identity of the coalitions usually emerges only after the war has begun. Thus we view the coalition question as more important to who wins the war than to why the wars began.

5. Innovation, Decline, and War

1. A useful overview of long-wave theoretical debates can be found in Goldstein 1988.

2. See Schumpeter 1939; Mensch 1979; Hartman and Wheeler 1979; Bousquet 1980; Kleinknecht 1981, 1987; Freeman, Clark, and Soete 1982; and Kogane 1988.

3. See Mandel 1975, 1980; Gordon 1980; and Boswell 1987.

4. See Kondratieff 1984; Graham and Senge 1980; Forrester 1981; and Sterman 1985.

5. Examples include Rostow 1978, 1985; Lewis 1978; Marchetti 1980; Modelski 1981, 1982; and Volland 1987.

6. See, for example, Thompson and Zuk 1982 and Thompson 1988.

7. Examples of this type of argument can be found in Kondratieff [1935] 1979; Imbert 1959; Vayrynen 1983; Craig and Watt 1985; and Goldstein 1988.

8. See Hohenberg and Lees 1985 and Goldstone 1991 for arguments bestowing primacy on population changes as the primary driver of long waves.

9. Rostow (1978) does not elaborate on why this should be the case. Presumably an aging sector has had time to become critical to a large proportion of the economy. Another possibility is that large and mature industries make it difficult for new, more innovative firms to emerge. Suppliers and the general economic infrastructure are geared to the older ways of doing things. In addition, venture capital may also be difficult to obtain within a decaying environment. Hoerr (1988: 592-93) applies these arguments to the decline of American steel in the Pittsburgh area.

10. The "active zone" concept is from Perroux 1979. See, in addition, Thompson 1988: 113-24, for a discussion of system leader definitions articulated by Modelski (1981, 1982, 1987), Keohane (1984), and Wallerstein (1984). One of the arguments of that analysis is that leading sectors lie at the heart of these definitions as well.

11. Modelski (1987: 217-33) provides a fuller discussion of the prerequisites for system leadership. Modelski and Thompson (1988) explore five hundred years of concentration and deconcentration in naval global-reach capabilities. For different theoretical slants on the rise of a globally oriented ruling coalition, see Modelski 1987: 161-93, and Frieden 1988.

12. Olson's (1982) thesis on distributional coalitions raises the interesting question of whether vested interests are a significant cause of decline or simply more likely to increase their political activities in the context of sectoral decline. Olson argues for the former interpretation, but we are inclined toward the latter view.

13. By 1914 the United States was producing 95 percent or more of the world's motor vehicles. The proportion remained above 50 percent until 1958.

14. The growth-slowing processes and practices that are intrinsic in aging industrial sectors are no less complicated than the other facets of systemic leadership decline. Some useful discussions of the nineteenth-century British case can be found in Levine 1967 and Elbaum and Lazonick 1986.

15. The primary data sources for Rostow's indicators include Mitchell 1980, 1982; U.S. Department of Commerce 1975; and several different United Nations yearbooks. Hammond 1897, Hammond and Hammond 1926, Plummer 1937, Svennilson 1954, Lamar 1957, Koh 1966, Deane and Cole 1967, Aldcroft 1970, Banks 1971, Price 1981, and U.S. Office of the President 1988 were used as supplementary sources. Motor Vehicle Manufacturers Association 1981 is the principal source for the motor vehicles information. Tilton 1971, Malerba 1985, and Organization for Economic Cooperation and Development 1985 were used to estimate semiconductor production. *Economist* 1986 provided the jet aircraft data. While this data proved useful in calculating relative leading-sector shares, the purpose for which the data were collected originally, the often negative growth rates performed erratically and appeared to depress or elevate average growth rates unduly. Their analytical usefulness is also compromised to some extent by the large, continuing American production share. Consequently, the aerospace indicator was not used in computing the average leading-sector scores analyzed in this chapter.

16. The U.S. military expenditure and GNP data are based on information reported in U.S. Department of Commerce 1975, Berry 1978, and U.S. Office of the President 1988. The British data are taken from Mitchell (1988). The Goldstein series is logged great power battle fatalities based on Levy's (1983) data.

17. In our experience, focusing on both cross-correlation and Granger causality is not a redundant exercise because it is possible for different conclusions to emerge from the two types of analysis. It is true that cross-correlations cannot account for internal or self-driven variable responses, but the advantage of cross-correlation is that it gives us some idea of the degree of instantaneous correlation among the variables. Nevertheless, the strength of our findings will be enhanced to the extent that the two approaches to the data produce compatible results. All reported findings were computed using MicroTSP software.

6. Perspectives on Overconsumption and Decline

1. See Yoffee 1991 for the Babylonian interpretation.

2. The Greek authors reviewed by de Romilly (1977) do not encompass the full life of the Roman Empire. The emphasis on the corruptions of prosperity, however, was continued by later Roman writers. See Walbank 1969 and Ferrill 1986 for brief overviews. Pelikan (1987: 3-12) also discusses the influence of interpretations of Roman decline on the writings of Edmund Burke, Adam Smith, Alexander Hamilton, James Madison, Alexis de Tocqueville, Karl Marx, Oswald Spengler, and Hannah Arendt. Gibbon, the eighteenth-century historian of Rome, clearly fits into this group as well: "The decline of Rome was the natural and inevitable effect of immoderate greatness. Prosperity ripened the principle of decay; the causes of destruction multiplied with the extent of conquest; and as soon as time or accident had removed the artificial supports, the stupendous fabric yielded to the pressure of its own weight" (1960: 524).

3. Tainter (1988) acknowledges fourteenth- and fifteenth-century decline explanations by Petrarch, Flavio Biondo, Leonardo Bruni Aretino, Antonio Agostino, and Machiavelli. But these were Roman-specific explanations and not general models of decline. One indication of the staying power of Ibn Khaldun's argument is the existence of strong parallels in Reischauer and Fairbanks's (1960) model for Chinese dynasties.

4. See Eisenstadt 1963 for a much different interpretation of imperial public consumption. Eisenstadt argues that decline is brought on by rulers who exhaust the resources that remain accessible to them.

5. For example, compare Chace 1988 and Kahler 1988. Chace argues for a particular approach to the restoration of solvency, while Kahler argues that the effect of an ambitious foreign policy on economic performance depends in part on a state's position in the system. Hegemons are more likely to suffer negative effects than are middle-ranking states, such as pre-World War II Japan.

6. See Block 1987 for a similar position, but one expressed within a fuller theoretical argument about why the linkages between investment and productivity growth should not be overemphasized.

7. In contrast, Block (1987) argues that there is little empirical basis for claims that high social welfare spending has sapped the vitality of the U.S. economy, or that cutbacks are a precondition for further economic growth. He contends that an expan-

sion of social welfare spending might well be the best way to restore U.S. economic strength.

8. See Friedman 1985, 1988; Friedman and Friedman 1981; Scott 1985; Thurow 1985; Peterson 1987; Peterson and Howe 1988.

9. A more thorough discussion of the relevant radical literature on this issue can be found in Burris 1984. It should be noted that Bowles, Gordon and Weisskipf (1983) acknowledge the role of U.S. hegemonic decline as a factor in declining productivity. Despite this overlap with leadership decline viewpoints, their positions are similar to those of scholars whose explanations emphasize falling profit rates (Glyn and Sutcliffe 1972; Boddy and Crotty 1975; and Castells 1980).

10. See O'Connor 1973, 1981; Offe 1975, 1984; Wright 1979; and Cox 1987.

7. The Case against Tradeoffs as a Primary Cause of Decline

1. The first four waves were 1957-58 with Soviet missile launches and *Sputnik*, the late 1960s with Nixon and détente, 1973 with the OPEC oil embargo, and the end of the 1970s with Soviet expansion in Afghanistan, Angola, and Mozambique.

2. Along similar lines, Doran (1971: 16-17) points out that there is a critical difference between empire and what he calls hegemony. Empires involve direct attempts to control a given imperial territory. Hegemony (or system leadership), however, is more likely to emphasize indirect control through the radiated influence of concentrated wealth and military power. Presumably, the formal institutions of empire need not behave in the same way as the more informal institutions of systemic leadership. For more discussion of the unique character of the modern system leaders, see Modelski 1987: 217-33.

3. While the standard operating procedures usually have been reinstated in a post-global war era, governmental activities do not return to the prewar level (Rasler and Thompson 1989).

4. A different type of illustration is provided by Barnett (1986), who traces British decline to World War II and its immediate aftermath.

5. Here and elsewhere in this examination, nonmilitary public consumption estimates are created by subtracting military expenditures from public consumption accounts. Technically, this is not entirely appropriate, because all public or military consumption cannot be regarded as consumption. Some of it is investment. Some compromises with accuracy, however, can be expected in creating longitudinal series.

6. Some of the complications inherent to modeling consumption are well illustrated by Hall (1978). We regard these complications as well as the question of how consumers determine their appropriate consumption levels as distant from our immediate concerns with whether or not evidence exists for a negative relationship between types of consumption and especially investment.

7. Relevant data are simply not available for the Dutch case. See Riley 1984 and Israel 1989 for discussions of the complications associated with treating this early case. Schama (1988), on the other hand, discusses the collective angst associated with the Dutch embarrassment of riches.

8. Addressing the specific problems of American decline, Gilpin (1987) modifies his 1981 causal chain somewhat but retains a similar form. Increased protection costs owing to the Soviet military threat, increased competition from newly indus-

trialized economies, and losses of energy, technological, and agricultural monopolies have diminished the hegemon's capacity. In particular, though, the Reagan administration budget deficits are singled out as responsible for accelerating the positional deterioration of the United States. Savings are reduced, domestic investment declines, and capital accumulation suffers as a consequence. A decline in capital accumulation leads to slower productivity growth and accelerated deindustrialization. Although we are most unlikely to capture any long-term effects of deficit spending, this type of consumption is examined in order to be as fair as possible to Gilpin's argument. See, as well, Calleo 1992.

9. This is the same measure used in Rasler 1990, but it differs from the crude indicator of investment, gross fixed capital formation, employed in Rasler and Thompson 1988. Nevertheless, the two indicators are better than moderately correlated. For our theoretical purposes, it is clear that a net measure is preferable to a gross investment indicator.

10. These transformations are generally required in Granger causality analyses. The log transformation ensures that all of the variables are linear covariance, stationary, stochastic time series. Differencing preserves stationarity by eliminating trend in the data. It also frequently removes the presence of first-order autocorrelation from the residuals. In this instance, the transformations yield white-noise time series.

11. The literature is not specific about what lag structure best captures the relationships. We initiated each examination using a conventional, symmetrical (both endogenous and exogenous variables) lag structure of four years. If no or few significant relationships emerged, we then tried six- and eight-year symmetrical lags. Less conservative, asymmetrical lags (four and six years lagged on two years) constituted the third and final trial. Obviously, an element of subjectivity is introduced by this lag search strategy. It is our responsibility to report any major deviations from the reported findings that are associated with lag structures that are not discussed. As it happens, there are no major deviations associated with our two system leader cases to report. As in chapter 6, here the vector autoregression results were obtained from the MicroTSP econometrics package. Chi-square statistics were calculated for the residuals of each bivariate equation. The statistics showed that the residuals were characterized by a white-noise process. Moreover, the first two rho values were zero or less than 0.30. A few data points were removed selectively from some series to avoid serious problems with residual outliers. Seemingly unrelated regression estimation is used in the event that there is residual correlation across the equations.

12. No significant instantaneous relationships emerged in the nineteenth-century British case.

13. Quarterly data on all of the American economic performance variables could not be found, in part because they are not calculated on that type of temporal basis. Since our primary interest is focused on the consumption-investment relationships, finding a similar investment variable was considered crucial to making the quarterly undertaking worthwhile. The net investment measure that we have used for the annual analyses is one of those categories that is not calculated quarterly because it involves capital depreciation corrections. With the assistance of analysts in the Department of Commerce's Bureau of Economic Analysis and the Federal Reserve Board, we were able to locate Federal Reserve Board Flow of Funds data, from which we could construct a close equivalent to our principal annual dependent vari-

able. This measure corrects gross, private, fixed, nonresidential plant and equipment investment by first removing the financial corporation portion and then subtracting total capital consumption with capital consumption adjustments after removing the owner-occupied homes and financial business subcategories. We are grateful to Betsy Fogler of the Board of Governors of the Federal Reserve System for making available the raw data in a timely fashion. We are solely responsible for what was done subsequently with the data.

14. The statistical results associated with our net investment variable (net non-residential, nonfinancial, fixed domestic investment as a proportion of net domestic product of nonfinancial corporate business) do hinge on employing an indicator that removes as much of the "noise" in the investment concept as possible. Somewhat late in our data analysis, we discovered that different results emerge when one employs a gross fixed investment indicator. Simple tests of antecedence do not reveal any tradeoff relationships between gross fixed investment and any of the three main consumption variables. Instantaneous tests, however, do pinpoint two-way, negative relationships between private nonmilitary consumption and gross fixed investment. We interpret these particular findings more as supporting the Keynesian accounting identity on which Gilpin's argument is based than as a serious contradiction of the findings associated with our net investment measure.

15. Another research design element is the question of appropriate level of analysis. Commenting on an earlier version of this chapter, Christopher Chase-Dunn noted that we approached the question of overconsumption strictly from a societal perspective, thereby overlooking the possibility that consumption problems are segmented by class. Rather than looking at whole societies overconsuming, we should expect such behavior to be concentrated within the upper classes. While we are unwilling to dismiss this observation out of hand, our own view, admittedly one that we have yet to test, is that relative decline processes accentuate class polarization rather than the other way around. Nonetheless, there does seem to be some room for a reciprocal relationship. One examination of the inequality consequences of American decline is Blumberg 1980.

16. We can stipulate that Britain after World War I and even more clearly after World War II was no longer engaged in systemic leadership decline per se. This observation is not meant to suggest that Britain ceased to experience relative decline. Positional erosion continued, but the question of systemic leadership was no longer involved. Nevertheless, more than one economic historian has confessed to feelings of déjà vu when confronted with analyzing British political economy developments since the late 1940s. As Kirby put it, "The literature on Britain's postwar economic ills is vast: managerial weaknesses, excessive trade union power and restrictive practices, an anachronistic social structure, an inadequate education system. The rising tide of government expenditure and weaknesses in government economic policy generally—all of these hypotheses and more have their supporters and all of them, either singly or in some combination, are regarded as primarily responsible for Britain's alleged failures as an industrial and trading actor. The element of déjà vu lies in the fact that a substantially similar list of weaknesses can and . . . has been applied to the British economy in the 1870-1914 period" (1981: 105-6).

Kirby goes on to suggest that a number of post-World War II analyses of Britain's problems are ahistorical in the sense that the direct link between post-1945 policy problems and pre-1914 problem origins is too often overlooked. The historical continuity emphasis on British decline problems is not unique to Kirby. Adams (1982), Eatwell (1982), Gamble (1981), and Weiner (1981) also take this approach in a variety of ways. For alternative views, see Pollard (1982, 1989); and Barnett (1986).

17. The three consumption variables are expressed annually as proportions of GNP (Mitchell 1988). Investment, from the same source, is fixed domestic capital as a proportion of GNP. Economic growth is measured in GDP per capita (Maddison 1979, 1982, 1987). Each variable is logged and first differenced. The findings reported in this part of the chapter represent a structure involving six values of the antecedent variable linked to two values of the variable that it is predicting. Once a choice is made as to which lagged results should be reported, it is our responsibility to note any major deviations associated with different lag structures. We have none to report. Finally, the separate tests for instantaneous relationships revealed new information in only two cases. Consequently, we report only the two exceptions.

18. The easiest explanation for the limited impact of British military spending before World War I is Britain's exploitation of inexpensive Indian troops for many of its imperial undertakings. The topic is discussed further in Thompson and Zuk (1986).

For more general literature on military spending tradeoffs, see Lindgren (1984), Chan (1985), Kupchan (1989), and Gold (1990). Empirical analyses of British military spending include Smith (1977, 1978, 1980, 1992); Chester (1978); Hartley and McLean (1978); and Cappelen, Gleditsch, and Bjerkholt (1984).

19. Maddison (1991: 160) suggests quite tentatively that the explanation for the empirical difficulties in modeling U.S. productivity slowdown is that "there has been a slow-down in the rate of technical progress" that would account for other economic factors not explaining leader slowdown while capturing follower slowdown reasonably well.

8. Observations on Overextension and Territorial Traps

1. The interpretation advanced in this chapter may appear to disagree with Kennedy's more generic approach to imperial overstretch. But in a 1990 letter to one of the authors (Thompson), Kennedy acknowledged that a state's capacities and obligations logically can become imbalanced either by increasing the state's ends (as in intensive war participation) or by experiencing shrinking means (as in the loss of economic competitiveness) or both. He referred to the first type as the German variant and to the second type as the British variant. Thus, the amount of overlap in the two interpretations is in fact greater than might otherwise appear to be the case.

2. In addition to paying the charges for military operations within India, the Indian government also helped defray the costs of nineteenth-century campaigns in Afghanistan, China, Persia, Abyssinia, Egypt, and Sudan (Mukerjee 1972: 200). Data on the expenditures of the British Indian government were obtained from United Kingdom, Parliament, Sessional Papers 1857-58 to 1914-16 and Dutt 1956. British naval spending information is found in Chandaman 1975 and Mitchell with Deane 1962.

3. Some analysts might prefer an allegedly more discriminating measure, such as battle deaths, but in much British imperial warfare, casualties were concentrated on the opposing side.

4. The Soviet outcome resembles in some respects the earlier Spanish decline

discussed by Phillips (1987), among others. We realize that this is a complex phenomenon. For a review of a number of the available explanations and their ingredients, see Deudney and Ikenberry 1991, 1992.

9. The Model Recapitulated

1. Goldstein also suggests that lateral pressure conflicts increase on the economic upswing, as do psychological moods favoring expansionary activity (1988: 262-64).

2. See, as well, Conybeare 1990, 1992; Williams, McGinnis, and Thomas 1992; and Williams 1993.

3. A third cluster of analyses with some degree of compatibility with our model is geopolitical studies that continue to stress the distinction between land and sea powers. These analysts would certainly contend that some aspects of our argument are likely to remain meaningful in the next century. The most recent example of such work is Arquilla 1992.

10. The Future of Transitional Warfare

1. The term *endism* is taken from Huntington (1989a), who looks at some of the same arguments but from a much different theoretical stance. Our employment of the term is also meant to be more neutral than was the case in the Huntington article. The six perspectives we examine do not exhaust the field of possible explanations. See, for example, Singer (1991), who lists twelve alternative hypotheses for the post-1945 "long peace," and Sanders (1992), who discusses some interpretations not reviewed here. For an emphasis on the role of norms in ending war, see Ray 1989, 1991.

2. We rely heavily on Doyle's (1986) review of the Kantian argument. For a different interpretation that is less optimistic about the likely pace of the pacifying influence of democratization, see Lake 1992.

3. For instance, readers may not need reminding that many of these arguments have been made before. Kant wrote in the late eighteenth century. Hegel first pronounced the end of history in the early nineteenth century. Manchester liberals stressed the pacifying effects of commercial interdependence in the mid-nineteenth century (Blainey 1973). Angell (1914) emphasized the prohibitive escalation in war costs. Bloch (1914) predicted that changes in military technology and strategy had made war impossible.

4. We should not even assume that a practice as odious as slavery is irreversible. For that matter, it is not all that clear that slavery and its functional equivalents have been as effectively eliminated as we might like to think. It should also be noted that the elimination of slavery that has been accomplished required armed force (British naval patrols) and war (the American Civil War), among other factors. See Eltis 1987 for a good discussion of the complicated processes surrounding the nineteenth-century suppression of the slave trade.

5. Rosenau (1992: 5) is one partial exception. He mentions the traditional conflict-inhibiting role of hegemons, but he assumes the future will be too complex to produce hegemonies (another endism?). Even if such a concentration of power

were to emerge, its decision makers would be constrained from using military force to resist challenges. In another article, Jervis (1993) discusses the end of primacy. Because of nuclear weapons, the spread of liberal democracy, and the decline of nationalism, war among the developed powers is said to be unlikely. Therefore, there is much less reason to seek primacy. Yet the reasoning here seems convoluted. Is primacy sought because of the need to fight wars, or are wars a by-product of the struggles for primacy? Jervis's preference for the former interpretation emphasizes insecurity as the root of war. But there is much more at stake in the global competition for primacy than simply security. See Layne 1993 and Huntington 1993 for two alternatives to Jervis's views that are more compatible with the interpretations advanced in this study.

6. See Weigley's (1991) recent argument that between 1631 and 1815, in an era thought to be conducive to effective and decisive warfare, European wars actually resulted in few clear winners and losers.

7. Curiously, no endism argument reviewed here presents systematic evidence of changes in mass or elite attitudes toward war.

8. From different perspectives, Goldstein (1988) and Chase-Dunn and O'Reilly (1989) arrive at similarly pessimistic conclusions.

Appendix B. Identifying Systemic Wars

1. For instance, explanations of hegemonic war with definite functional flavors can be found in Chase-Dunn 1981, Gilpin 1981, and Modelski 1987.

2. See, for example, Wallerstein, who gravitated toward the position that "hegemonic powers were primarily sea (now sea-air) powers" (1984: 41).

3. Detailed evidence on the number of cannon carried by Dutch ships at various times is available in de Jonge 1869.

4. Modelski and Thompson (1988) spend some time discussing several states that do not meet the criteria.

5. Purging the war years from the series does not always leave ten to fifteen years to examine. The most obvious case is the Jenkins's Ear/Austrian Succession fighting (1739-48) and the Seven Years' War (1755-63), when only six years are available between the two conflicts. Consequently, the ten- and fifteen-year examinations assess impacts on only as many years as are available and appropriate per war. The Box-Tiao model parameters are computed with the assistance of the Scientific Computing Associates (SCA) Statistical System (Liu et al. 1985).

6. The Thirty Years' War was principally a regional European war in which the Dutch finally defeated the Spanish in one dimension of the multiple conflicts involved in the war. The Dutch chose to demobilize their naval forces at war's end, only to be almost immediately beset by a series of inconclusive English challenges (1652-54, 1663-67, and 1672-74).

References

Abu-Lughod, J. 1989. *Before European Hegemony.* New York: Oxford Univ. Press.

Adams, R.N. 1982. *Paradoxical Harvest: Energy and Explanation in British History, 1870-1914.* Cambridge: Cambridge Univ. Press.

Adams, S. 1990. "Tactics or Politics? 'The Military Revolution' and the Hapsburg Hegemony, 1525-1648." In *Tools of War: Instruments, Ideas and Institutions of Warfare, 1445-1871.* Edited by J.A. Lynn. Urbana: Univ. of Illinois Press.

Addington, L.H. 1984. *The Patterns of War since the Eighteenth Century.* Bloomington: Indiana Univ. Press.

Adelman, J.R. 1985. *Revolution, Armies, and War.* Boulder, Colo.: Lynne Rienner.

Aldcroft, D.H. 1970. *The Inter-War Economy: Britain, 1919-1939.* London: B.T. Batsford.

Aldrich, John H., and Forrest D. Nelson. 1984. *Linear Probability, Logit and Probit Models.* Beverly Hills, Calif.: Sage.

Alexander, J.T. 1989. *Catherine the Great.* New York: Oxford Univ. Press.

Alexinsky, G. 1915. *Russia and the Great War.* Translated by B. Miall. New York: Charles Scribner's Sons.

Ambler, J.S. 1968. *Soldiers against the State: The French Army in Politics.* Garden City, N.Y.: Doubleday.

Anderson, M.S. 1971. "Russia under Peter the Great and the Changed Relations of East and West." In *The New Cambridge Modern History.* Vol. 6, *The Rise of Great Britain and Russia, 1688-1725.* Edited by J.S. Bromley. Cambridge: Cambridge Univ. Press.

———. 1984. *War and Society in Europe of the Old Regime, 1618-1789.* Leicester: Leicester Univ. Press.

Andrews, K.R. 1984. *Trade, Plunder and Settlement: Maritime Enterprise and the Genesis of the British Empire, 1480-1630.* Cambridge: Cambridge Univ. Press.

Angell, N. 1914. *The Great Illusion: A Study of the Relation of Military Power to National Advantage.* London: Heinemann.

Arquilla, J. 1992. *Dubious Battles: Aggression, Defeat, and the International System.* Washington, D.C.: Crane Russak.

Askenazy, S. 1907. "Russia." In *The Cambridge Modern History.* Vol. 10, *The Restoration.* Edited by A.W. Ward, G.W. Prothero, and S. Leathes. Cambridge: Cambridge Univ. Press.

Baily, M.N. 1981. "Productivity and the Services of Capital and Labor." *Brookings Papers on Economic Activity* 1: 1-66.

Baily, M.N., and A.K. Chakrabarti. 1988. *Innovation and the Productivity Crisis.* Washington, D.C.: Brookings Institution.

Bain, R.N. 1908. "Peter the Great and His Pupils." In *The Cambridge Modern History.* Vol. 5, *The Age of Louis XIV.* Edited by A.W. Ward, G.W. Prothero, and S. Leathes. Cambridge: Cambridge Univ. Press.

Baldwin, D. 1979. "Power Analysis and World Politics." *World Politics* 31: 161-94.

———. 1989. *Paradoxes of Power.* New York: Basil Blackwell.

Baldwin, H.W. 1962. *World War I.* New York: Grove Press.

Banks, A.S. 1971. *Cross-Polity Time-Series Data.* Cambridge, Mass.: MIT Press.

Barker, A.J. 1980. *Japanese Army Handbook, 1939-1945.* London: Ian Allen.

Barker, J.E. 1906. *The Rise and Decline of the Netherlands.* London: Smith Elder and Co.

Barker, T.M. 1982. *Army, Aristocracy, Monarchy: Essays on War, Society and Government in Austria, 1618-1780.* New York: Columbia Univ. Press.

Barnett, C. 1970. *Britain and Her Army, 1509-1970.* New York: William Morrow.

———. 1986. *The Pride and the Fall: The Dream and Illusion of Britain as a Great Nation.* New York: Free Press.

Baumgart, W. 1982. *Imperialism: The Idea and Reality of British and French Colonial Expansion, 1880-1914.* New York: Oxford Univ. Press.

Baumol, W.J., S.A.B. Blackman, and E.N. Wolff. 1989. *Productivity and American Leadership.* Cambridge, Mass.: MIT Press.

Beasley, W.G. 1963. *The Modern History of Japan.* London: Weidenfeld and Nicolson.

———. 1987. *Japanese Imperialism, 1894-1945.* Oxford: Clarendon Press.

Beck, N. 1991. "The Illusion of Cycles in International Relations." *International Studies Quarterly* 35: 455-76.

Bergesen, A. 1985. "Cycles of War in the Reproduction of the World Economy." In *Rhythms in Politics and Economics.* Edited by P.M. Johnson and W.R. Thompson. New York: Praeger.

Bergesen, A., and R. Schoenberg. 1980. "Long Waves of Colonial Expansion and Contraction, 1415-1969." In *Studies of the Modern World-System.* Edited by A. Bergesen. New York: Academic Press.

Berry, B.J.L. 1991. *Long-Wave Rhythms in Economic Development and Political Behavior.* Baltimore: Johns Hopkins Univ. Press.

Berry, T.S. 1978. *Revised Annual Estimates of American Gross National Product: Preliminary Estimates of Four Major Components of Demand, 1789-1889.* Richmond, Va.: Bostwick Press.

Best, G. 1982. *War and Society in Revolutionary Europe, 1770-1870.* New York: St. Martin's Press.

Betts, R.R. 1961. "The Habsburg Lands." In *The New Cambridge Modern History.* Vol. 5, *The Ascendancy of France.* Edited by F.L. Carsten. Cambridge: Cambridge Univ. Press.

Black, J. 1991. *A Military Revolution? Military Change and European Society, 1550-1800.* Atlantic Highlands, N.J.: Humanities Press International.

Blainey, G. 1973. *The Causes of War.* New York: Free Press.

Bloch, J. de. 1914. *The Future of War.* Boston: World Peace Foundation.

Block, F. 1987. "Rethinking the Political Economy of the Welfare State." In *The*

Mean Season: The Attack on the Welfare State. Edited by F. Block, R.N. Cloward, B. Ehrenreich, and F.F. Piven. New York: Pantheon.

Bloomfield, L., W. Clemens, and F. Griffiths. 1974. *Khrushchev and the Arms Race.* Cambridge, Mass.: MIT Press.

Blumberg, P. 1980. *Inequality in an Age of Decline.* Oxford: Oxford Univ. Press.

Boddy, R., and J. Crotty. 1975. "Class Conflict and Macro-Policy: The Political Business Cycle." *Review of Radical Political Economics* 7: 1-19.

Bond, B. 1980. *British Military Policy between the Two World Wars.* Oxford: Clarendon Press.

Boswell, T. 1987. "Accumulation Innovations in the American Economy: The Affinity for Japanese Solutions to the Current Crisis." In *America's Changing Role in the World-System.* Edited by T. Boswell and A. Bergesen. New York: Praeger.

Boswell, T., and M. Sweat. 1991. "Hegemony, Long Waves and Major Wars." *International Studies Quarterly* 35: 123-49.

Boswell, T., M. Sweat, and J. Brueggemann. 1989. "War in the Core of the World-System: Testing the Goldstein Thesis." In *War in the World-System.* Edited by R. Shaeffer. New York: Greenwood Press.

Bousquet, N. 1979. "Esquisse d'une théorie de l'alternance de concurrence et d'hégémonie au centre de l'économie-monde capitaliste." *Review* 2: 501-17.

———. 1980. "From Hegemony to Competition: Cycles of the Core?" In *Processes of the World-System.* Edited by T.K. Hopkins and I. Wallerstein. Beverly Hills, Calif.: Sage.

Bowles, S., and H. Gintis. 1982. "The Crisis of Liberal Democratic Capitalism: The Case of the United States." *Politics and Society* 11: 51-93.

Bowles, S., D.M. Gordon, and T.E. Weisskopf, 1983. *Beyond the Waste Land.* New York: Doubleday.

Box, G.E.P., and G.M. Jenkins. 1970. *Time Series Analysis.* San Francisco: Holden-Day.

Box, G.E.P., and G.C. Tiao. 1975. "Intervention Analysis with Applications to Economic and Environmental Problems." *Journal of the American Statistical Association* 70: 70-92.

Boxer, C.R. 1965. *The Dutch Seaborne Empire, 1600-1800.* New York: Knopf.

———. 1969. *The Portuguese Seaborne Empire, 1415-1825.* New York: Knopf.

Boyd, C. 1988. "Japanese Military Effectiveness: The Interwar Period." In *Military Effectiveness.* Vol. 2, *The Interwar Years.* Edited by A.R. Millett and W. Murray. Boston: Allen and Unwin.

Brainard, W.C., and G.L. Perry, eds. 1981. *Brookings Papers on Economic Activity* 1: vii-xxi.

Bremer, S.A. 1992. "Dangerous Dyads: Interstate Wars, 1816-1965." *Journal of Conflict Resolution* 36: 309-41.

Brittan, S. 1975. "The Economic Contradictions of Democracy." *British Journal of Political Science* 15: 129-59.

Bueno de Mesquita, B. 1981. *The War Trap.* New Haven, Ct.: Yale Univ. Press.

Bueno de Mesquita, B. and D. Lalman. 1988. "Empirical Support for Systemic and Dyadic Explanations of International Conflict." *World Politics* 41: 1-20.

Burris, V. 1984. "The Politics of Marxist Crisis Theory." In *Research in Political Theory* Vol. 7. Edited by P. Zarembka, Greenwich, Ct.: JAI Press.

Butow, R.J.C. 1961. *Tojo and the Coming of the War.* Stanford, Calif.: Stanford Univ. Press.

Calleo, D.P. 1982. *The Imperious Economy*. Cambridge, Mass.: Harvard Univ. Press.
———. 1984. "Since 1961: American Power in a New World." In *Economics and World Power*. Edited by W.H. Becker and S.F. Wells, Jr. New York: Columbia Univ. Press.
———. 1987. *Beyond American Hegemony: The Future of the Western Alliance*. New York: Basic Books.
———. 1992. *The Bankrupting of America: How the Federal Budget Is Impoverishing the Nation*. New York: William Morrow.
Cappelen, A., N.P. Gleditsch, and O. Bjerkholt. 1984. "Military Spending and Economic Growth in the OECD Countries." *Journal of Peace Research* 21: 361-73.
Carsten, F.L. 1961. "The Rise of Brandenburg." In *The New Cambridge Modern History*. Vol. 5, *The Ascendancy of France*. Edited by F.L. Carsten. Cambridge: Cambridge Univ. Press.
Carter, A.C. 1971. *The Dutch Republic in Europe in the Seven Years War*. Coral Gables, Fla.: Univ. of Miami Press.
Castells, M. 1980. *The Economic Crisis and American Society*. Princeton, N.J.: Princeton Univ. Press.
Chace, J. 1988. "A New Grand Strategy." *Foreign Policy* 70: 3-25.
Chan, S. 1985. "The Impact of Defense Spending on Economic Performance: A Survey of Evidence and Problems." *Orbis* 29: 403-34.
Chandaman, C.D. 1975. *The English Public Revenue, 1600-1688*. London: Oxford Univ. Press.
Chandler, D.G. 1971. "Armies and Navies: The Art of War on Land." In *The New Cambridge Modern History*. Vol. 6, *The Rise of Great Britain and Russia, 1688-1725*. Edited by J.S. Bromley. Cambridge: Cambridge Univ. Press.
Chase-Dunn, C. 1981. "Interstate System and Capitalist World-Economy: One Logic or Two?" *International Studies Quarterly* 25: 19-42.
———. 1989. *Global Formation: Structures of the World-Economy*. New York: Basil Blackwell.
Chase-Dunn, C., and K. O'Reilly. 1989. "Core Wars of the Future." In *War in the World-System*. Edited by R. Shaeffer. New York: Greenwood Press.
Chase-Dunn, C., and R. Rubinson. 1977. "Toward a Structural Perspective on the World-System." *Politics and Society* 7: 453-76.
Chester, E. 1978. "Military Spending and Capitalist Stability." *Cambridge Journal of Economics* 2: 293-98.
Childs, J. 1982. *Armies and Warfare in Europe, 1648-1789*. Manchester: Manchester Univ. Press.
Choucri, N., and R.C. North. 1975. *Nations in Conflict: National Growth and International Violence*. San Francisco: W.H. Freeman.
———. 1989. "Lateral Pressure in International Relations: Concept and Theory." In *Handbook of War Studies*. Edited by M. Midlarsky. Boston: Unwin Hyman.
Cipolla, C.M. 1965. *Guns, Sails and Empires: Technological Innovation and the Early Phases of European Expansion, 1400-1700*. New York: Minerva Press.
———. 1970. "Editor's Introduction." In *The Economic Decline of Empires*. Edited by C.M. Cipolla. London: Methuen.
Clark, G. 1961. "The Social Foundations of States." In *The New Cambridge Modern History*. Vol. 5, *The Ascendancy of France*. Edited by F.L. Carsten. Cambridge: Cambridge Univ. Press.
———. 1971a. "From the Nine Years War to the War of the Spanish Succession." In

The New Cambridge Modern History. Vol. 6, *The Rise of Great Britain and Russia, 1688-1725.* Edited by J.S. Bromley. Cambridge: Cambridge Univ. Press.

———. 1971b. "The Nine Years War, 1688-1697." In *The New Cambridge Modern History.* Vol. 6, *The Rise of Great Britain and Russia, 1688-1725.* Edited by J.S. Bromley. Cambridge: Cambridge Univ. Press.

Clark, P.K. 1979. "Investment in the 1970s: Theory, Performance and Prediction." *Brookings Papers on Economic Activity* 1: 73-124.

Collins, J.M. 1980. *U.S.-Soviet Military Balance: Concepts and Capabilities, 1960-1980.* New York: McGraw-Hill.

———. 1985. *U.S.-Soviet Military Balance, 1980-1985.* Washington, D.C.: Pergamon Brassy's.

Connelly, O., H.T. Parker, P.W. Becker, and J.K. Burton, eds. 1985. *Historical Dictionary of Napoleonic France, 1799-1815.* Westport, Conn.: Greenwood Press.

Conybeare, J.A.C. 1990. "A Random Walk Down the Road to War." *Defense Economics* 1: 329-37.

———. 1992. "Weak Cycles, Length and Magnitude of War: Duration Dependence in International Conflict." *Conflict Management and Peace Science* 12: 99-116.

Cooper, M. 1978. *The German Army, 1933-1945: Its Political and Military Failure.* New York: Stein and Day.

Coox, A.D. 1988. "The Effectiveness of the Japanese Military Establishment in the Second World War." In *Military Effectiveness.* Vol. 3, *The Second World War.* Edited by A.R. Millett and W. Murray. Boston: Allen and Unwin.

Corvisier, A. 1979. *Armies and Societies in Europe, 1494-1789.* Translated by A.T. Siddall. Bloomington: Indiana Univ. Press.

Cox, R. 1987. *Production, Power, and World Order: Social Forces in the Making of History.* New York: Columbia Univ. Press.

Craig, G.A. 1956. *The Politics of the Prussian Army, 1640-1945.* New York: Oxford Univ. Press.

Craig, P.P., and K.E.F. Watt. 1985. "The Kondratieff Cycle and War." *Futurist* 19: 25-27.

Cronin, J.E. 1979. *Industrial Conflict in Modern Britain.* London: Croom Helm.

Dahl, R.A. 1970. *Modern Political Analysis.* 2d ed. Englewood Cliffs, N.J.: Prentice-Hall.

Danvers, F.C. 1966. *The Portuguese in India.* 2 vols. New York: Octagon Books.

Deane, P., and W.A. Cole. 1967. *British Economic Growth, 1688-1959: Trends and Structure.* 2d ed. Cambridge: Cambridge Univ. Press.

Dehio, L. 1962. *The Precarious Balance.* New York: Vintage.

———. 1967. *Germany and World Politics in the Twentieth Century.* Translated by D. Persner. New York: Norton.

Delbruck, H. 1985. *History of the Art of War.* Vol. 4. Translated by W.J. Renfoe, Jr. Westport, Conn.: Greenwood Press.

Denison, E.F. 1980. "The Contribution of Capital to Economic Growth." *American Economic Review* 70: 220-24.

———. 1985. *Trends in American Economic Growth, 1929-1982.* Washington, D.C.: Brookings Institution.

de Jonge, J.C. 1869. *Geschiedenis van het Niederländsche Zeewezen.* 6 vols. Zwolle, Neth.: Van Hogstraten und Gorter.

de Romilly, J. 1977. *The Rise and Fall of States according to Greek Authors.* Ann Arbor: Univ. of Michigan Press.

de Schweinitz, K., Jr. 1983. *The Rise and Fall of British India: Imperialism as Inequality*. London: Methuen.

Deudney, D., and G.J. Ikenberry. 1991. "Soviet Reform and the End of the Cold War: Explaining Large-Scale Historical Change." *Review of International Studies* 17: 225-50.

———. 1992. "Who Won the Cold War?" *Foreign Policy* 87: 123-38.

Deutsch, K.W., and J.D. Singer. 1964. "Multipolar Power Systems and International Stability." *World Politics* 16 (April): 390-406.

Diffie, B.W., and G.D. Winius. 1977. *Foundations of the Portuguese Empire, 1415-1580*. Minneapolis: Univ. of Minnesota Press.

Dmytryshyn, B. 1977. *A History of Russia*. Englewood Cliffs, N.J.: Prentice-Hall.

Doran, C.F. 1971. *The Politics of Assimilation: Hegemony and Its Aftermath*. Baltimore: Johns Hopkins Univ. Press.

———. 1989a. "Power Cycle Theory of Systems Structure and Stability: Commonalities and Complementarities." In *Handbook of War Studies*. Edited by M. Midlarsky. Boston: Unwin Hyman.

———. 1989b. "Systemic Disequilibrium, Foreign Policy Role, and the Power Cycle: Challenges for Research Design." *Journal of Conflict Resolution* 33: 371-401.

———. 1991. *Systems in Crisis*. Cambridge: Cambridge Univ. Press.

Doran, C.F., and W. Parsons. 1980. "War and the Cycle of Relative Power." *American Political Science Review* 74: 947-65.

Dorn, W.L. 1940. *Competition for Europe, 1740-1763*. New York: Harper and Row.

Doyle, M. 1986. "Liberalism and World Politics." *American Political Science Review* 80: 1151-69.

Doyle, W. 1978. *The Old European Order, 1660-1800*. Oxford: Oxford Univ. Press.

Duffy, C. 1974. *The Army of Frederick the Great*. New York: Hippocrene Books.

———. 1977. *The Army of Maria Theresa*. New York: Hippocrene Books.

———. 1981. *Russia's Military Way to the West: Origins and Nature of Russian Military Power, 1700-1800*. London: Routledge and Kegan Paul.

———. 1987. *The Military Experience in the Age of Reason*. London: Routledge and Kegan Paul.

Dukes, P. 1990. *The Making of Russian Absolutism, 1613-1801*. 2d ed. London: Longman.

Dupuy, R.E., and T.N. Dupuy. 1977. *The Encyclopedia of Military History*. Rev. ed. New York: Harper and Row.

Dutt, R. 1956. *The Economic History of India in the Victorian Age*. London: Routledge and Kegan Paul.

Eatwell, J. 1982. *Whatever Happened to Britain? The Economics of Decline*. New York: Oxford Univ. Press.

Economist. 1986. "The Big Six: A Survey of the World's Aircraft Industry." 295 (June 1-7): 1-24.

Edelstein, M. 1982. *Overseas Investment in the Age of High Imperialism: The United Kingdom, 1850-1914*. New York: Columbia Univ. Press.

Ehrman, J. 1956. *Grand Strategy*. Vol. 6, *Oct. 1955-Aug. 1945*. London: HMSO.

Eisenstadt, S.N. 1963. *The Political Systems of Empires: The Rise and Fall of the Historical Bureaucratic Empires*. New York: Free Press.

Elbaum, B., and W. Lazonick, eds. 1986. *The Decline of the British Economy*. Oxford: Oxford Univ. Press.

Ellis, J. 1973. *Armies in Revolution*. London: Croom Helm.

Elting, J.R. 1988. *Swords around a Throne: Napoleon's Grande Armée*. New York: Free Press.

Eltis, D. 1987. *Economic Growth and the Ending of the Transatlantic Slave Trade*. New York: Oxford Univ. Press.

Erickson, J. 1962. *The Soviet High Command*. London: St. Martin's Press.

Erickson, J., L. Hansen, and W. Schneider. 1986. *Soviet Ground Forces: An Operational Assessment*. Boulder, Colo.: Westview Press.

Ferrill, A. 1986. *The Fall of the Roman Empire: The Military Explanation*. New York: Thames and Hudson.

Fieldhouse, D.K. 1966. *The Colonial Empires: A Comparative Survey from the Eighteenth Century*. New York: Delacorte Press.

———. 1973. *Economics and Empire, 1830-1914*. Ithaca, N.Y.: Cornell Univ. Press.

Fisher, H.A.L. 1906. "The First Restoration." In *The Cambridge Modern History*. Vol. 9, *Napoleon*. Edited by A.W. Ward, G.W. Prothero, and S. Leathes. Cambridge: Cambridge Univ. Press.

Flora, P., J. Alber, R. Eichenberg, T. Kohl, F. Kraus, W. Pfenning, K. Seebohm. 1983. *State, Economy, and Society in Western Europe, 1815-1975*. Vol. 1: *The Growth of Mass Democracies and Welfare States*. Chicago, Il.: St. James Press.

Flora, P., F. Kraus, and W. Pfenning. 1987. *State, Economy and Society in Western Europe, 1815-1975*. Vol. 2, *The Growth of Industrial Societies and Capitalist Economies*. Chicago: St. James Press.

Forrester, J.W. 1981. "Innovation and Economic Change." *Futures* 13: 323-31.

Forster, J.E. 1988. "The Dynamics of Volsgemeinschaft: The Effectiveness of the German Military Establishment in the Second World War." In *Military Effectiveness*. Vol. 3, *The Second World War*. Edited by A.R. Millett and W. Murray. Boston: Allen and Unwin.

Fortescue, J.W. 1911. *A History of the British Army*, Vol. 3 (1763-1793). London: Macmillan.

Freeman, C., J. Clark, and L. Soete. 1982. *Unemployment and Technical Innovation*. London: Frances Pinter.

Freeman, C., and C. Perez. 1988. "Structural Crises of Adjustment, Business Cycles and Investment Behavior." In *Technical Change and Economic Theory*. Edited by G. Dosi, C. Freeman, R. Nelson, G. Silverberg, and L. Soete. London: Frances Pinter.

Freeman, J.R. 1983. "Granger Causality and the Time Series Analysis of Political Relationships." *American Journal of Political Science* 27: 327-58.

French, D. 1990. *The British Way in Warfare, 1688-2000*. London: Unwin Hyman.

Frieden, J. 1988. "Sectoral Conflict and Foreign Economic Policy, 1914-1940." *International Organization* 42: 59-90.

Friedman, B.M. 1985. "Saving, Investment and Government Deficits in the 1980s." In *U.S. Competitiveness in the World Economy*. Edited by B.R. Scott and G.C. Lodge. Boston: Harvard Business School Press.

———. 1988. *Day of Judgement: The Consequences of American Economic Policy under Reagan and After*. New York: Random House.

Friedman, M., and R. Friedman. 1981. *Free to Choose: A Personal Statement*. New York: Avon Books.

Fukuyama, F. 1989. "The End of History?" *National Interest* 16: 3-18.

Fuller, W.C., Jr. 1984. "The Russian Empire." In *Knowing One's Enemies: Intelligence Assessment before the Two World Wars*. Edited by E.R. May. Princeton, N.J.: Princeton Univ. Press.

————. 1985. *Civil-Military Conflict in Imperial Russia, 1881-1914*. Princeton, N.J.: Princeton Univ. Press.

Galbraith, J.S. 1960. "The 'Turbulent Frontier' as a Factor in British Expansion." *Comparative Studies in Society and History* 2: 150-68.

Gallagher, J., and R. Robinson. 1953. "The Imperialism of Free Trade." *Economic History Review*, 2d series, 6: 1-15.

Gamble, A. 1981. *Britain in Decline: Economic Policy, Political Strategy and the British State*. Boston: Beacon Press.

Garder, M. 1966. *A History of the Soviet Army*. New York: Praeger.

Garvey, G. 1943. "Kondratieff's Theory of Long Cycles." *Review of Economic Statistics* 25: 203-20.

Geller, D.S. 1992a. "Capability Concentration, Power Transition, and War." *International Interactions* 17: 269-84.

————. 1992b. "Power Transition and Conflict Initiation." *Conflict Management and Peace Science* 12: 1-16.

Gibbon, E. 1960. *The Decline and Fall of the Roman Empire*. Abridged by D.M. Low. New York: Harcourt, Brace.

Gibbs, N.H. 1965. "Armed Forces and the Art of War." In *The New Cambridge Modern History*. Vol. 9, *War and Peace in an Age of Upheaval, 1793-1830*. Edited by C.W. Crawley. Cambridge: Cambridge Univ. Press.

————. 1976. *Grand Strategy*. Vol. 1, *Rearmament Policy*. London: HMSO.

Gilpin, R. 1975. *U.S. Power and the Multinational Corporations: The Political Economy of U.S. Foreign Direct Investment*. New York: Basic Books.

————. 1981. *War and Change in World Politics*. New York: Cambridge Univ. Press.

————. 1987. *The Political Economy of International Relations*. Princeton, N.J.: Princeton Univ. Press.

Glyn, A., and B. Sutcliffe. 1972. *Capitalism in Crisis*. New York: Pantheon Books.

Godechot, J., B.F. Hyslop, and D.L. Dowd. 1971. *The Napoleonic Era in Europe*. New York: Holt, Rinehart and Winston.

Goerlitz, W. 1975. *History of the German General Staff, 1657-1945*. Translated by B. Battleshaw. Westport, Conn.: Greenwood Press.

Gold, D. 1990. *The Impact of Defense Spending on Investment, Productivity and Economic Growth*. Washington, D.C.: Defense Budget Project.

Goldstein, J.S. 1988. *Long Cycles: Prosperity and War in the Modern Age*. New Haven, Conn.: Yale Univ. Press.

————. 1991a. "The Possibility of Cycles in International Relations." *International Studies Quarterly* 35: 477-80.

————. 1991b. "A War-Economy Theory of the Long Wave." In *Business Cycles: Theories, Evidence and Analysis*. Edited by N. Thygesen, K. Velupillai, and S. Zambelli. London: Macmillan.

Goldstone, J.A. 1991. "The Causes of Long Waves in Early Modern Economic History." In *Research in Economic History*. Supplement 6. Edited by J. Mokyr. Greenwich, Conn.: JAI Press.

Golovine, N.N. 1931. *The Russian Army in the World War*. New Haven, Conn.: Yale Univ. Press.

Gooch, J. 1984. "Italy before 1915: The Quandary of the Vulnerable." In *Knowing One's Enemies: Intelligence Assessment before the Two World Wars*. Edited by E.R. May. Princeton, N.J.: Princeton Univ. Press.

Gordon, D.M. 1980. "Stages of Accumulation and Long Economic Cycles." In *Processes of the World-System*. Edited by T. Hopkins and I. Wallerstein. Beverly Hills, Calif.: Sage.

Gould, S.J. 1987. *Time's Arrow, Time's Cycle: Myth and Metaphor in the Discovery of Geological Time*. Cambridge, Mass.: Harvard Univ. Press.

Graham, A.K., and P.M. Senge. 1980. "A Long Wave Hypothesis of Innovation." *Technological Forecasting and Social Change* 17: 283-311.

Granger, C.W.J. 1969. "Investigating Causal Relations by Econometric Models and Cross-Spectral Methods." *Econometrics* 37: 424-38.

Ha, Y-S. 1983. *Nuclear Proliferation: World Order and Korea*. Seoul: Seoul National Univ. Press.

Hale, J.R. 1985. *War and Society in Renaissance Europe, 1450-1620*. Baltimore: Johns Hopkins Univ. Press.

Hall, R.E. 1978. "Stochastic Implications of the Life Cycle-Permanent Income Hypothesis: Theory and Evidence." *Journal of Political Economy* 86: 971-87.

Hammond, J.L., and B. Hammond. 1926. *The Rise of Modern Industry*. New York: Harcourt, Brace and Co.

Hammond, M.B. 1897. *The Cotton Industry*. New York: Macmillan.

Hartley, K., and P. McLean. 1978. "Military Expenditure and Capitalism: A Comment." *Cambridge Journal of Economics* 2: 287-92.

Hartman, R.S., and D.R. Wheeler. 1979. "Schumpeterian Waves of Innovation and Infrastructure Development in Great Britain and the United States: The Kondratieff Cycle Revisited." *Research in Economic History* 4: 37-85.

Hatton, R. 1971. "Charles XII and the Great Northern War." In *The New Cambridge Modern History*. Vol. 6, *The Rise of Great Britain and Russia, 1688-1725*. Edited by J.S. Bromley. Cambridge: Cambridge Univ. Press.

Haumant, E. N.d. *La Russie au XVIIIe siècle*. Paris: L. Henry-May.

Hayter, T. 1978. The Army and the Crowd in Mid-Georgia England. Tototowa, N.J.: Rowan and Littlefield.

Headrick, D.R. 1981. *The Tools of Empire: Technology and European Imperialism in the Nineteenth Century*. New York: Oxford Univ. Press.

Herodotus. 1972. *The Histories*. Translated by A. de Selincourt and A.R. Burns. London: Penguin Books.

Herwig, H.H. 1984. "Imperial Germany." In *Knowing One's Enemies: Intelligence Assessment before the Two World Wars*. Edited by E.R. May. Princeton, N.J.: Princeton Univ. Press.

————. 1988. "The Dynamics of Necessity: German Military Policy during the First World War." In *Military Effectiveness*. Vol. 1, *The First World War*. Edited by A.R. Millett and W. Murray. Boston: Allen and Unwin.

Hobsbawm, E.J. 1969. *Industry and Empire*. London: Pelican.

Hoerr, J.P. 1988. *And the Wolf Finally Came: The Decline of the American Steel Industry*. Pittsburgh: Univ. of Pittsburgh Press.

Hohenberg, P.M., and L.H. Lees. 1985. *The Making of Urban Europe, 1500-1950*. Cambridge, Mass.: Harvard Univ. Press.

Holsti, K.J. 1985. *The Dividing Discipline: Hegemony and Diversity in International Theory*. Boston: Allen and Unwin.

————. 1991. *Peace and War: Armed Conflicts and International Order, 1648-1989.* Cambridge: Cambridge Univ. Press.

Hood, R.C., III. 1988. "Bitter Victory: French Military Effectiveness during the Second World War." In *Military Effectiveness.* Vol. 3, *The Second World War.* Edited by A.R. Millett and W. Murray. Boston: Allen and Unwin.

Houweling, H., and J.G. Siccama. 1988. *Studies of War.* Boston: Kluwer.

Howard, M. 1972. *Grand Strategy.* Vol. 4, *Aug. 1942-Sept. 1943.* London: HMSO.

————. 1976. *War in European History.* London: Oxford Univ. Press.

Hufton, O. 1980. *Europe: Privilege and Protest, 1730-1789.* Ithaca, N.Y.: Cornell Univ. Press.

Huntington, S.P. 1975. "The United States." In *The Crisis of Democracy.* Edited by M. Crozier, S.P. Huntington, and J. Watanuki. New York: New York Univ. Press.

————. 1988. "Coping with the Lippmann Gap." *Foreign Affairs* 66: 453-74.

————. 1989a. "No Exit: The Errors of Endism." *National Interest* 17: 3-11.

————. 1989b. "The U.S.: Decline or Renewal?" *Foreign Affairs* 67: 76-96.

————. 1993. "Why International Primacy Matters." *International Security* 17: 68-83.

Ibn Khaldun. 1967. *The Muqaddimah: An Introduction to History.* Translated by Franz Rosenthal, edited and abridged by N.J. Dawood. Princeton, N.J.: Princeton Univ. Press.

Imbert, G. 1959. *Des Mouvements de longue durée Kondratieff.* Aix-en-Provence: La Pensée Universitaire.

Institute for Strategic Studies. 1959-1988-89. *The Military Balance.* Multiple Volumes. London: Institute for Strategic Studies.

Irving, D. 1977. *Hitler's War.* New York: Viking Press.

Israel, J.I. 1982. *The Dutch Republic and the Hispanic World, 1606-1661.* Oxford: Clarendon Press.

————. 1989. *Dutch Primacy in World Trade, 1585-1740.* Oxford: Clarendon Press.

Jervis, Robert. 1991-92. "The Future of World Politics: Will It Resemble the Past?" *International Security* 16: 39-78.

————. 1993. "International Primacy: Is the Game Worth the Candle?" *International Security* 17: 52-67.

Jessup, J.E. 1988. "The Soviet Armed Forces in the Great Patriotic War, 1941-5." In *Military Effectiveness.* Vol. 3, *The Second World War.* Edited by A.R. Millett and W. Murray. Boston: Allen and Unwin.

Jones, A.H.M. 1964. *The Later Roman Empire, 284-602.* Vol. 2. Norman: Univ. of Oklahoma Press.

Jones, C. 1981. "The Military Revolution and the Professionalization of the French Army under the Ancien Régime." In *The Military Revolution and the State, 1500-1800.* Edited by M. Duffy. Exeter: Univ. of Exeter.

Jones, D.R. 1988. "Imperial Russia's Forces at War." In *Military Effectiveness.* Vol. 1, *The First World War.* Edited by A.R. Millett and W. Murray. Boston: Allen and Unwin.

Kahler, M. 1988. "External Ambition and Economic Performance." *World Politics* 60: 419-51.

Kaiser, D. 1990. *Politics and War: European Conflict from Philip II to Hitler.* Cambridge, Mass.: Harvard Univ. Press.

Kamen, H. 1969. *The War of Succession in Spain, 1700-15.* Bloomington: Indiana Univ. Press.

————. 1980. *Spain in the Later Seventeenth Century, 1665-1700.* New York: Longman.

Kann, R.A. 1974. *A History of the Habsburg Empire, 1526-1918*. Berkeley: Univ. of California Press.

Kant, I. 1970. *Kant's Political Writings*. Edited by H. Reiss, translated by H.B. Nisbet. Cambridge: Cambridge Univ. Press.

Katz, S. 1982. *The Decline of Rome and the Rise of Mediaeval Europe*. Westport, Conn.: Greenwood Press.

Kaysen, C. 1990. "Is War Obsolete? A Review Essay." *International Security* 14: 42-69.

Keep, J.L.H. 1985. *Soldiers of the Tsar: Army and Society in Russia, 1462-1874*. Oxford: Clarendon Press.

Keim, A. 1906. "The War of 1809." In *The Cambridge Modern History*. Vol. 9, *Napoleon*. Edited by A.W. Ward, G.W. Prothero, and S. Leathes. Cambridge: Cambridge Univ. Press.

Kennedy, M.D. 1924. *The Military Side of Japanese Life*. London: Constable and Co.

Kennedy, P.M. 1976. *The Rise and Fall of British Naval Mastery*. New York: Charles Scribner's Sons.

———. 1983. *Strategy and Diplomacy, 1870-1945*. London: George Allen and Unwin.

———. 1987a. "The Decline of America." *Atlantic* 260: 29-38.

———. 1987b. *The Rise and Fall of the Great Powers*. New York: Random House.

Kennett, L.B. 1967. *The French Armies in the Seven Years' War: A Study in Military Organization and Administration*. Durham, N.C.: Duke Univ. Press.

Keohane, R.O. 1984. *After Hegemony: Cooperation and Discord in the World Political Economy*. Princeton, N.J.: Princeton Univ. Press.

Kim, W. 1989. "Power, Alliance and Major Wars, 1816-1975." *Journal of Conflict Resolution* 33: 255-73.

———. 1991. "Alliance Transitions and Great Power War." *American Journal of Political Science* 35: 833-50.

———. 1992. "Power Transitions and Great Power War from Westphalia to Waterloo." *World Politics* 45: 153-72.

Kim, W., and J.D. Morrow. 1992. "When Do Power Shifts Lead to War?" *American Journal of Political Science* 36: 896-922.

King, G. 1989. *Unifying Political Methodology*. Cambridge: Cambridge Univ. Press.

Kirby, M.W. 1981. *The Decline of British Economic Power since 1870*. London: Allen and Unwin.

Kleinknecht, A. 1981. "Innovation, Accumulation, and Crisis: Waves in Economic Development." *Review* 4: 687-711.

———. 1987. *Innovation Patterns in Crisis and Prosperity: Schumpeter's Long Cycle Reconsidered*. New York: St. Martin's Press.

Knox, M. 1988. "The Italian Armed Forces, 1940-3." In *Military Effectiveness*. Vol. 3, *The Second World War*. Edited by A.R. Millett and W. Murray. Boston: Allen and Unwin.

Koch, H.W. 1978. *A History of Prussia*. London: Longman.

———. 1981. *The Rise of Modern Warfare, 1618-1815*. Englewood Cliffs, N.J.: Prentice-Hall.

Kogane, Y. 1988. "Long Waves of Economic Growth: Past and Future." *Futures* 20: 532-50.

Koh, S.J. 1966. *Stages of Industrial Development in Asia*. Philadelphia Pa.: Univ. of Pennsylvania Press.

Kondratieff, N. [1935] 1979. "The Long Waves in Economic Life." *Review of Economic Statistics* 17 (1935): 105-15. Reprinted in *Review* 2 (1979): 519-62.

———. 1984. *The Long Wave Cycle.* Translated by Guy Daniels. New York: Richardson and Snyder.

Kossmann, E.H. 1970. "The Low Countries." In *The New Cambridge Modern History.* Vol. 4, *The Decline of Spain and the Thirty Years War, 1609.* Edited by J.P. Cooper. Cambridge: Cambridge Univ. Press.

Kuczynski, T. 1982. "Leads and Lags in an Escalation Model of Capitalist Development: Kondratieff Cycles Reconsidered." *Proceedings of the Eighth International Economic History Congress, Budapest* B3: 27.

Kugler, J., and D. Lemke, eds. Forthcoming. *Parity and War: A Critical Reevaluation of the Power Transition.* Ann Arbor: Univ. of Michigan Press.

Kugler, J., and A.F.K. Organski. 1989. "The Power Transition: A Retrospective and Prospective Evaluation." In *Handbook of War Studies.* Edited by M. Midlarsky. Boston: Unwin Hyman.

Kupchan, C. 1989. "Defense Spending and Economic Performance." *Survival* 31: 447-61.

Lake, D.A. 1992. "Powerful Pacifists: Democratic States and War." *American Political Science Review* 86: 24-37.

Lamar, M. 1957. *The World Fertilizer Economy.* Stanford, Calif.: Stanford Univ. Press.

Lambi, I.N. 1984. *The Navy and German Power Politics, 1861-1914.* Boston: Allen and Unwin.

Lane, R. 1990. "Concrete Theory: An Emerging Political Method." *American Political Science Review* 84: 927-40.

Lasswell, H.D., and A. Kaplan. 1950. *Power and Society: A Framework for Political Inquiry.* New Haven, Conn.: Yale Univ. Press.

Layne, C. 1993. "The Unipolar Illusion: Why New Great Powers Will Arise." *International Security* 17: 5-51.

Lee, K. 1967. *The French Armies in the Seven Years' War.* Durham, N.C.: Duke Univ. Press.

Levine, A.L. 1967. *Industrial Retardation in Britain, 1880-1914.* New York: Basic Books.

Levy, J.S. 1983. *War in the Modern Great Power System, 1495-1975.* Lexington: Univ. Press of Kentucky.

———. 1985. "Theories of General War." *World Politics* 37: 344-74.

———. 1987. "Declining Power and the Preventive Motivation for War." *World Politics* 40: 82-107.

———. 1990-91. "Preferences, Constraints, and Choices in July 1914." *International Security* 15: 151-86.

———. 1991. "Long Cycles, Hegemonic Transitions and the Long Peace." In *The Long Postwar Peace.* Edited by C.W. Kegley, Jr. New York: Harper Collins.

Lewis, W.A. 1978. *Growth and Fluctuations, 1870-1913.* London: Allen and Unwin.

Liddell Hart, B.H. 1960. "Armed Forces and the Art of War: Armies." In *The New Cambridge Modern History.* Vol. 10, *The Zenith of European Order.* Edited by J.P.T. Bury. Cambridge: Cambridge Univ. Press.

Lindgren, G. 1984. "Review Essay: Armaments and Economic Performance in Industrialized Economies." *Journal of Peace Research* 21: 375-87.

Lippmann, W. 1943. *U.S. Foreign Policy: Shield of the Republic.* Boston: Little, Brown.

Liska, G. 1978. *Career of Empire: America and Imperial Expansion over Land and Sea.* Baltimore: Johns Hopkins Univ. Press.

Liu, L-M, and G.B. Hudak, with G.E.P. Box, M.E. Muller, and G.C. Tiao. 1985. *The SCA Statistical System Reference Manual.* DeKalb, Ill.: Scientific Computing Associates.

Lloyd, T.O. 1984. *The British Empire, 1558-1983.* New York: Oxford Univ. Press.

Luard, E. 1986. *War in International Society: A Study in International Sociology.* London: Tauris.

Lundkvist, S. 1973. "The Experience of Empire: Sweden as a Great Power." In *Sweden's Age of Greatness, 1632-1718.* Edited by M. Roberts. New York: St. Martin's Press.

Lutz, R.H., ed. 1969. *The Causes of the German Collapse in 1918.* Translated by W.L. Campbell. Hamden, Conn.: Archon Books.

Lybyer, A.H. 1913. *The Government of the Ottoman Empire in the Time of Suleiman the Magnificent.* Cambridge, Mass.: Harvard Univ. Press.

Lynn, J.A. 1980. "The Growth of the French Army during the Seventeenth Century." *Armed Forces and Society* 6: 568-85.

———. 1984. *The Bayonets of the Republic.* Urbana: Univ. of Illinois Press.

———. 1990. "The Pattern of Army Growth, 1445-1945." In *Tools of War: Instruments, Ideas and Institutions of Warfare, 1445-1871.* Edited by J.A. Lynn. Urbana: Univ. of Illinois Press.

McCleary, R., and R.A. Hay, Jr. 1980. *Applied Time Series Analysis for the Social Sciences.* Beverly Hills, Calif.: Sage.

McEvedy, C., and R. Jones. 1978. *Atlas of World Population History.* New York: Facts on File.

McGovern, W. 1920. *Modern Japan.* New York: Charles Scribner's Sons.

McKay, D., and H.M. Scott. 1983. *The Rise of the Great Powers, 1648-1815.* London: Longman.

Maddison, A. 1979. "Per Capita Output in the Long Run." *Kyklos* 32: 412-25.

———. 1982. *Phases of Capitalist Development.* New York: Oxford Univ. Press.

———. 1987. "Growth and Slowdown in Advanced Capitalist Economies: Techniques of Quantitative Assessment." *Journal of Economic Literature* 25: 649-98.

———. 1991. *Dynamic Forces in Capitalist Development: A Long-Run Comparative View.* Oxford: Oxford Univ. Press.

Magaziner, I.C., and R.B. Reich. 1982. *Minding America's Business: The Decline and Rise of the American Economy.* New York: Harcourt, Brace, Jovanovich.

Mahan, A.T. 1890. *The Influence of Sea Power upon History, 1660-1783.* New York: Holland Wang.

Maland, D. 1983. *Europe in the Seventeenth Century.* London: Macmillan Education.

Malerba, F. 1985. *The Semiconductor Business: The Economics of Rapid Growth and Decline.* Madison: Univ. of Wisconsin Press.

Mallett, M.E., and J.R. Hale. 1984. *The Military Organization of a Renaissance State: Venice c. 1400 to 1617.* Cambridge: Cambridge Univ. Press.

Mandel, E. 1975. *Late Capitalism.* London: New Left Books.

———. 1980. *Long Waves of Capitalist Development: The Marxist Interpretation.* Cambridge: Cambridge Univ. Press.

Marchetti, C. 1980. "Society as a Learning System: Discovery, Invention and Innovation Cycles Revisited." *Technological Forecasting and Social Change* 18: 267-82.

Martin, A. 1977. "Political Constraints on Economic Strategies in Advanced Industrial Societies." *Comparative Political Studies* 10: 323-54.

Mazzarino, S. 1966. *The End of the Ancient World.* Translated by G. Holmes. New York: Knopf.

Mead, W.R. 1987. *Mortal Splendor: The American Empire in Transition.* Boston: Houghton Mifflin.

Mearsheimer, J.J. 1990. "Back to the Future: Instability in Europe after the Cold War." *International Security* 15: 5-56.

Mensch, G. 1979. *Stalemate in Technology: Innovations Overcome the Depression.* Cambridge, Mass.: Ballinger.

Michel, H. 1975. *The Second World War.* Translated by D. Parmée. London: André Deutsch.

Midlarsky, M. 1984. "Some Uniformities in the Origin of Systemic War." Paper presented at the annual meeting of the American Political Science Association, Washington, D.C., September.

———. 1988. *The Onset of World War.* Boston: Unwin Hyman.

———, ed. 1990. *Big Wars, Little Wars: A Single Theory?* Special issue of *International Interactions* 16: 157-224.

Mitchell, A. 1984. *Victors and Vanquished: The German Influence on Army and Church in France after 1870.* Chapel Hill: Univ. of North Carolina Press.

Mitchell, B.R. 1980. *European Historical Statistics, 1750-1975.* 2d rev. ed. New York: Facts on File.

———. 1982. *International Historical Statistics, Africa and Asia.* New York: New York Univ. Press.

———. 1988. *British Historical Statistics.* Cambridge: Cambridge Univ. Press.

Mjoset, L. 1990. "The Turn of Two Centuries: A Comparison of British and U.S. Hegemonies." In *World Leadership and Hegemony.* Edited by D.P. Rapkin. Boulder, Colo.: Lynne Rienner.

Modelski, G. 1974. *World Power Concentrations: Typology, Data, Explanatory Frameworks.* Morristown, N.J.: General Learning Press.

———. 1978. "The Long Cycle of Global Politics and the Nation State." *Comparative Studies in Society and History* 20: 214-35.

———. 1981. "Long Cycles, Kondratieffs and Alternating Innovations: Implications for U.S. Foreign Policy." In *The Political Economy of Foreign Policy Behavior.* Edited by C.W. Kegley, Jr., and P.J. McGowan. Beverly Hills, Calif.: Sage.

———. 1982. "Long Cycles and the Strategy of U.S. International Political Economy." In *America in a Changing World Political Economy.* Edited by W. Avery and D.P. Rapkin. New York: Longman.

———. 1984. "Global Wars and World Leadership Selection." Paper presented at the second World Peace Science Society Congress, Rotterdam.

———. 1987. *Long Cycles in World Politics.* London: Macmillan.

———. 1990. "Is World Politics Evolutionary Learning?" *International Organization* 44: 1-24.

Modelski, G., and G. Perry. 1991. "Democratization in Long Perspective." *Technological Forecasting and Social Change* 39: 23-34.

Modelski, G., and W.R. Thompson. 1988. *Seapower and Global Politics, 1494-1993.* London: Macmillan.

———. 1992. "K-Waves, the Evolving Global Economy, and World Politics: The

Problem of Coordination." Paper presented at the annual meeting of the International Studies Association, Atlanta, March.

———. forthcoming. *Leading Sectors and World Politics: The Co-Evolution of Global Economics and Politics*. Columbia: Univ. of South Carolina Press.

Motor Vehicle Manufacturers Association. 1981. *World Motor Vehicle Data*. Detroit: Motor Vehicle Manufacturers Association.

Mueller, J. 1989. *Retreat from Doomsday: The Obsolescence of Major War*. New York: Basic Books.

Mukerjee, T. 1972. "Theory of Economic Drain: Impact of British Rule on the Indian Economy, 1840-1900." In *Economic Imperialism*. Edited by K. Boulding and T. Mukerjee. Ann Arbor: Univ. of Michigan Press.

Mulhall, M.G. 1903. *The Dictionary of Statistics*. London: George Routledge and Sons.

Muller-Hillebrand, B. 1969. *Das Heer, 1933-1945: Der Zweifrontenkrieg*. Vol. 3. Frankfurt: E.S. Mittler und Sohn.

Nye, J.S., Jr. 1990a. *Bound to Lead: The Changing Nature of American Power*. New York: Basic Books.

———. 1990b. "The Changing Nature of World Powers." *Political Science Quarterly* 105: 177-92.

O'Connor, J. 1973. *The Fiscal Crisis of the State*. New York: St. Martin's Press.

———. 1981. "The Fiscal Crisis of the State Revisited." *Kapitaliste* 9: 41-61.

Offe, C. 1975. "The Theory of the Capitalist State and the Problem of Policy Formation." In *Stress and Contradiction in Modern Capitalism*. Edited by L. Lindberg, R. Alford, C. Crouch, and C. Offe. Lexington, Mass.: Lexington Books.

———. 1984. *Contradictions of the Welfare State*. Cambridge, Mass.: MIT Press.

Olson, M. 1982. *The Rise and Decline of Nations: Economic Growth, Stagflation, and Social Rigidities*. New Haven, Conn.: Yale Univ. Press.

Oman, C. 1937. *A History of the Art of War in the Sixteenth Century*. London: Methuen.

Organization for Economic Cooperation and Development. 1980-87. *Main Economic Indicators*. Quarterly Volumes. Paris: OECD.

———. 1985. *The Semi-Conductor Industry: Trade Related Issues*. Paris: OECD.

Organski, A.F.K. 1958. *World Politics*. New York: Knopf.

Organski, A.F.K., and J. Kugler. 1980. *The War Ledger*. Chicago: Univ. of Chicago Press.

Parker, G. 1972. *The Army of Flanders and the Spanish Road, 1567-1659*. Cambridge: Cambridge Univ. Press.

———. 1978. "The Dutch Revolt and the Polarization of International Politics." In *The General Crisis of the Seventeenth Century*. Edited by Parker and L. Smith. Boston, Ma.: Routledge and Kegan Paul.

———. 1979a. *Europe in Crisis, 1598-1648*. Ithaca, N.Y.: Cornell Univ. Press.

———. 1979b. "Warfare." In *The New Cambridge Modern History*. Vol. 13, *Companion Volume*. Edited by P. Burke. Cambridge: Cambridge Univ. Press.

———, ed. 1987. *The Thirty Years War*. Rev. ed. London: Routledge and Kegan Paul.

———. 1988. *The Military Revolution*. Cambridge: Cambridge Univ. Press.

Parker, H.M.D. 1957. *Manpower: A Study of War-Time Policy and Administration*. London: HMSO.

Pelikan, J. 1987. *The Excellent Empire: The Fall of Rome and the Triumph of the Church*. San Francisco: Harper and Row.

Pennington, D.H. 1989. *Europe in the Seventeenth Century*. London: Longman.

Perroux, F. 1979. "An Outline of a Theory of the Dominant Economy." In *Transnational Corporations and World Order*. Edited by G. Modelski. San Francisco: W.H. Freeman.

Peterson, P.G. 1987. "The Morning After." *Atlantic* 260: 43-69.

Peterson, P.G., and N. Howe. 1988. *On Borrowed Time: How the Growth in Entitlement Spending Threatens America's Future*. San Francisco: ICS Press.

Phillips, C.R. 1987. "Time and Duration: A Model for the Economy of Early Modern Spain." *American Historical Review* 93: 531-62.

Pindyck, R.S., and D.L. Rubinfeld. 1981. *Econometric Models and Economic Forecasts*. New York: McGraw-Hill.

Plummer, A. 1937. *New British Industries in the Twentieth Century*. London: Pitman and Sons.

Pollard, R.A., and S.F. Wells, Jr. 1984. "1945-1960: The Era of American Economic Hegemony." In *Economics and World Power*. Edited by W.H. Becker and S.F. Wells, Jr. New York: Columbia Univ. Press.

Pollard, S. 1982. *The Wasting of the British Economy: British Economic Policy, 1945 to the Present*. London: Croom Helm.

———. 1989. *Britain's Prime and Britain's Decline: The British Economy, 1870-1914*. London: Edward Arnold.

Porch, D. 1976. "Making an Army Revolutionary: France, 1815-48." In *War, Economy and the Military Mind*. Edited by G. Best and A. Wheatcroft. London: Croom Helm.

Porter, B. 1975. *The Lion's Share: A Short History of British Imperialism, 1850-1970*. London: Longman.

Price, R. 1981. *An Economic History of Modern France, 1730-1914*. New York: St. Martin's Press.

Rapkin, D.P., and W.R. Thompson, with J.A. Christopherson. 1979. "Bipolarity and Bipolarization in the Cold War Era." *Journal of Conflict Resolution* 23: 261-95.

Rasler, K.A. 1990. "Spending, Deficits and Welfare-Investment Tradeoffs: Cause or Effect of Leadership Decline?" In *World Leadership and Hegemony*. Edited by D.P. Rapkin. Boulder, Colo.: Lynne Rienner.

Rasler, K.A., and W.R. Thompson. 1983. "Global Wars, Public Debts and the Long Cycle." *World Politics* 35: 489-516.

———. 1985. "War Making and State Making: Governmental Expenditures, Tax Revenues and Global Wars." *American Political Science Review* 79: 491-507.

———. 1988. "Defense Burdens, Capital Formation and Economic Growth: The Systemic Leader Case." *Journal of Conflict Resolution* 32: 61-86.

———. 1989. *War and State Making: The Shaping of the Global Powers*. Boston: Unwin Hyman.

———. 1992. "Assessing the Costs of War: A Preliminary Cut." In *Effects of War on Society*. Edited by G. Ausenda. Republic of San Marino: Center for Interdisciplinary Research on Social Stress.

Ray, J.L. 1989. "The Abolition of Slavery and the End of International War." *International Organization* 43: 405-39.

———. 1991. "The Future of International War." Paper presented at the annual meeting of the American Political Science Association, Washington, D.C., August.

Ray, J.L., and J.D. Singer. 1973. "Measuring the Concentration of Power in the International System." *Sociological Methods and Research* 1: 403-37.

Reddaway, W.F. 1908. "The Scandinavian Kingdoms." In *The Cambridge Modern History.* Vol. 5, *The Age of Louis XIV.* Edited by A.W. Ward, G.W. Prothero, and S. Leathes. Cambridge: Cambridge Univ. Press.

Reischauer, E.O., and J.K. Fairbanks. 1960. *East Asia: The Great Tradition.* Boston: Houghton Mifflin.

Research Working Group on Cyclical Rhythms and Secular Trends. 1979. "Cyclical Rhythms and Secular Trends of the Capitalist World-Economy: Some Premises, Hypotheses, and Questions." *Review* 2: 483-500.

Riley, J.C. 1984. "The Dutch Economy after 1650: Decline or Growth?" *Journal of European Economic History* 13: 521-69.

———. 1986. *The Seven Years War and the Old Regime in France.* Princeton, N.J.: Princeton Univ. Press.

Roberts, J.M. 1967. *Europe, 1880-1945.* New York: Holt, Rinehart and Winston.

Roberts, P. 1947. *The Quest for Security, 1715-1740.* New York: Harper and Row.

Rose, A. 1941. "Wars, Innovations and Long Cycles: A Brief Comment." *American Economic Review* 31: 105-7.

Rose, R. 1975. "Overloaded Government: The Problem Outlined." *European Studies Newsletter* 5: 13-18.

Rosecrance, R.N. 1987. "Long Cycle Theory and International Relations." *International Organization* 41: 283-301.

———. 1990. *America's Economic Resurgence: A Bold New Strategy.* New York: Harper and Row.

Rosen, J. 1961. "Scandinavia and the Baltic." In *The New Cambridge Modern History.* Vol. 5, *The Ascendancy of France.* Edited by F.L. Carsten. Cambridge: Cambridge Univ. Press.

Rosenau, J.N. 1990. *Turbulence in World Politics: A Theory of Change and Continuity.* Princeton, N.J.: Princeton Univ. Press.

———. 1992. "A Wherewithal for Revulsion: Notes on the Obsolescence of Interstate War." Paper presented at the Conference on Peace and Conflict in International Relations, Peace Research Institute, Frankfurt, May.

Rostow, W.W. 1978. *The World Economy: History and Prospect.* Austin: Univ. of Texas Press.

———. 1985. "The World Economy since 1945: A Stylized Historical Analysis." *Economic History Review* 38: 252-75.

Rothenberg, G.E. 1976. *The Army of Francis Joseph.* West Lafayette, Ind.: Purdue Univ. Press.

———. 1978. *The Art of Warfare in the Age of Napoleon.* Bloomington: Indiana Univ. Press.

———. 1982. *Napoleon's Great Adversaries: The Archduke Charles and the Austrian Army, 1792-1814.* London: B.T. Batsford.

Rude, G. 1964. *Revolutionary Europe, 1783-1815.* New York: Harper and Row.

Rupert, M.E., and D.P. Rapkin. 1985. "The Erosion of U.S. Leadership Capabilities." In *Rhythms in Politics and Economics.* Edited by P.M. Johnson and W.R. Thompson. New York: Praeger.

Sabrosky, A.N. 1985. "Alliance Aggregation, Capability Distribution, and the Expansion of Interstate War." In *Polarity and War.* Edited by A.N. Sabrosky. Boulder, Colo.: Westview Press.

Sanders, J.W. 1992. "The War of Historical Interpretation and the Prospects for Peace in the Post-Cold War Era." In *Research in Social Movements, Conflicts and Change*. Edited by L. Kriesberg and D. Segal. Greenwich, Conn.: JAI Press.

Schama, S. 1988. *The Embarrassment of Riches*. Berkeley: Univ. of California Press.

Schumpeter, J.A. 1939. *Business Cycles: A Theoretical, Historical and Statistical Analysis of the Capitalist Process*. New York: McGraw-Hill.

Scott, B.R. 1985. "National Strategies: Key to International Competition." In *U.S. Competitiveness in the World Economy*. Edited by B.R. Scott and G.C. Lodge. Boston: Harvard Business School Press.

Scott, H.F., and W.F. Scott. 1979. *The Armed Forces of the USSR*. Boulder, Colo.: Westview Press.

Scouller, R.E. 1966. *The Armies of Queen Anne*. Oxford: Clarendon Press.

Seaton, A. 1971. *The Russo-German War, 1941-45*. London: Arthur Barker.

———. 1981. *The Fall of Fortress Europe, 1943-1945*. London: B.T. Batsford.

———. 1982. *The German Army, 1933-45*. London: Weidenfeld and Nicolson.

Shanahan, W.O. 1945. *Prussian Military Reforms, 1786-1813*. New York: Columbia Univ. Press.

Sheppard, E.W. 1974. *A Short History of the British Army*. 4th ed. Westport, Conn.: Greenwood Press.

Shinohara, M. 1982. *Industrial Growth, Trade and Dynamic Patterns in the Japanese Economy*. Tokyo: Univ. of Tokyo Press.

Sims, C. 1972. "Money, Income and Causality." *American Economic Review* 62: 540-52.

———. 1977. "Exogeneity and Causal Ordering in Macroeconomic Models." In *New Methods of Business Cycle Research: Proceedings from a Conference*. Edited by C. Sims. Minneapolis: Federal Reserve Bank of Minneapolis.

———. 1980. "Macroeconomics and Reality." *Econometrica* 48: 1-48.

Singer, J.D. 1991. "Peace in the Global System: Displacement, Interregnum or Transformation?" In *The Long Postwar Peace: Contending Explanations and Projections*. Edited by C.W. Kegley, Jr. New York: Harper Collins.

Singer, J.D., S.A. Bremer, and J. Stuckey. 1972. "Capability Distribution, Uncertainty, and Major Power War, 1820-1965." In *Peace, War and Numbers*. Edited by B.M. Russett. Beverly Hills, Calif.: Sage.

Singer, J.D. and M. Small. 1972. *The Wages of War*. New York: Wiley.

Siverson, R.M. 1980. "War and Change in the International System." In *Change in the International System*. Edited by O.R. Holsti, R.M. Siverson, and A.L. George. Boulder, Colo.: Westview Press.

Siverson, R.M., and M.P. Sullivan. 1983. "The Distribution of Power and the Onset of War." *Journal of Conflict Resolution* 17: 473-94.

Sked, A. 1979. *The Survival of the Habsburg Empire: Radetzky, the Imperial Army and the Class War, 1848*. London: Longman.

Smith, R.P. 1977. "Military Expenditures and Capitalism." *Cambridge Journal of Economics* 1: 61-76.

———. 1978. "Military Expenditure and Capitalism: A Reply." *Cambridge Journal of Economics* 2: 299-304.

———. 1980. "Military Expenditures and Investment in OECD Countries, 1954-1973." *Journal of Comparative Economics* 4: 19-32.

Snyder, J. 1984. *The Ideology of the Offensive*. Ithaca, N.Y.: Cornell Univ. Press.

————. 1991. *Myths of Empire: Domestic Politics and International Ambition.* Ithaca, NY: Cornell Univ. Press.

Sommers, A.T. 1975. "Social Goals and Economic Growth: The Policy Problem in Capital Formation." *Conference Board Record* 12: 17-26.

Sonnino, P. 1987. "The Origin of Louis XIV's Wars." In *The Origins of War in Early Modern Europe.* Edited by J. Black. Edinburgh: John Donald Publishers.

————. 1988. *Louis XIV and the Origins of the Dutch War.* Cambridge: Cambridge Univ. Press.

Spiers, E.M. 1980. *The Army and Society, 1815-1914.* London: Longman.

Sprout, H., and M. Sprout. 1968. "The Dilemma of Rising Demands and Insufficient Resources." *World Politics* 20: 660-93.

St. Augustine. 1957. *The City of God.* 2 vols. Translated by John Healy. New York: E.P. Dutton.

Stein, A.A., and B.M. Russett. 1980. "Evaluating War: Outcomes and Consequences." In *Handbook of Political Conflict: Theory and Research.* Edited by T.R. Gurr. New York: Free Press.

Sterman, J.D. 1985. "An Integrated Theory of the Economic Long Wave." *Futures* 17: 104-31.

Stone, N. 1975. *The Eastern Front, 1914-1917.* New York: Charles Scribner's Sons.

Stoye, J.W. 1971. "Armies and Navies: Soldiers and Civilians." In *The New Cambridge Modern History.* Vol. 6, *The Rise of Great Britain and Russia, 1688-1725.* Edited by J.S. Bromley. Cambridge: Cambridge Univ. Press.

Strachan, H. 1983. *European Armies and the Conduct of War.* London: Allen and Unwin.

————. 1984. *Wellington's Legacy: The Reform of the British Army, 1830-54.* Manchester: Manchester Univ. Press.

Stradling, R.A. 1981. *Europe and the Decline of Spain.* London: Allen and Unwin.

Stschepkin, E. 1906. "Russia under Alexander I and the Invasion of 1812." In *The Cambridge Modern History.* Vol. 9, *Napoleon.* Edited by A.W. Ward, G.W. Prothero, and S. Leathes. Cambridge: Cambridge Univ. Press.

Sullivan, B.R. 1988. "The Italian Armed Forces, 1918-40." In *Military Effectiveness.* Vol. 2, *The Interwar Years.* Edited by A.R. Millett and W. Murray. Boston: Allen and Unwin.

Svennilson, I. 1954. *Growth and Stagnation in the European Economy.* Geneva: United Nations.

Tainter, J.A. 1988. *The Collapse of Complex Societies.* Cambridge: Cambridge Univ. Press.

Thompson, I.A.A. 1976. *War and Government in Habsburg Spain, 1560-1620.* London: Athlone Press.

Thompson, W.R. 1983a. "Cycles, Capabilities and War: An Ecumenical View." In *Contending Approaches to World System Analysis.* Edited by W.R. Thompson. Beverly Hills, Calif.: Sage.

————. 1983b. "Succession Crises in the Global Political System: A Test of the Transitional Model." In *Crises in the World-System.* Edited by A. Bergesen. Beverly Hills, Calif.: Sage.

————. 1985. "Cycles of General, Hegemonic and Global War." In *Dynamic Models of International Conflict.* Edited by U. Luterbacher and M.D. Ward. Boulder, Colo.: Lynne Rienner.

————. 1988. *On Global War: Historical-Structural Approaches to World Politics.* Columbia: Univ. of South Carolina Press.

————. 1990a. "Long Waves, Technological Innovation and Relative Decline." *International Organization* 44: 201-33.

————. 1990b. "The Size of War, Structural and Geopolitical Contexts, and Theory Building/Testing." *International Interactions* 16: 183-99.

————. 1992. "Systemic Leadership and Growth Waves in the Long Run." *International Studies Quarterly* 36: 25-48.

Thompson, W.R., and L. Vescera. 1992. "Growth Waves, Systemic Openness, and Protectionism." *International Organization* 46: 493-532.

Thompson, W.R., and G. Zuk. 1982. "War, Inflation and Kondratieff's Long Waves." *Journal of Conflict Resolution* 26: 621-44.

————. 1986. "World Power and the Strategic Trap of Territorial Commitments." *International Studies Quarterly* 30: 249-67.

Thucydides. 1954. *The Peloponnesian War.* Translated by R. Warner. Harmondsworth, Eng.: Pelican.

Thurow, L. 1985. *The Zero-Sum Solution.* New York: Simon and Schuster.

Tilly, C. 1990. *Coercion, Capital and European States, AD 990-1990.* Cambridge, Mass.: Basil Blackwell.

Tilton, J.E. 1971. *International Diffusion of Technology: The Case of Semiconductors.* Washington, D.C.: Brookings Institution.

Tinbergen, J. 1981. "Kondratiev Cycles and So-Called Long Waves: The Early Research." *Futures* 13: 258-63.

Treasure, G. 1985. *The Making of Modern Europe, 1648-1780.* London: Methuen.

Trevelyan, M.C. 1934. *William the Third and the Defense of Holland, 1672-1674.* London: Longmans, Green and Co.

United Kingdom. Parliament. Sessional Papers. 1857-58 to 1914-16. *Statistical Abstract of British India.* London: HMSO.

United Nations. 1948-1985. *U.N. Statistical Yearbook.* Annual Volumes. New York: United Nations.

United States. Department of Commerce. 1910-1990. *Statistical Abstract of the United States.* Annual Volumes. Washington, D.C.: GPO.

————. 1975. *Historical Statistics of the United States: Colonial Times to 1970.* Washington, D.C.: GPO.

————. Office of the President. 1988. *Economic Report of the President.* Washington, D.C.: GPO.

Vagts, A. 1959. *A History of Militarism.* Rev. ed. New York: Free Press.

van Creveld, M. 1982. *Fighting Power: German and U.S. Army Performance, 1939-1945.* Westport, Conn.: Greenwood Press.

Vayrynen, R. 1983. "Economic Cycles, Power Transitions, Political Management and War between the Major Powers." *International Studies Quarterly* 27: 389-418.

Veenendaal, A.J. 1971. "The War of the Spanish Succession in Europe." In *The New Cambridge Modern History.* Vol. 6, *The Rise of Great Britain and Russia, 1688-1725.* Edited by J.S. Bromley. Cambridge: Cambridge Univ. Press.

Volland, C.S. 1987. "A Comprehensive Theory of Long Wave Cycles." *Technological Forecasting and Social Change* 32: 123-45.

von Pflugk-Harttung, J. 1906. "The War of Liberation." In *The Cambridge Modern History.* Vol. 9, *Napoleon.* Edited by A.W. Ward, G.W. Prothero, and S. Leathes. Cambridge: Cambridge Univ. Press.

Walbank, F.W. 1969. *The Awful Revolution: The Decline of the Roman Empire in the West.* Toronto: Univ. of Toronto Press.

Walker, W.B. 1980. "Britain's Industrial Performance, 1850-1950: A Failure to Adjust." In *Technological Innovation and British Economic Performance.* Edited by K. Pavitt. London: Macmillan.

Wallerstein, I. 1984. *The Politics of the World-Economy.* Cambridge: Cambridge Univ. Press.

Waltz, K. 1979. *Theory of International Politics.* Reading, Mass.: Addison-Wesley.

Ward, A.W. 1908. "The Great Elector and the First Prussian King." In *The Cambridge Modern History.* Vol. 5, *The Age of Louis XIV.* Edited by A.W. Ward, G.W. Prothero, and S. Leathes. Cambridge: Cambridge Univ. Press.

Ward, M.D. 1984. "Differential Paths to Parity: A Study of the Contemporary Arms Race." *American Political Science Review* 78: 287-317.

Warner, P. 1973. *The Crimean War: A Reappraisal.* New York: Taplinger Publishing Co.

Webb, A.D. 1911. *The New Dictionary of Statistics.* London: Routledge and Sons.

Weigley, R.E. 1991. *The Age of Battles: The Quest for Decisive Warfare from Breitenfeld to Waterloo.* Bloomington: Indiana Univ. Press.

Weiner, M.J. 1981. *English Culture and the Decline of the Industrial Spirit, 1850-1980.* Cambridge: Cambridge Univ. Press.

Weisskopf, T. 1981. "The Current Economic Crisis in Historical Perspective." *Socialist Review* 57: 9-54.

Weisskopf, T., S. Bowles, and D.M. Gordon. 1983. "Hearts and Minds: A Social Model of U.S. Productivity." *Brookings Papers on Economic Activity* 2: 381-450.

Werth, A. 1964. *Russia at War, 1941-1945.* New York: E.P. Dutton.

Western, J.R. 1968. "Armies." In *The New Cambridge Modern History.* Vol. 8, *The American and French Revolutions, 1763-93.* Edited by A. Goodwin. Cambridge: Cambridge Univ. Press.

Westphal, S. 1951. *The German Army in the West.* London: Cassell and Co.

Weygand, M. 1953. *Histoire de l'armée française.* Montrouge, France: Draeger Frères.

Whittam, J. 1977. *The Politics of the Italian Army, 1861-1918.* London: Croom Helm.

Wijn, J.W. 1970. "Military Forces and Warfare, 1618-1648." In *The New Cambridge Modern History.* Vol. 4, *The Decline of Spain and the Thirty Years War, 1609^{48}/$_{59}$.* Edited by J.P. Cooper. Cambridge: Cambridge Univ. Press.

Willems, E. 1986. *A Way of Life and Death: Three Centuries of Prussian-German Militarism.* Nashville: Vanderbilt Univ. Press.

Williams, J. 1993. "Evaluating Long Cycle Theory Using Time-Varying Bayesian Vector Autoregression." *Political Analysis* 4: 97-125.

———. M. McGinnia, and J.C. Thomas, 1992. "Breaking the War-Economy Link." Paper presented at the annual meeting of the International Studies Association. Atlanta, March.

Wilson, C.H. 1965. *England's Apprenticeship, 1603-1763.* London: Longmans, Green and Co.

Wilson, T. 1986. *The Myriad Faces of War: Britain and the Great War, 1914-1918.* Cambridge: Polity Press.

Wohlforth, W.C. 1987. "The Perception of Power: Russia in the Pre-1914 Balance." *World Politics* 39: 353-81.

Wolf, C., Jr. 1985. "The Costs of the Soviet Empire." *Science* 230: 997-1002.

Wolf, J.B. 1951. *The Emergence of the Great Powers, 1685-1715.* New York: Harper and Row.

Wolfe, A. 1981. *America's Impasse: The Rise and Fall of the Politics of Growth.* Boston: South End Press.

Wolfe, T.W. 1970. *Soviet Power and Europe.* Baltimore: Johns Hopkins Univ. Press.

Wright, E.O. 1979. *Class, Crisis and the State.* London: Verso.

Wright, Q. 1965. *A Study of War.* 2d ed. Chicago: Univ. of Chicago Press.

Yoffee, N. 1991. "The Collapse of Ancient Mesopotamian States and Civilization." In *The Collapse of Ancient States and Civilizations.* Edited by N. Yoffee and G.C. Cowgill. Tucson: Univ. of Arizona Press.

Young, P. and J.P. Lawford. 1975. *History of the British Army.* New York: Putnam.

Ziemke, E.F. 1988. "The Soviet Armed Forces in the Interwar Period." In *Military Effectiveness.* Vol. 2, *The Interwar Years.* Edited by A.R. Millett and W. Murray. Boston: Allen and Unwin.

Zolberg, A.R. 1981. "Origins of the Modern World System: A Missing Link." *World Politics* 33: 253-81.

———. 1983. "'World' and 'System': A Misalliance." In *Contending Approaches to World System Analysis.* Edited by W.R. Thompson. Beverly Hills, Calif.: Sage.

Index

DATE DUE

GAYLORD			PRINTED IN U.S.A.